D0397925

TERRI | THE TRUTH

Dutton

TERRI

THE TRUTH

MICHAEL SCHIAVO

with Michael Hirsh

DUTTON
Published by Penguin Group (USA) Inc.
375 Hudson Street, New York, New York 10014, U.S.A.
Penguin Group (Canada), 90 Eglinton Avenue East, Suite 700, Toronto, Ontario M4P 2Y3, Canada (a division of Pearson Penguin Canada Inc.); Penguin Books Ltd, 80 Strand, London WC2R 0RL, England; Penguin Ireland, 25 St Stephen's Green, Dublin 2, Ireland (a division of Penguin Books Ltd); Penguin Group (Australia), 250 Camberwell Road, Camberwell, Victoria 3124, Australia (a division of Pearson Australia Group Pty Ltd); Penguin Books India Pvt Ltd, 11 Community Centre, Panchsheel Park, New Delhi – 110 017, India; Penguin Group (NZ), cnr Airborne and Rosedale Roads, Albany, Auckland 1310, New Zealand (a division of Pearson New Zealand Ltd); Penguin Books (South Africa) (Pty) Ltd, 24 Sturdee Avenue, Rosebank, Johannesburg 2196, South Africa

Penguin Books Ltd, Registered Offices: 80 Strand, London WC2R 0RL, England

Published by Dutton, a member of Penguin Group (USA) Inc.

First printing, March 2006
10   9   8   7   6   5   4   3   2   1

 REGISTERED TRADEMARK—MARCA REGISTRADA

LIBRARY OF CONGRESS CATALOGING-IN-PUBLICATION DATA
has been applied for.

ISBN 0–525–94946–1

Printed in the United States of America
Set in Dante with Agenda
Designed by Carla Bolte

While the author has made every effort to provide accurate telephone numbers and Internet addresses at the time of publication, neither the publisher nor the author assumes any responsibility for errors, or for changes that occur after publication. Further, the publisher does not have any control over and does not assume any responsibility for author or third-party Web sites or their content.

For the two loves of my life

This book is dedicated to the memory of

TERRI

who will always be part of me

and to

JODI

my wife, my friend, my rock

The truth is incontrovertible; malice may attack it, ignorance may deride it, but in the end; there it is.

— Sir Winston Churchill

Everyone is entitled to their own opinion, but not their own facts.

— Daniel Patrick Moynihan

Contents

Preface

This is a story I never wanted to tell. I'm a very private person. I'd be happy if no one outside my immediate circle of friends and coworkers knew my name. I would have been much happier if I had nothing of interest to say to anyone but my wife and kids and friends. But we don't always get to choose the road we'll travel or, for that matter, the companions who will be with us for the length of the journey.

Over the last fifteen years I've learned that there are forces over which we have no control; forces that will influence our lives in the most unexpected ways. The story you're about to read begins in my twenty-first year and goes through my forty-second. It starts when I was still pretty much a kid, someone who was about to fall in love for the first time with one woman, and ends with my public, legal, and religious proclamation of love and fidelity to another woman, to the mother of our two children, Jodi Centonze.

For twelve of the last fifteen years, Jodi was by my side, quietly, sometimes almost invisibly, supporting my every effort to do the right thing for the first love of my life, Theresa Marie Schiavo. Jodi is the unsung hero of those troubled times.

This book has been written with the presumption that you know the headlines of the tragedy of Terri Schiavo, who lived for fifteen years in a persistent vegetative state. I initially thought that I could tell this story chapter by chapter, taking a literary approach, writing it as though I didn't know where it was going and how it was going to get there. I was wrong. It became impossible for me to detail critical events without telling you right then why they would prove to be significant years later. In these pages, then, you'll learn new things about *what* happened, and many more details about *why*.

By now you know that one of the most thorough autopsies ever performed in the state of Florida—perhaps in the country—put the lie to the constant din of the Schindler family and their faith-based, moralist supporters claiming that Terri had cognition; that she could speak, could see, could hear, and could interact with visitors to the extent that not long before her death she supposedly cried, "I want to live." The autopsy report, which was released on June 15, 2005, proved everything I—and her doctors—knew to be true about Terri's condition. She would have never gotten better; not even a little bit. She had no cognition. She could not hear. She could not see. She could not feel pain. There was no doubt whatsoever.

You also may know that an investigation by the local state attorney absolutely exonerated me of the preposterous charges made by my in-laws, radical priests, and ambitious politicians—both indicted and not—as well as a racist ex-detective now flacking for my in-laws, that I caused Terri's collapse, and therefore, I was a murderer.

You are also probably aware that although Terri had left no written advance directives about her end-of-life wishes—how many twenty-six-year-olds do?—Pinellas County circuit court judge George Greer determined that there was clear and convincing evidence of her desires as required by the laws and judicial decisions of the state of Florida. Judge Greer reached that conclusion early in 2000, and it was on the basis of that original decision that we were able to remove Terri's feeding tube and allow her to go to her final rest on March 31, 2005.

The appendix of this book contains the three documents essential to knowing the legal truth about the Terri Schiavo case. You'll find critical excerpts from medical examiner Dr. Jon Thogmartin's autopsy report; State Attorney Bernie McCabe's report to Governor Jeb Bush, which answered with finality the governor's questions about my possible complicity in Terri's death; and Judge George Greer's original order that explained why he authorized removal of artificial life support. My detractors and accusers still deny the truths contained in these three documents.

This is an emotional book, and for that I make no apologies. After everything I went through, I could not write it any other way. I have no argument with those who may honestly disagree with me and the choices I made over the last fifteen years. But honest disagreement over principle is not what has characterized what became known worldwide as "The Schiavo Case," in my opinion.

Instead of honest disagreement there were repeated distortions of the facts by people high and low with both personal and political axes to grind. The facts have been twisted—and continue to be twisted—by Terri's parents, Robert Schindler, Sr., and Mary Schindler; by her brother, Bobby; and by her sister, Suzanne. The facts have been twisted by politicians, including the governor of Florida, the majority leaders of the United States House and Senate, by one of my own senators in Florida, and by the president of the United States. The facts have been twisted by medical practitioners who diagnosed by television and by attorneys who appear to have placed their religious beliefs above their sworn duty as officers of the court to uphold the Constitution of the United States. The facts have also been utterly disregarded by religious leaders who would prefer to see our country turned into a theocracy, but only so long as the divine guidance of our leaders comes from *their* God, interpreted *their* way. Strange, but isn't that precisely what we're fighting in Iraq and Afghanistan and in the war on terrorism?

Even as I worked with my coauthor, Michael Hirsh, on this book, the facts about The Schiavo Case were still being distorted. Terri's parents, firmly in the clutches of the moral troglodytes of the religious right, are saying that my wife's death came as a result of *the forces of euthanasia*. They dishonor their own daughter's memory by allowing her to be used by those waging a culture war on America. You doubt that? Maybe you didn't know that on their Web site, Terri's parents sold the wretched videotape of her in the hospice for one hundred dollars a copy. Do you think they cared whether that's the way she'd like to be remembered?

That said, I still have empathy for the Schindlers. I have a little girl; I can't begin to imagine the pain I'd feel if something happened to her. There's no question that the grief they've endured with the loss of Terri demands compassion. Several times during this saga, before it became ugly and bitter as well as after, I suggested that counseling was available to help them deal with the loss. One of the advantages of having Terri in a hospice instead of a nursing home is that a hospice has people who are trained to help grieving moms and dads, and sons and daughters, learn how to accept their loss. But every time that I knew it was offered to the Schindlers, they declined. There does come a point, then, where I had to say, "I tried, I offered. They're adults, they've made a conscious choice to deny the reality of Terri's condition." The help they needed was not to fight a war, but to recover from their wounds. I wish someone whom they trust, who truly loves and cares for them, would suggest that it is never too late to get help and move beyond the pain of our loss.

If you want to trace the cause of Terri's collapse, you begin with an eating disorder, bulimia, and work backward. When Terri collapsed, she weighed about 115 pounds. When we married, she was approximately 130 pounds. She was losing weight so quickly before our wedding that between the second fitting of her gown and our ceremony, the dress had to be pinned into place. When we met, she was approximately 160 pounds. When she was in high school, she had ballooned to nearly 250 pounds. The questions that have to be asked are *why* did she lose all that weight? And *how* did she lose all that weight?

There's no doubt in my mind that Terri was suffering from bulimia nervosa. The experts don't know the causes of the disorder with any degree of certainty, but they do know that if an individual is vulnerable to the disease, environmental factors such as verbal abuse can trigger it.

Terri told me that from the time she was in seventh or eighth grade through high school, her father ridiculed her about her weight. The older she got, the worse the ridicule. It was so intense, she often ran to her room in tears and cried herself to sleep.

Daughters want to hear expressions of unconditional love and support from their fathers, not put-downs because of the way they look. The damage done is long-term.

And that is perhaps the lesson to be learned from Terri. The intense pressure in our society on young girls to conform to the Eva Longoria–size double-zero standard of beauty is destroying lives. One of my trial attorneys, Gary D. Fox, saw this clearly as he learned about Terri's life. Gary has three kids, two of whom, Keaton and Kalle, were pre-adolescent girls when he wrote in a commentary, "It sends chills down my spine when I hear my daughters reading the calorie content from the side of cereal boxes." Gary remains distressed that "well-intentioned but uninformed parents may make mistakes dealing with adolescent weight issues that can have profound consequences for their children." I'll give Robert Schindler, Sr., "uninformed," but not "well-intentioned."

Turning to the political atmosphere surrounding The Schiavo Case, we find the other looming lesson from this saga: If it could happen to me, it can happen to you. There are forces in our country who believe it is their right to tell you how to live, how to behave, and what to believe. They wouldn't hesitate for a second to codify their religious beliefs in our country's laws; they insist that our right to life, liberty, and the pursuit of happiness is not only *what* they say it is, but *how* they say it is. Their number includes craven politicians who want their votes, religious leaders who take their money, nuts who offer bounties and threaten death, and lawyers who have no regard for the facts, and even one lawyer who made a death threat reported to the court.

I would be remiss if I didn't make clear that *Terri: The Truth* is not a comprehensive legal history of The Schiavo Case, nor is it an exposé of how backers of the extreme religious right funded the Schindlers' court battles. The book you're holding is my personal account of the lengthy battle that I fought to see that Terri's wishes were fulfilled. This book does go into detail about the trials I participated in, but I would suggest that those of you interested in the complete legal history or those other aspects of the story read *Using Terri*, written by Jon Eisenberg, one of our volunteer appellate attorneys.

If there's one word that characterizes The Schiavo Case over the years, it's *conflict*. I don't know what's in the minds of the Schindlers or their attorneys or supporters, but if anyone knows the facts of this case, I do. And while living The Schiavo Case, I've arrived at certain opinions about the events and the people who were participants in them. Read the book and decide for yourself whether or not you agree with me. The point of writing this book was to tell you the truth as I saw it. You may read things here that confirm your beliefs about The Schiavo Case, or you might be confronted with facts and opinions that are at odds with everything you thought you knew. And that may cause you to wonder who was telling the truth, and who wasn't. If I've done my job writing this book, you'll have to make a choice. Both sides can't be right. But I didn't presume to tell anyone what to think over the past fifteen years; I'm not going to start now.

One of my great frustrations over the past few years is that there were all sorts of people pretending to know Terri; to know what she was like, to know what she would have wanted. I'm sure you heard politicians, religious leaders, and even media types talk about Terri as though they were on first-name terms with her. They didn't know *my* Terri. This book is my opportunity to introduce the real Terri Schiavo to you.

Finally, if *Terri: The Truth* does nothing else, my hope is that it mobilizes those of you who have been sitting on the sidelines to get involved in the effort to defeat the forces that were arrayed against me and my family during the final years of Terri's life. The legal manpower, the public relations effort, and the money to pay for both that they were able to bring to bear is scary—and need to be confronted with numbers, strength, and passion. The politicians didn't wait for the polls to tell them that there are more of *us* than *them* out there (there are); the politicians acted based on who was shouting the loudest at the time of the vote. We need to start shouting sooner. The worst thing you could do after reading my book is nothing.

Michael Schiavo
Clearwater, Florida
January 21, 2006
mike@terripac.com

TERRI | THE TRUTH

Prologue

"Agostino's, good evening," I said, grabbing a handful of menus as I eyed another large group coming in the door. Even for a Saturday night at the height of snowbird season in Clearwater, Florida, the place was unusually busy. I'd been here since early afternoon, and it looked as though I wouldn't get out for another three hours. Twelve-hour shifts in the restaurant business were normal, especially when you're the dining room manager.

A soft, sweet voice on the other end of the line said, "Hi, honey. When are you coming home?"

"I don't think I can get out of here till we close. Probably be home after midnight. Did you do it?"

"You'll just have to wait and see," Terri said with a giggle. She'd had an appointment to get her hair cut— "real short" is what she'd told me she wanted. "I just got home from having dinner with the folks. Now, I've got to go over to Bobby's and iron his pants."

Bobby Schindler was her brother. He was thirteen months younger than Terri, who'd turned twenty-six a couple of months earlier. Bobby lived in the same St. Petersburg apartment complex we did, and we saw him often. Actually, our relationship with Bobby was a little closer than I would have preferred. Because a business venture—a futon store—with his dad had gone south, all the Schindlers except Suzanne had declared personal bankruptcy. Bobby needed to use one of Terri and my credit cards while he was traveling for a national soft-pretzel company because he didn't want the owners, who were friends of the family, to know that he couldn't get credit.

"You're ironing his pants? You gonna do his shorts, too? He's a grown boy; can't he iron his own pants?" I asked, laughing.

Terri ignored the questions. "Wake me when you get home, okay?" We said good-bye and I went back to three more hours of dealing with people who thought that overcooked fettuccini was proof that our civilization was doomed.

By the time I climbed the stairs to our fourth-floor apartment, my tux jacket was off and I'd begun unbuttoning my shirt. It was somewhere between 12:30 and 1:00 A.M. when I let myself in, knowing that Terri would be sound asleep.

The apartment was one of two on the fourth floor. Terri had fallen in love with it because the rooms were large, and with its cathedral ceilings the place felt very roomy. We didn't need much furniture when we moved in, but we'd found this great antiques store on Fourth Street called Karen's Antiques and got a great deal on a two-hundred-year-old dining table with a hutch that matched. The place was also large enough that we finally had room to hang up the set of four decorative plates we'd gotten as an engagement present. Terri really liked decorating with little odds and ends that she picked up. We even had her grandmother's hope chest, which fit against the same wall the plates were on.

I was tiptoeing around the place and draped my coat over one of the dining room chairs. I didn't turn on a lot of lights. As usual, Terri had left the stove light on, and that was bright enough for me. I ate the peanut-butter-and-crackers snack she always left on the kitchen counter, then brushed my teeth, slipped on a pair of gym shorts, and, exhausted, walked into the bedroom and crawled into bed, trying hard not to wake her. Problem is, a six-foot-six-inch guy climbing under the covers is about as subtle as a gentle earthquake. Terri turned toward me and mumbled a sleepy "Hello," adding, "See you in the morning.

I love you." We kissed, said good night, and in seconds, were both asleep.

Sometime after 5:30 A.M. I woke up because I needed to go to the bathroom. I wasn't wearing a watch and never looked at the alarm clock beside the bed, which is why I can't recall the precise time. And I wouldn't be making a big deal of it if, fifteen years later, it hadn't become a matter of concern for all sorts of people, including the governor of Florida.

As I started to get out of bed, it didn't even register that Terri wasn't there. And then I heard a thud. I threw off the sheet, got up, and ran out into the hall. The bathroom lights were on and I could see Terri on the floor, sort of on her left side facing the closet door, in the hallway outside the bathroom. She had one arm by her side and the other arm over her head—almost in a ballerina's pose. I got down on my knees, rolled her over so that she was facing me, and scooped her into my arms. "Terri, Terri, are you all right? What happened? What's going on?"

She didn't respond. All I heard were weird noises coming out of her mouth. She seemed to be breathing, but she wasn't answering. Then I heard this sharp intake of breath and it scared the crap out of me. I immediately laid her down, ran through the living room to the table phone that was about twenty feet away, and dialed 911. The cord on the phone wasn't long enough for me to keep an eye on Terri while I was talking to the operator. I was frantic on the phone, just screaming at the operator. "My wife isn't responding to me—I don't know what's going on." Truth is, I don't remember precisely what I said. The one thing I do recall is the operator asking me if I wanted her to stay on the line with me till the paramedics got there. I said no, and shouted something like "Get here!" Then I hung up the phone and ran back to the hallway.

The police department records indicate that I made the call at 05:40 on Sunday, February 25, 1990. I'll take their word for it. All I'm certain of is that I called them less than a minute after finding Terri on the floor. I did not delay calling the paramedics—no matter what Governor Jeb Bush apparently still believes.

When I got back to Terri, I picked her up again, hoping that she'd say something. "Terri, talk to me. What's wrong? What're you doing?" Nothing. I put her back down and called her parents.

Terri's father, Robert Schindler, Sr., picked up the phone. "Dad, something's wrong with Terri. I called 911." From before we were married I had called him Dad and Mrs. Schindler Mom.

"Well, call 911," he said.

"I already did; they're on their way," I said, and hung up.

I ran back to Terri, then ran back to the phone and called Bobby. "Your sister's collapsed, she's not doing anything. She's on the floor." He said he'd be right over.

In what seemed like seconds, Bobby was there. He walked over to Terri, looked down at her, and said, "Terri, wake up." I thought it was strange that he didn't kneel down, didn't touch her at all. All he said was, "Terri, wake up." Just moments later, I heard the fire paramedics coming up the stairs and I just turned and opened the door. Everything was that close—the bathroom, the front door, the door to the bedroom.

The first two guys saw Terri on the floor as they came into the apartment. They both knelt down next to Terri, who was laying there in a tank top and sweatpants. They went through the mental checklist of things to do to get an unconscious patient to respond— they tapped her, and then did a sternal rub. That's where you take your knuckles and rub the breastbone really hard. If you're able, you'll respond to it. Next thing I knew, I heard someone saying, "No heart rate; start CPR." They cut her tank top open. And as soon as a couple more rescue guys showed up, they began putting monitor leads on her and starting IVs. All I could see were these guys jumping all over my wife, and me standing there holding my head, saying, "Oh, my God, what the hell are you doing? What's going on here? I just talked to her last night. She said 'good night' to me." It was awful.

I think that the first two guys in were off a fire truck. Two paramedics arrived in the ambulance next. And I think the cops got there last.

One of the EMT guys started blaming me—or at least that's how I felt. "What kind of drugs does she take?" he asked.

"She doesn't take any drugs" I responded, clearly getting angry.

"Don't make me search this house."

"Go ahead and search the fucking house. There aren't any drugs here," I yelled at him. He just kept pushing the issue, pissing me off more and more. "She doesn't take any drugs. We don't do drugs." There I was, twenty-six years old, sitting there, my wife's chest exposed, they've started IVs, they've got a bag over her mouth and nose trying to force air into her lungs, and the next thing I knew, they were zapping her with the paddles to try and start her heart. I tried to comprehend what the hell had just happened, and he was arguing with me about drugs. I'm pretty sure there were a few "fuck yous" tossed around.

The cops managed to get me back in the living room, saying, "Calm down, they're just doing their job." I wasn't in the medical field at that time, so to see a couple of guys pounding on Terri's chest was a shock. CPR isn't a gentle procedure; you can break ribs. And Terri was incredibly thin. You could see her collarbones and ribs, and there they were, pounding on her.

I don't know whether they really believed Terri had OD'd, or just did it as a precaution, but they administered Narcan, a drug that causes reversal of narcotic depression, including respiratory depression induced by opioids.

While all this was going on I was pacing between the kitchen where I could watch the paramedics, and the living room, where Bobby sat in a chair. At one point he looked up and said to me, "Oh, she'll be all right, Mike." How the hell would he know? He didn't even care enough to stay with Terri while they were working on her.

My mind was still racing, not coming to any rational explanation of what was going on in the next room. I was crying; sort of shaking all over. Anxious; agitated. You can imagine.

By that time, one of the firemen had run downstairs and come back up with a backboard, and they were strapping Terri to it. It was all happening very, very quickly. Someone said, "We've got to load and go." It was a term I learned a few years later when I became a certified EMT, and then got further medical training in order to help care for Terri. Six of them picked up Terri and headed for the stairs. I tried to stay with her, but then realized I wasn't wearing anything but gym shorts. I dashed back to our bedroom, threw on my shirt and a pair of shorts, grabbed my wallet, and then ran back to the front door, where I slipped into a pair of deck shoes. They were no more than a couple of seconds ahead of me, carrying her down the stairs, continuing CPR and feeding her pure oxygen through the ambu-bag as they moved. Bobby stayed behind to lock up, and then drove to the hospital.

At one point, I heard someone say, "Stop CPR, we need to shock her again." Or maybe they said "defibrillate." I think this was while they were still trying to maneuver her down the stairs, but I'm not certain. The turns were so tight, sometimes they almost had to stand the backboard vertically. I followed them down the stairwell with one of the cops, and I still didn't understand what was happening to Terri. When they got to the back of the ambulance and stopped, someone checked her pulse and they shocked her again.

I tried to climb into the rear of the ambulance, but one of the guys said, "Why don't you sit up front?" and led me over to the passenger seat in the front of this high-tech Sunstar ambulance. Maybe they didn't want me to see what was happening. I don't know. There were already four guys in the back continuing to work on her, so I didn't argue. I do remember this paramedic coming up to the side of the ambulance, and as he was closing the door, he stuck his hand in and patted me on the shoulder. At the time, I just thought that maybe he was just being nice, his way of saying "good luck," but now I think he was saying that he was sorry, that he probably knew Terri wasn't going to make it.

Then he slammed the door, ran around to the other side, climbed in, and we took off for Humana Northside Hospital.

1 | In the Beginning

Five growing boys, each approximately two years apart, in a four-bedroom house. That's about all you need to know in order to understand what life was like for me growing up in Levittown, Pennsylvania. Oh, yeah. One more thing. I was the youngest.

Our father, Bill, was a safety engineer for Western Electric in Hopewell, New Jersey. He taught first aid, he monitored OSHA compliance—anything that had to do with safety was his job. He worked for them for thirty-two years.

Our mom, Claire—*not* Clara, even though it was her real name—was a full-time homemaker for most of the time we were being raised. Then she worked for Gimbel's department store in Bucks County, Pennsylvania. She'd been hired as a cashier, but during the training period they asked her to become assistant to the personnel director.

All the boys turned out to be big, even though our parents were average in height. I'm 6' 6", my oldest brother Bill is 6' 1", next comes Steve at 6' 5", Brian's next at 6' 3", then Scott at 6' 2". Strangely, the only one who showed any real athletic skill was Brian. I played Little League, but never got into high school sports.

Brian says that when I was a kid, I was actually a bit of a mama's boy. I don't remember it that way, but why would I? Scott confirms the mama's boy thing—and since he has the reputation of being the guy in the family with a memory like an elephant, I suppose I have to go along with it.

Mom was a great cook, and she cooked in massive quantities. Chicken, meat loaf, spaghetti, pancakes—whatever five growing boys would eat, she cooked it. Brian tells the story of bringing a good friend home from college for dinner, and the kid was amazed to see that we had two whole hams on the table. He'd never seen anything like that in his life. Brian recalls that "it was a timing thing to put your hand in so you didn't get stuck by someone's incoming fork."

Dinnertime could be absolutely hilarious, depending on what was going on during the day—who got into trouble at school, all the stuff that goes on with basically good kids. My brother Steve hated string beans; just absolutely hated them. We had the same dining room table for years, and when the kids started leaving home, my parents wanted new furniture. One day they were dismantling the dining room table and discovered dozens of rolled up napkins stuck underneath, filled with dehydrated string beans.

What I realize as I'm trying to tell you the story of growing up with the Schiavos is that we were absolutely normal. We were not the dysfunctional American family. Sure, my older brothers would pound on me when they thought I deserved it, and I even think Mom may have known about some of it and had let it happen. But she and Dad never let us forget that there's strength in family: We might have our disagreements with our brothers, but it's our job to stick together against the world if necessary. That's how it was then and, thankfully, that's still how it is now. Everyone talked to each other when we were young; until our folks died, we all talked to them regularly. Now that it's just the boys and our wives, we're all still close. I know that doesn't make for exciting reading, but it's the truth.

We had our scrapes as kids. I'll never forget the day my oldest brother, Bill, got his BB gun back from the repair shop and decided to try it out. He and Steve were hanging out the back window shooting at cats on the fence. Before we knew it, the police were at our front door saying that the neighbors were complaining that they were under attack. But that was about as bad as we got.

I know there's a story that went around the blogs attacking me, claiming that at a family picnic, all five of us boys got up on a bench to see who could pee the farthest. It never happened. It couldn't have. There wasn't a picnic bench built that the five Schiavo boys could stand on without breaking it. There may have been the occasional mooning, but we never did anything really gross.

We were raised to be respectful of adults and respectful of women. We respected our parents and respected our grandparents. That's something Mom and Dad taught us, and in thinking about it, it probably made my split with Mr. and Mrs. Schindler that much more difficult, because it went against how I was raised.

In 1983, I began attending a community college in Bucks County. I dated a couple of different girls; nothing special, no long-term commitments. But one day at the beginning of a new semester—I believe I was sitting in a psychology class—I heard this laugh behind me. It was sort of muffled, as though the laugher had placed a hand over her mouth in an attempt to lower the volume.

When I turned around I saw a young lady with big brown eyes, soft, shoulder-length brown hair, and smooth skin with a beautiful olive complexion. When she removed her hand from her mouth, I could see a radiant smile. This was a smile I couldn't resist. We began to chat a little bit until class began. Then I tried to focus on taking notes, but couldn't. All I could think of was the girl seated behind me. I'd never been struck this way by a girl, and I wanted to get to know her.

After class, we met outside and talked until we were both almost late for our next classes. I felt nervous with her, and could sense that she was a little apprehensive as well, but I managed not to say anything that would turn her off, and we agreed to talk again before our next psych class.

Two days later, I walked into the classroom and immediately began looking for her. I didn't want to be too obvious about it, but apparently that wasn't a problem for Terri. She'd saved the seat next to her for me. There was that smile again; it conveyed sweetness and warmth and was irresistible. I made it through that period, but if the instructor had given a pop quiz on the lecture, I'd have tanked.

The third time Terri and I met, I planned to ask her out. My sister-in-law Joan was having a surprise birthday party for Bill on Saturday, and I thought this would be a good first date. Don't ask me why. Clearly, I wasn't thinking straight when it came to Terri. My brothers and I have a good time when we all get together—maybe even a little too good—and I wasn't sure I wanted to expose her to that. But I got over my nerves and after class invited her to come with me to the party.

She said she would—but I'd have to meet her father and mother beforehand. That made me really nervous, but I agreed and we exchanged phone numbers. That night I called her home and she answered the phone. We talked for a good while—for much of the time I could hear her family teasing her—and got to know each other a little better. What I didn't know at the time was that this was going to be the first date Terri ever had.

I'd warned my family that Terri was a little shy, hoping that they'd restrain themselves and not do anything that might embarrass me or her. I should have known better, but I figured it was worth a shot.

I got out of the car at the Schindlers', and as I walked to the front door, I could hear giggling coming off to the side of the house. It turned out to be Terri's younger brother, Bobby, and his friends. I rang the doorbell and Terri greeted me with the same shy smile I'd grown accustomed to seeing. Her father wasn't home from work yet, which I thought was a real break, so I just made small talk with Terri's mom, Mary, while Terri finished getting ready. Frankly, I think it was a preplanned stalling maneuver so that her mom could give me the third degree.

We were about to walk out the door when in came Mr. Schindler. I began sweating bullets, but managed to act as though nothing was wrong. He seemed sort of gruff, not nearly as warm as Terri's mom, who was outgoing and friendly. If I had to pick one word to describe Mary Schindler, it would be sweet. She was a much easier person to like than her husband. Nevertheless, by the time Terri and I left for the party, I was actually feeling pretty comfortable with both of her parents.

When we got to Bill and Joan's house, I introduced Terri to everyone, and as expected, they welcomed her with open arms. That didn't mean that some craziness wasn't going to erupt without notice—but at least things were starting off on the right foot. Terri was her usual shy self for a short period of time, but then began opening up with everyone, especially my sisters-in-law.

Initially I tried to stay close to her, figuring that it would make her more comfortable since she didn't know anyone but me. This gave me a chance to watch her talking with my family, laughing, making little gestures that I came to realize were part of her. With every new discovery about this girl, I found myself feeling very warm inside. It suddenly dawned on me that I was really falling for Terri; that I was possibly about to find out what love was all about.

A couple of hours into the party, everyone was getting raucous. I was thinking that it might be best for us to leave, but it was too late. My oldest brother Bill walked out the front door at one point and said, "Hey everybody, time to drop your pants." He loosened his belt as though he was going to do it, and that's when I saw Terri start cracking up. That changed my mind about leaving, and we stayed and enjoyed the rest of the night.

I took the long way home so the two of us would have some time to talk. We shared more laughs about the party, and then talked about our pasts, growing up, schools, families, graduations. Much too soon, we got to Terri's house. I walked her to the front door where she told me she'd had a good time, thanked me, and gave me a kiss on the cheek. I asked her if she would like to go to the movies the next evening and she said yes. I was in heaven the entire ride home.

A few weeks after the party, my family and I were headed home after a funeral for my great-uncle. During the gathering afterward,

Brian had spilled something on his pants. The route home took us past the dry cleaners where Terri worked. When I mentioned that Terri worked there, Brian asked us to stop so he could get the pants cleaned. It was a cold day and Brian was wearing a trench coat. That was a good thing, because as soon as he walked into the cleaners, he went over to the counter, took his pants off, handed them to Terri, and asked how long it would take. We were all watching from the car. My mother, of course, was mortified, but this was one for *America's Funniest Home Videos*. Terri didn't recognize Brian, and the look on her face before she ran to the back of the store was priceless. Then a minute or so later, she realized who it was and became hysterical with laughter. That's when I came into the store. She was laughing so hard there were tears rolling down her face. Terri came over, gave me a hug, and told me that my family was nuts.

Over time, Terri and I became very close. We would see each other at school during the week, and usually every weekend. Terri confided in me a lot, telling me that she'd been very heavy as a kid. In high school, her weight topped out at around 250 pounds, and she never went to any dances or proms. It sort of explained why she'd never gone out with anyone until she met me.

When I met Terri, she weighed about 160 pounds. When our relationship became serious, I asked her about losing so much weight. She told me that she'd grown tired of being made fun of by people—especially by her father and brother. Once Terri and I were engaged, Terri revealed to me the extent of the ridicule she'd taken from her father. Instead of getting help and support from him, she got fat jokes and offers of money to slim down. She said that her brother Bobby managed to get hold of her driver's license with its photo of her as an overweight teenager, and when visitors would come to the house, he and her father got big laughs out of showing it around. Terri told me that while her mom would yell at Bobby and even whack him with a broomstick for doing it, she never put a stop to it: She never stepped in to protect her daughter from the ridicule of her father, and she never took the damned photo away from them.

According to Pauline Powers, M.D., a Tampa psychiatrist who is the president of the National Eating Disorders Association, consistent ridicule won't cause a teenage girl to become bulimic, but it could very well be a precipitating factor. She says, "When negative comments are made to people about their appearance, this can cause negative feelings toward the self—sometimes seeing yourself as larger than you are in reality. And this is one of the factors that predisposes one to eating disorders."

Throughout the years of The Schiavo Case, I always felt that Robert Schindler's ridicule of Terri because of her weight had to be one of the clues to why she developed bulimia, which is what led to her collapse and, ultimately, to her death.

Terri always said she loved her father, but didn't feel she could talk to him very easily. And her mom pretty much did what her father wanted. Think of Archie and Edith Bunker. Bob Schindler would come home, plunk down in his recliner, and shout, "Mare! Bring me this," and "Mare! Bring me that." And Mary would serve him.

Before I met her, Terri had gone on the NutriSystem diet to lose weight. When we met, she was probably a size 14 or 16, and I could see that she was still self-conscious about her appearance. She watched everything she ate, but never gave any indication that she was doing anything unhealthy in order to keep her weight in check.

Early in our relationship, Terri and my sisters-in-law became very close. My father usually referred to them as the awesome foursome (Brian was still single at the time). She and Joan were extremely friendly, spending a lot of time together. Joan said that she fell in love with Terri at that raucous birthday party. "The instant I saw her cracking up when Bill threatened to drop his pants, I knew she fit in with this crazy family." On weekends that I worked, Terri and Joan would hang out or go shopping—just do girl stuff.

Terri and I were engaged to be married after dating for about a year. I proposed to her at a local restaurant that we went to on special occasions. I can still remember her face when I asked her. She lit up, she was so excited. We didn't say anything to our families until the next morning, when Terri told her mom that I'd asked her. Mary was excited and happy for her, but said that I would have to ask her father for her hand.

That night I went to the Schindler house to ask. Everyone knew why I was there, and I think that probably made me even more nervous. Terri and I sat side by side on the couch, while Mr. Schindler sat in his recliner watching TV. Finally, her mom broke the ice by blurting out, "Bob, Mike and Terri have something to talk about with you."

I took a deep breath and told Mr. Schindler that I loved his daughter and wanted his blessing to get married. Terri held my hand through the entire conversation. He was hesitant at first, saying, "Don't you think you're too young?" I was twenty and Terri was nineteen. Terri jumped in. "No younger than you and Mom were."

Her dad went on to tell us about the ups and downs of marriage, but in the end, he gave us his blessing. We set our date for November 10, 1984, and started planning what was going to be a big wedding. Neither of us finished college. We both took full-time jobs. I began working for a local fast-food restaurant as a manager, and Terri took a job with Prudential Insurance.

I spent a lot of evenings at the Schindlers' house, and most of the times I'd stay the night, sleeping downstairs on the couch. Against her father's wishes, Terri would sneak downstairs late at night, snuggle next to me for a while, and then sneak back upstairs before it became light outside. She told me that it would be well worth it even if she did get caught by her dad. I didn't want to find out.

My family is Lutheran, but not especially religious. Terri was Catholic, and there was no question that Terri and I would be married in a Catholic church, although don't jump to the conclusion that her family were practicing Catholics. Terri had gone to Catholic school because the family could afford to send her there and it was better than public school. But they were "EC Catholics"—they attended Mass on Easter and Christmas; that's it. As for me not being Catholic and getting married in the church—it wasn't a problem as long as I took the required premarriage classes and we agreed to raise our children Catholic.

Once the whole Schindler-Schiavo dispute turned into a war, all sorts of distortions began to fly around. One of them was that the Schindlers were *devoutly Catholic*. Those were the exact words used by writer Joan Didion in a *New York Review of Books* article titled "The Case of Theresa Schiavo." She was wrong.

Besides me, I'd have to say that my sister-in-law Joan knew Terri best. She said on the subject of the Schindlers' religiosity, "The Schindlers never went to church on Sunday. They never even had a crucifix or statue in the house. Terri never spoke to me about religion. I'd put my life on the line that they were not religious people at all."

Even though she never exercised, Terri had continued to lose weight throughout our engagement, and I never thought to ask if she was on any sort of diet plan. I do recall that when she had her last fitting for her wedding dress, my mother went with her and was surprised to learn that Terri had dropped more weight in the three months between her first fitting and that one. Mom said she was down to a size 10 or 12 and the dress was now way too big for her, and it was too late to get it fixed. She had no choice but to wear it, and in some of our album pictures you can see that the dress was just floating on her.

Finally, the wedding day arrived. We'd planned a morning ceremony at the nearby Catholic church. It rained early that morning, but by the time the guests began to arrive, the sun had come out and it was turning into a beautiful day. There were two-hundred-fifty invited guests, and the church was full. When the time for the ceremony arrived, my brother Steve, who was best man, and I were led out to the pulpit with the priest. We stood there watching the bridesmaids walk down the aisle. As the last one got to the altar, Terri and her father came through the doors. I was stunned. Terri was breathtaking; she was absolutely beautiful, wearing a white gown, and instead of a traditional veil had chosen a fashionable hat for herself and each of her attendants.

One of the things that puzzled me about the ceremony was that Terri had felt obligated to choose her sister Suzanne as maid of honor. Terri and Suzanne were not close. Suzanne was eight years younger than Terri and was Mrs. Schindler's baby. It was Joan who explained to me that Terri asked her kid sister to be maid of honor because she said it was the right thing to do, which probably means she thought it would make her mother happy.

What I prefer to remember about the wedding is how happy Terri was. I can distinctly remember her smile as she came down the aisle; it was big as life itself. At last we were married; we danced and partied for hours afterward. The next day we went to Florida on our honeymoon, staying at the Schindlers' condo in St. Petersburg, taking day trips to Disney World and around the islands.

We spent a lot of time together by the pool, watching the incredible sunsets over the Gulf of Mexico. It was the first time in Terri's entire life that she had worn a two-piece. She was so proud of the fact that she'd lost so much weight for the wedding, and I was happy for her. After a week in the sun, we returned to Huntingdon Valley, Pennsylvania, and moved into the apartment that we'd rented, around the corner from her parents.

Everything was great, but Terri and I hated living in cold weather and were ready for a permanent change. A weeklong Florida vacation in the wintertime just wasn't going to do it. On top of that, I wasn't happy with my job. I was working long hours and not making much money, so it seemed like a good time to do what we'd actually discussed before we got married—move to Florida.

When we discussed this with the Schindlers, they offered us the use of their St. Petersburg condo if we wanted to make the move. It didn't take long for us to take them up on the offer. We broke our lease at the apartment and temporarily moved into the Schindlers' basement until we could complete arrangements for the move—about three or four months.

Around the same time, Terri's father was having difficulties at the industrial equipment company he co-owned. He was staying home from work a lot, which was very odd for him, and he ultimately acknowledged that he sold his equity in the firm.

The upshot of all this was that the Schindlers also decided to move to Florida, but it would take them longer to execute the plan. They had a house to sell and a lot more stuff to pack than we did.

All the Schiavos gave us a surprise going-away party, which turned into a very emotional event. Terri had become so close to my family and she knew she'd miss them terribly—especially Joan. The two women promised to stay in close touch. In Schiavo-speak, that meant they'd talk on the phone at least once a day—maybe more.

When the day finally came to leave, we packed our new car with clothes and personal items, and headed south on I-95. It was a long drive, and Terri did most of it. She loved to drive. The trip gave us lots of time to talk about our future together, and one of the major topics was having children. Terri loved kids and wanted to have a houseful, but we were both realistic. We had to get established financially, so we agreed to wait at least five years before starting a family.

As soon as we settled into the condo, I began looking for a job. Because of my experience in the restaurant business, it didn't take me long to find something. Terri, on the other hand, was having a problem finding work, and it depressed her. There's not much to do when you don't have a lot of money and your husband takes your only car to work.

One of the bright spots about living in Florida is that there's usually no shortage of visitors from the North. Terri loved when we had company, but once they left, she'd slip back into her depression. At some point, she received a bequest from her grandmother's estate, and we decided that the most sensible thing to do would be to use it to buy a second car, an Olds Cutlass. It would give Terri more flexibility in looking for a job.

She applied at a Prudential Insurance branch nearby, and since she'd worked for the company in Philadelphia, they accepted her as a transfer. It didn't take long for the old Terri to come back. The job gave her a renewed sense of self-worth, as she had the opportunity to meet and make new friends.

A few months later, Mr. and Mrs. Schindler, along with Bobby and Suzanne, moved to Florida, renting a three-story townhome in the upscale community of Tierra Verde, not far from where we lived. While I was working evenings, Terri spent time with her family—at the pool, going out to dinner, and hanging out at a local hotel where the Schindlers had a longtime friend who had a pool and lounge membership. With both of us happy, family nearby, and two incomes, Terri and I began talking about moving up the timetable for having children.

That's when reality struck. Mr. Schindler had not worked since moving to Florida. The family was living off the money he'd received from the buyout of his share of the equipment business, but the money was running out and they could no longer afford to live in the style they'd grown accustomed to. The end result was that they had to give up the fancy townhome. Their solution was to move into the condo that they owned, the one that Terri and I had been living in.

The timing wasn't great, because I was in the middle of changing jobs again, so money was tight and both of us were worried about it. The fact is that this kind of job-switching is normal for the restaurant business. As soon as you get a job, you begin looking for a better one, something higher up the food chain. I finally took a job at Agostino's, a well-known, upscale restaurant owned by a family, not a huge corporation. We were both excited about it because it was the best paying job I'd ever had. Starting a family was now possible.

This made Terri incredibly happy; she couldn't wait to become a mother. It was a constant topic of conversation between her and Joan. What I didn't know right away, but she'd previously discussed with Joan, was that Terri had always had trouble with her menstrual periods. She was usually late and occasionally missed periods.

A couple years earlier, we'd gone back to Philadelphia for a wedding and everyone was pretty shocked at how much weight Terri had lost. It hadn't registered with me, because I saw her every day. But when you haven't seen someone for a long time, it has an impact. As Joan described it, "I expected Terri to be thinner, because she'd told me that she'd lost weight, but when she got here, I looked at her and asked if she was all right. She was sickly thin. Her color didn't look good, her cheeks were sunken. She'd lost some hair and her fingernails were somewhat discolored. All she said was, 'I'm fine.' And she'd change the subject.

"At the time I was pregnant with my third child, Tommy, but nobody in the family knew it yet. I hadn't had any morning sickness with the other kids, but this time it got me. Terri and I had made plans to go to the mall the next morning, but when she called me to find out when I'd be ready to leave, I told her that I was sick to my stomach and felt like I was going to throw up.

"She said, 'Why don't you put your finger down your throat like I do when I'm sick to my stomach? I feel so much better when I stick my finger down my throat and throw up.' "

Joan never repeated that story until after Terri's death. When she originally had that conversation, it never dawned on her that Terri had an eating disorder. "You hear about eating disorders, throwing up, bingeing, but you never think someone that you know is doing it. And I never put it together," Joan said. "I was worried about her because she was so thin."

My aunt, Carol Schiavo, actually suspected that Terri had bulimia as early as 1986. She told Terri that she was getting too thin, that she was a beautiful girl, but she had to stop losing weight. But what convinced her that Terri had a problem was what occurred at a big family dinner at a restaurant. Aunt Carol said, "We ate soup to nuts; appetizers through desserts and drinks. And Terri went in the bathroom and threw up. I didn't see it, but when she came back, she was gray and she was sweating and she was not well. I said to my husband, 'She's been sick,' and he said, 'Maybe she got a bad shrimp.' We kind of blew it off. But I always had in the back of my mind that this child wants to be thin so bad, she won't eat. I didn't want to be the old fart buttinski aunt; I didn't want to be the nag."

In any event, we continued trying to get pregnant, and also decided that we wanted to move to a larger place in a new apartment complex down the road from where we were living. We agreed on a great apartment with vaulted ceilings. The only downside was that it was on the fourth floor, and there was no elevator.

I was finally in a job that I really liked. The difficulty for the two of us was that I worked nights as the dining room manager and Terri worked days for Prudential. It meant that we didn't get to spend a whole lot of time with each other during the week, although we talked on the phone an awful lot. Nevertheless, we really began trying to have a baby.

After the first month, Terri missed her period and I got very excited. But Terri told me that her period was usually late, so we waited. Time passed, and still no period. We purchased a home pregnancy test. That had to have been the longest three minutes in the world. The test was negative and Terri was devastated. She never did get her period that month. It never crossed my mind, or apparently hers, that her loss of weight might have something to do with her irregular periods. I remembered hearing a story about Olympic gymnasts being so thin, having so little body fat, that they never got periods—but that's not something you connect with your own wife.

The next month, we tried again with the same results. That's when Terri decided that she should see a doctor. We belonged to an HMO, and Terri had to see her primary care physician, Dr. Joel S. Prawer, for a referral to a gynecologist.

He sent her to see Dr. G. Stephen Igel, who asked her if she had any bleeding at all in the past month. She told him that she'd only had a spot or two of blood. The doctor advised her that the spotting had been her period, and told her not to worry about it. He did a pelvic exam, apparently found nothing abnormal, and that was the end of the visit. Neither doctor took a complete medical history; neither asked her about her weight loss.

Month after month for about a year we had the same experience. Terri had once thought she'd be a mom by this time, and the fact that we were making no progress was depressing. She discussed it with her doctor, and at one point he suggested that maybe I should be tested. It wasn't male vanity that made me react negatively—well, maybe a little bit—to the suggestion, just common sense. If she's not getting her period, she's not going to get pregnant. Solve that problem first, and then let's see what happens.

On Friday, February 23, 1990, we talked about the situation and decided that it was time to seek the advice of another physician. We agreed that on Monday she'd take a look at the HMO's listing of member practitioners and choose one. On Saturday, I went to work as usual, and Terri went to get her hair cut, and then went out with her parents for an Italian dinner. When she got home she called to tell me that she couldn't wait for me to see her new hairstyle. It was a busy night, so after telling me that she was going to iron Bobby's pants, we said good-bye and hung up.

Around nine o'clock, Terri called Joan in Philadelphia, excited about her new hairstyle. It was their last conversation ever.

2 | Terri's Coming Home

As darkness gave way to twilight, the streets were still empty on this Sunday morning, but the ambulance carrying Terri to Humana North-side Hospital was lit up like a Christmas tree, and the driver leaned on the siren. Other than telling me to hang on, I don't recall him saying much. There was this little window between the cab and the back, and I tried looking through it to see what they were doing. At one point one of the guys in back shouted to the driver, "Slow down, I have to shock."

My mind was a jumbled mess. None of this made any sense whatsoever. Except for the problem with her periods, Terri was healthy. All sorts of things went through my head. Maybe she ate something when she was out with her folks last night. But that didn't make sense. Food poisoning makes you sick to your stomach—it doesn't make your heart stop. I couldn't figure out why she'd gotten out of bed.

All I knew at that point was that something was wrong with Terri, but we were on our way to the hospital, the doctors were going to fix her up, and I'd bring her home later in the day. It wasn't a denial of reality; it was just a reflection of my understanding of the situation at that moment. Since there was no reason that I knew of for her collapse, it had to be something that they could take care of quickly, and send us on our way.

The ride through the early morning St. Petersburg streets took about ten minutes. When we got there, they took Terri through the ambulance entrance and sent me around to the door that leads to the ER waiting room. It was empty—no one was even on duty at the little cubicles where the admitting clerks sit and gather information.

It was like any hospital waiting room you've ever been in: uncomfortable chairs, old magazines, and vending machines selling the usual stuff. I didn't sit; I paced. When someone from the hospital walked through, I asked if I could use a phone to call my folks, and she pointed to one on the information desk. Finishing the call to my dad in Pennsylvania, I looked out the double doors and saw Terri's parents walking up underneath the big canopy. I was in tears; they were both dry-eyed. Mary came up and started rubbing my back, saying it would be all right.

"Yeah, but they had to do CPR on her."

Mr. Schindler just wasn't getting it. He said, "She probably just fainted." I wasn't in the mood to argue with him. Truth is, I probably wasn't getting it either. It's amazing what your mind does. Even though I knew they did CPR, I knew they shocked her, some part of me was still saying, "They're going to fix her and I'll take her home."

Every so often I'd ask whether I could go back and see Terri. All the nurses would say was, "No. They're still working with her. The doctor will be out." After a while someone came and got me, and I went inside to give them whatever information they needed. I kept asking what was going on, and they just kept repeating the standard line, "Someone will be out in a little while to talk to you." Now that I'm in the medical field, I know that a statement like that under circumstances like these is not good news. If things are going well, a nurse will usually say, "She's okay," or "She's doing fine," or "She's stable." But when they don't say anything, it's bad.

After what seemed like hours I heard someone say, "Mr. Schiavo?" I turned around and ran up to him. We stood there facing each other and he told me that Terri was in very critical condition. She'd been shocked seven times before they got her heart beating and her blood pressure up. He said the next twenty-four hours would be touch-and-go. They had no idea why she ended up like this; they were doing further testing. I kept asking, "Is she gonna die?" And he kept saying that the next twenty-four hours were critical.

Tears were pouring out of my eyes, and I must have had this dumbfounded look on my face. "Why is this happening? Why are we here?"

Much, much later I learned that one of the reasons it was taking so long for them to transfer Terri to the cardiac care unit was that they were looking for evidence of physical abuse. Of course, they never found any. Let's be perfectly clear—there wasn't any to be found because there had been no abuse, but they looked, and they documented everything they did to rule it out. So we waited. I wasn't a heavy smoker, but that morning I must have smoked a pack of cigarettes.

I finally went over and sat down next to the Schindlers. Nothing was said, just complete silence while we waited for her to leave the ER. I'm not sure how long we sat there, but eventually they rolled her down this long corridor, almost to the other end of the building. Finally, they told me I could go in and see her.

I walked over to the bed, bent down, and if it was possible to get even more terrified than I'd been in the apartment, that's what I did. She needed a ventilator to breathe; she had IVs dripping into her; she had a monitor tracking her vital signs. It was unbelievable. I was living in this weird dream, one of those this-isn't-really-happening type of dreams.

After a while her admitting physician, Dr. Samir Shah, came in and asked me a bunch of questions: Was Terri dieting? Did she have any medical problems or unusual medical history? I told him she'd been back and forth to her obstetrician for about a year because she wasn't getting her period and they hadn't been able to figure out why, but other than that, Terri was healthy. He asked about medication she might be taking; just standard history. He told us they were still waiting for lab results and X-rays, and then he left.

A few minutes later a nurse came in and asked, "Do you want a priest?" Talk about a question that hits you like a sucker punch. I was crying my eyes out. Can you imagine being in a world that you just don't want to be in? "Why am I here? Why is Terri lying here? Am I dreaming?" A while later, a priest came in and I stood there with Mrs. Schindler while he administered last rites to my wife. When he finished, he shook my hand, said he was sorry, and "God bless." Mr. Schindler stayed outside.

During the last rites was when I first noticed Terri's new, short haircut. Throughout everything that had already happened that day, it hadn't registered at all.

It was all so unreal. We were both twenty-six-year-old kids. You come home one night and your wife says "Good night" and "I love you," the two of you kiss, and ten hours later there's a priest standing at her bedside giving her last rites. I didn't have a very good grasp of reality then. I still was thinking that I was going to be able to bring her home. She's here in the ER, they moved her to the ICU, she's sick, so they'll make her better. That's what they do in hospitals. It was a strange, strange world to be living in.

That marked the beginning of my camping in the ICU waiting room for sixteen days.

The waiting room was just outside the ICU, and there was a row of chairs up against one wall. The other side of that wall was Terri's room, and they pretty much let me go in and out whenever I wanted to. All we had were questions. No answers. They wanted to get her off the ventilator and breathing on her own. But they just kept testing her, evaluating her brain functions. Doctors would come up to me and tell me things, and I didn't know what the hell they were talking about.

If it's possible to have a surreal experience within an already surreal experience, it happened during Terri's second day in the hospital. Her sister Suzanne showed up all atwitter. She'd just gotten engaged and thought there was no reason not to share the news with her family members gathered around the bed where her sister lay in a coma, on a ventilator, and had been given last rites. Not only did she not have the decency to delay her engagement until she knew whether

her sister was going to live or die, she was quite indignant that the family wasn't prepared to leave the hospital and join her and her fiancé for a celebratory dinner. But after Suzanne talked to them about it, her parents *did* leave the hospital for that dinner after all. I'm sure that Terri would not have believed this.

At one point during those first few days, someone on the medical team mentioned anorexia. Then, when we were meeting with Dr. Shah a couple of days later, he said they believed Terri was a mild bulimic. She wasn't showing definite signs, because they usually have overdeveloped neck muscles from throwing up. Someone said that even as a family member I probably wouldn't have known that she was bulimic because it's a very secretive disease. It was in that first detailed conversation with Dr. Shah that we learned her potassium level was low.

They asked me if she'd been taking diuretics or laxatives, and I said she hadn't. I mentioned that she drank an awful lot of iced tea, maybe a gallon a day, but I was sure she wasn't taking any kind of diet drugs. They told me that bulimics often hide things. So Brian and I drove back to the apartment to search it just in case. We went through everything—her clothes, all her pockets, her shoes—everything I could think of. I went through her purses. Nothing. I even had the manager at work search her desk to see if maybe she was keeping something there. Still nothing.

A consulting gynecologist was called in and we discussed the fact that she'd been missing her periods. That's when I learned that amenorrhea could be an indicator of dozens of things, from bulimia to a brain tumor. But Terri's own doctors never checked this out properly, which is what eventually led to the malpractice suit that we filed against Doctors Prawer and Igel. It was during one of the conversations with doctors at Humana Northside when I remembered that Terri had had a bout of dizziness and almost fainted. We had been at Disney World with my brother Steve and his wife. When it happened, I thought it was because it was hot and we were in the middle of a crowd. Actually, Terri had little bouts of lightheadedness, but we'd always say it was because she stood up too fast. I suppose if we'd been walking around with a Bulimia Symptoms Checklist we might have figured out what was going on, but no one ever believes that someone they know has got an eating disorder, especially when you regularly see them eat a lot of food.

For about a week, maybe a little longer, Terri's eyes were completely closed. Then, one day, she opened them. I had just walked into her room and the nurse was there. She looked up as I came in, and seeing that I'd spotted Terri's eyes, she said, "Yeah, she just opened them."

My reaction was predictable. I thought *This is great,* and I began talking to Terri, thinking, *She's awake!* But all I got in response was the moan that we would become so accustomed to over time. I was still looking for signs of progress, however, and if I'd seen her hand move, or see her move an arm or leg, even a toe, or her head would turn, I'd get excited. But the doctors said that these movements weren't significant.

During the first couple of weeks following Terri's collapse, I spent all my time at the hospital. My brother Brian had come down from Philadelphia to be with me, and when he thought I was getting too ripe, he'd drive me home for a shower and a change of clothes; but I didn't want to be away from Terri for very long.

About two weeks into it, Mr. Schindler and Brian took me to a nearby restaurant with an outdoor bar, the Tiki Hut. I was very quiet, just kind of looking around, wanting to get back to the hospital because I felt as though I shouldn't leave Terri just in case something happened. I had a couple of beers and the two of them had something to eat. I'd been surviving on hospital cafeteria food, but didn't feel like eating. It was actually a gorgeous day to be sitting outside—sunny, cool breeze, watching the boats. It was a Sunday and they had a band. One of those winter days that reminds you why you live in Florida.

I was extremely depressed. I couldn't sleep. And if I did it was in a chair in the ICU waiting room. I got up to go to the bathroom, leaving Brian sitting with Mr. Schindler. When I got back, there was a strange look on Brian's face. I sort of gave him a "What's goin' on?" look, but he just shook his head very slightly. Later in the day when Brian and I were alone, he told me that Terri's father had said that I—me—needed to go out and get laid.

Terri spent about forty-five days in intensive care, and the news never got better. The neurologist caring for Terri, Dr. Garcia J. De-sousa, would always tell me that it's a waiting game, that we have to wait three months before we can come to any conclusions. Apparently, with a head injury, if there's no recovery within three months, then there isn't likely to be any. They're looking for a patient to do something, such as follow a verbal command. And Terri wasn't doing that.

While Dr. Desousa told me that we had to wait and see, he would tell Brian that Terri would never progress. Brian didn't tell me, of course, but later I learned that the doctor had told him on several occasions that the only thing she'd do was open her eyes.

If he had told me directly, I wouldn't have believed him. I would have said, "Nope, that's not the way it's going to be. I'm going to get my wife back. I'm going to bring her home and we're just going to get on with our lives." I'd see her hand move and I'd just live on that for days, maybe weeks.

I used to interpret things that Terri would do in the most positive light. I'd put my fingers in her hand, across her palm, and her hand would close around it. It's a primitive instinct; it's lower brain stem. If you do it with an infant, the baby will close its hand. And that's what Terri was doing. But I'd be calling people and saying, "Hey, look at her! Look at this! All right, Terri, keep going."

Or her eyes would open and she'd appear to be looking around and I'd think, *Hey, this is all right*. We'd try the "blink once for yes, twice for no" thing, and there'd be those moments when I'd say, "Gosh, look at that. She did it," and it would get me psyched to the point where I was going to bring her home and she was going to be my wife again. Nobody was going to tell me any different.

If you sat there for five minutes and told Terri to do something, and all of a sudden she did it, the reaction was, "Oh, my God, she's doing it." Sometimes if I got no response, people would say, "Well, you have to keep doing it for a while so she can complete the thought process. Slow down, repeat it a few times. Don't say, 'Terri, move your arm once; okay, now move your leg; okay now do this.'" They'd tell me to continue the same thing over and over again, one command at a time.

If you can understand how much I wanted to believe that my Terri was in there, but just temporarily locked up and unable to communicate with me, you can see why I would have interpreted every coincidental reflex as a cognitive response. Eventually, however, after years of no progress and doctors telling us that "this is all there is," I had to believe them. Perhaps if the Schindlers had gotten some help dealing with the grief and loss, they might have come to accept it, too.

Mrs. Schindler spent a lot of time at the hospital. In the early years, we would hang out together all the time. She used to tell me things like, "Terri loved you a lot. She knows you're doing the proper thing for her." She'd even tell me that Terri would do the same for me if I were the one who had gotten sick.

I was very angry at God, because nothing that was happening to us made any sense. I was angry with him for a very long time. Why did he do this? Why is this happening? What did I do? What did Terri do? I believe in God. If you were rating religiosity on a scale from one to ten, with ten being going to Mass every day, I guess I'd be about a five. I believe God is here with us, but I don't believe that you have to go worship in a certain place in order to talk to him, which is why I didn't go to church very often.

————

While Terri was still in the ICU we began talking about a malpractice suit against the two doctors Terri had been seeing before her collapse. It was my boss at Agostino's, attorney Dan Grieco, who first broached the subject, but he wasn't the right kind of lawyer to handle something like that. When the time came, he said he'd refer me to someone.

After about forty-five days, the doctors decided that Terri could be moved to a regular floor and out of intensive care. They'd been able to take her off the ventilator. Her condition was stable. Her blood work was fine and she had no heart problems. She was still getting some IV fluids but nothing serious.

She'd been in a coma for several weeks, and had finally come out of it. I used to think that coming out of a coma was all good news. I was wrong. Terri awoke to a vegetative state, not to a state of consciousness. Her eyes were now open—and that was it. But I didn't believe it.

The first time the nurses sat Terri up and I got to see her sitting there, I got all excited. Her eyes got really big, and her head went back. I thought she was doing great, that she was even hearing us. One afternoon they put her in a wheelchair and took her out the back door where I met them with Terri's two cats. We put the cats in her lap, and I would have bet anything that she was responding to them and knew that they were there. Her eyes seemed to get really big—but they did that all the time. She would hyperextend and her legs would go straight out. Later on I learned that that's what happens when you don't use your muscles for a while. It's almost as though they go into spasm. But that session with the cats was the highlight of my life. I said to one of the nurses, "Terri is waking up. I told you I was going to take her home." The nurses didn't argue with me, but looking back, I'm sure that they knew the reality of the situation. They could read an absolutely flat EEG. It didn't take a neurologist to infer the truth.

Once Terri was stable, hospital staff began rehabilitation therapy with her. They'd come in and stretch her arms and legs, and they made splints to keep her hands from closing. They always made sure she had Podus Boots on to try to prevent foot drop. But I knew that sooner or later Terri would have to be moved to a nursing home that specialized in rehabilitation therapy.

I'd discovered that Prudential Insurance, which was paying for her health care, would regularly send a nurse around to find out what was being done, and what Terri's prognosis was. What the nurse learned was that the doctors didn't believe she was going to recover, and therefore, even though her insurance policy entitled her to three months of rehabilitation, Prudential didn't want to authorize it. What that meant was that I had to find a nursing home to move her to while I continued the fight for rehab.

On May 12, 1990, after ten weeks at Humana Northside Hospital, we moved Terri by ambulance to College Harbor, a skilled nursing home in St. Pete. While she'd been taken off the ventilator, she still had a trach collar on, which meant that she was getting oxygen directly through an opening cut into her neck, and not primarily by breathing in and out through her nose or mouth. Constant suctioning was essential because she generated a lot of mucous. She still had a catheter in her bladder, and of course she was being fed through a PEG tube—that's short for percutaneous (through the skin) endoscopic gastrotomy—that allowed them to feed liquid nutrients directly into Terri's stomach.

All the time I was off work staying with Terri, my paychecks from the restaurant continued, and eventually, Dan Grieco did as he had promised, and began helping us plan the initial legal moves that were essential. The first thing he did was tell us that we needed to file a guardianship petition so that I'd have the legal right to make all decisions for Terri. As the husband, I was able to approve her health-care treatment, but guardianship gave me power of attorney for her. Getting guardianship of another person means that you become that person. You are her mind and body. You speak for her legally.

Dan drew up the petition and we went before a judge. The court appointed a guardian *ad litem* to take Terri's side, but that person really doesn't do much in a case such as this. There was one court hearing, and on June 18, the court officially appointed me guardian.

The Schindlers, who would contest my guardianship a few years later, never voiced any objection. They knew I was the one who had to be guardian. They didn't even come to the hearing in court.

While she was at College Harbor, I used to spend twelve to fourteen hours a day with her, making sure they got her out of bed and sitting up in a chair; making sure she was getting her therapy; just being a very good watchdog. Prudential had taken the position that the doctors said rehabilitation therapy would do Terri no good, and they'd refused to authorize her transfer to a facility that specialized in that sort of thing. That's when I made my first contacts with the media.

I launched a media campaign to embarrass Prudential into paying for rehab by contacting the consumer help reporter at one of the local television stations. They came out and shot video of Terri sitting in a wheelchair, and if I recall correctly, that got one of the newspapers to cover the story. Our story was very simple: Terri had benefits coming that should pay for ninety days of rehab and Prudential was saying that they wouldn't pay because they didn't think she'd benefit from it. It was more than a bit uncomfortable because Prudential was the company she had worked for.

It's ironic that years later, I'd learn that Prudential's decision had been correct. Their medical people had looked at Terri's test results and knew that no amount of rehab would make a difference. However, when you know that their primary interest as an insurer is saving money, every decision they make on a claim is suspect. And that's the angle that the media readily accepted.

On June 30, after Prudential finally agreed to pay for rehab, we moved Terri to Bayfront Rehabilitation Center in St. Pete for intensive work. The rehab center is part of Bayfront Hospital. It's much more than a skilled-care nursing home where all they do is maintain a patient who needs special medical services. This was continuous rehab, all day long, under the supervision of Dr. David Baras, a physiatrist. Just moving her to Bayfront was a shot in the arm for me. I was still convinced that I'd be bringing Terri home.

About three or four months after her collapse, I had returned to work at Agostino's part-time. Early one evening at the restaurant, maybe about six o'clock, I got a call from the doctor. "We've got good news," he said. I thought that Terri had spoken, or responded in some positive way, and I was getting excited. Then he said, "We got her trach out."

It scared the hell out of me, and I started bawling. Tears were just pouring from my eyes and I was sobbing right in the middle of the restaurant. Dr. Baras asked, "What's wrong?"

And I said, "I'm afraid."

"Of what?" he responded.

"You took her trach out and I'm afraid she's not going to be able to breathe."

He reassured me that Terri was doing just fine. To me, it meant the world. It was the biggest milestone she'd achieved. The trach was something she had needed to help her breathe. They had put the collar around her neck and tons of mucous came out. They were always sticking tubes down her trach and sucking out that mucous. She'd cough and she'd gag—it would always make her gag.

The next morning, I walked into her room at Bayfront with raised expectations. Sure, it was foolish of me to think that just taking the trach out would really change her, but when you're looking for a sign—anything—that confirms your belief that she's getting better, you grab onto anything. For whatever reason, my expectation when I entered her room was that she'd be more aware; but she was the same. The only observable difference was that she had a little bandage over the hole in her neck to keep the wound clean until it closed naturally.

It was while Terri was at Bayfront that I had my first conversations with the attorneys who would ultimately file the malpractice suit against Doctors Prawer and Igel. My boss at Agostino's referred me to Glenn Woodworth, an attorney in St. Petersburg with a medical liability trial practice. Glenn brought in his partner at the time, Roland Lamb, and ultimately a Miami litigator named Gary Fox. I remember them telling me that it was a hard case, but they would have to review all the records before they could figure out what they believe would happen.

That meeting was very upsetting, and I broke down. Only a few months had passed since Terri's collapse, and I was feeling as though life had become one big battle. Everything was a fight, and I was filled with a lot of anger. I was especially angry with her doctor. I wanted to find out what happened, why he didn't treat her. Why didn't he notice the gynecological problems that were discovered in the hospital? It turned out that he had prescribed this cream for her to use and it literally burned her internally—she was all inflamed from it. At that point I was interested in finding out why this had happened to Terri and punishing both her doctors for not preventing it.

3 | Rehab

In the fall of 1990, about eight months after Terri collapsed, one of my cousins told me about an experimental program at the University of California at San Francisco Hospital that sounded as though it might help Terri. I contacted the doctor in charge, a neurologist named Yoshio Hosobuchi, and after he reviewed Terri's records, he said that she was definitely a candidate for his program.

Since the program was still experimental, there would be no cost for the procedure and follow-up care. However, we had to get Terri to San Francisco, and in her condition, that would prove to be expensive. We needed to raise at least $20,000, and I began working hard to do it. The resident association in our apartment complex raised some money at a dance, and I worked a deal that got us the loan of a hot dog stand on St. Pete Beach. For several weeks, my friends and I sold food and drinks to raise money for Terri. We got some publicity on local television, and that helped. It's worth mentioning, because of what eventually happened later; that while I was fund-raising by selling hot dogs on the beach, the only Schindler who ever showed up to help was Terri's mom. Suzanne was away at school, but neither Mr. Schindler nor Bobby could spare the time to help me raise money—or offered any—for Terri's care.

In November, I took Terri to San Francisco. The trip was extremely difficult, because we flew on a commercial airline with Terri on a stretcher. I had to buy four first-class tickets, one for me and another for the special nurse I'd hired to help. The airline removed two seats from the first-class section to accommodate Terri. We flew from Tampa to Minneapolis, where we had a long layover before going on to San Francisco.

Dr. Hosobuchi implanted a three-and-a-half-inch-long electronic lead into the thalamus in Terri's brain through a hole drilled in her skull. However, contrary to what I thought was his early enthusiasm, he wasn't terribly optimistic that it would help because her EEG showed minimal brain activity. We needed to stay in California for more than two months in order for the researchers to track whether adjustments in the strength of the electrical stimulus was having a positive effect on her brain cells. For me, it meant helping the paid staff care for her 24/7, and after a month, I was emotionally drained and physically exhausted.

I called Mrs. Schindler and asked if she could fly out to California to help me care for Terri, telling her that there was money left over in the fund-raising proceeds to pay for the plane ticket. For a woman who would spend years telling the world how much she wanted the opportunity to be a loving parent until Terri died naturally, the answer I got was shocking. She said she couldn't come, because there would be no one to take care of Terri's father.

I later learned that during that time Mrs. Schindler managed to take two weeks to help Suzanne move to Virginia with her new husband. Years later, in a sworn deposition, Mary Schindler would say that the reason she couldn't come to California was that she didn't have the money. In the same deposition, she acknowledged taking the trip to Virginia.

On January 29, 1991, I brought Terri back to Florida from California and after a few weeks of her living at home with us, had her admitted to Mediplex Rehab in Bradenton. Mediplex was accredited by the Commission on Accreditation of Rehabilitation Facilities for the comprehensive treatment of brain injury. It was the best rehab facility in our area, and it had a reputation as a very caring place.

Her admitting diagnosis was "Anoxia, secondary to Cardiac Arrest," which meant that her brain had been deprived of an adequate supply of oxygen for a devastatingly long time. The psychosocial history that was prepared for the staff members who would be treating Terri said, "The purpose of her admission is for Terri to be provided with an extensive rehabilitation program to potentiate any possible increase in functional and/or cognitive abilities. She is currently best described as a Level II–III on the Rancho Los Amigos scale of cognitive function."

That's medical-speak. What they told me in plain English was that they're going to do the best they could to see about bringing her to a higher level. But my desire to have Terri get better put a subconscious spin on what they'd said. What I heard was, "When Terri leaves Mediplex, she'll be talking to you."

At the time I was evaluating the situation as: *We've got the stimulator in her and it's going to work. She's going to be able to start responding to us. She's going to talk to me and I'll be able to bring her home, and we'll be together. Yes, she'll have a handicap, but she'll have her life back.*

Why shouldn't I think that way? Nobody ever told me anything different. What they told me was, "We'll *try.*" They didn't say "We *will.*" But it's how I heard it that gave me hope. They weren't the ones giving me undue hope. Now that I'm in the medical field, I understand it much better. M.D.s are trained to give you the worst scenario, not the best. In case nothing good happens, they're covered. But if things go well, hey, that's wonderful.

But let's look at reality. On admission to Mediplex, they said she was a Level II–III on the Rancho Los Amigos scale. This is a tool that was developed in 1972, and is widely used in this country. The scale ranges from Level I, where the patient shows no response and "appears to be in a deep sleep and is completely unresponsive to any stimuli," to Level VIII, where the patient's response is purposeful and appropriate. A Level VIII patient is "alert and oriented, able to recall and integrate past and recent events, and is aware of, and responsive to, his culture."

The admitting assessment evaluated Terri at somewhere between Level II and III. A Level II patient "reacts inconsistently and non-purposefully to stimuli in a non-specific manner. Responses are limited in nature and are often the same regardless of stimulus presented. Responses may be physiological changes, gross body movements, and/or vocalization. Often the earliest response is to deep pain. Responses are likely to be delayed."

A Level III patient has localized responses. "Patient reacts specifically, but inconsistently, to stimuli. Responses are directly related to the type of stimulus presented as in turning head toward a sound or focusing on an object presented. The patient may withdraw an extremity and/or vocalize when presented with a painful stimulus. He may follow simple commands in an inconsistent, delayed manner such as closing his eyes, squeezing or extending an extremity. Once external stimuli is removed, he may lie quietly. He may also show a vague awareness of self and body by responding to discomfort by pulling at nasogastric tube or catheter or resisting restraints. He may show a bias toward responding to some persons (especially family, friends) but not to others."

Terri's admitting history says that she was "currently non-ambulatory, non-verbal, opens her eyes to voice and appears to have a limited tracking ability. She appears to focus her eyes upon objects placed within her environment by her family for short periods of time. She is incontinent of bowel and bladder and has a gastrostomy tube for nutrition, hydration and ordered medications. She has bilateral foot drop and no apparent functional/purposeful movement of her extremities. She is able to turn her head towards sound."

That was just what they saw. That was their first impression of Terri. If you went into the room and you made a clucking noise, Terri's head would turn toward it. If you kept doing it but on the other side of the bed, Terri would still look in the other direction.

The records say, "Brain stem responses normal, showing auditory reception by brain stem." I learned that it meant her brain stem still had reflexes. Her ears worked, but since she had no way to understand what her ears were hearing because that part of her brain was damaged and eventually replaced with spinal fluid, she didn't really *hear*. If you walked into her room and clapped your hands loudly, she had a startle response. She may even have turned her head toward the sound. She would do the same thing on a very random basis with human voices. But she wasn't *hearing*. It was a reflex—just like blinking her eyes was a reflex. She had no idea what she was turning her head toward—or why.

The extensive history taken upon admission to Mediplex and included in Terri's records is based on interviews with Terri's mom and me. In the section on "Mental/Physical Health," it says, "Mary describes Terri as being 'always a quietly, happy person until she got thin then she came out of her shell.' Terri weighed 250 pounds when she graduated from high school. She went on the NutriSystem diet and lost 75 pounds initially then continued to lose down to the 126 pounds at the time of her cardiac arrest. There was a question raised as to whether Terri had been anorexic at the time of the cardiac arrest as Terri had a subtherapeutic Potassium level, which may have precipitated ventricular fibrillation resulting in the cardiac arrest. Mike denies Terri was anorexic but Mary Schindler feels there was a strong possibility that Terri was, in fact, Bulimic as opposed to Anorexic. (Mike does not agree with this.)"

Years later, when I was confronted with a list of symptoms and behavior patterns of bulimic patients—not even considering the potassium issue—I would change my position. I came to believe that Terri had suffered from this insidious eating disorder. As you can see from the comments written by our case manager at Mediplex, Mary Schindler was fairly convinced that Terri was bulimic. She'd done enough research about eating disorders to know and understand the differences between anorexia nervosa and bulimia. Mary's belief that Terri was bulimic was apparently nothing new. In going through

Terri's medical records, we found a consultation report from her time at Bayfront Rehabilitation Center, dated June 29, 1990, prepared by Dr. Felix Hernandez. Under "history of present illness," the doctor writes, ". . . the charge nurse today tells me that her mother had mentioned that she was bulimic and apparently aspirated on purging herself being the cause of her anoxia. This has not been confirmed by hospital records."

Ultimately, when it was strategically important for the Schindlers' case, Mary would somehow manage to forget that she'd ever gone on record as saying that Terri was bulimic.

Under "Family Expectations/Discharge Plans" the report reads, "Mike states 'I don't know right now what I want, right now I just want her to get better.' Mary states, 'I just want her to get better and we'll take it from there—to know me again. We'll take her home, ultimately.' "

The senior case manager writing the evaluation, Toni Luzier, a certified rehabilitation registered nurse (CRRN), notes, "Since the family has previously attempted (unsuccessfully) to care for Terri in the home setting, a question comes to mind as what would be different for them now."

She concludes, "Mike and Mary are involved, supportive and appear loving and very patiently caring . . . Length of stay is undetermined at this time pending Terri's response to her program and the Team's recommendations to her family. Projection is for a three month evaluation period."

Six weeks later, the summary prepared for the period from February 15 to March 15, 1991, appears neutral. The summary says that she was medically stable, that the implant stimulator continued on an 8 A.M. to 8 P.M. regimen, and that therapy continued on a 5½-day-per-week basis.

Because the Mediplex records provide the most objective and easy to understand glimpse at Terri's condition over a specific time period, I want to try to show how this sort of care worked with her, how she responded to it, and how I responded to it. Mediplex documented everything.

Let's start with the physical therapy department for that mid-February to mid-March period. "Terri continues physical therapy five times each week for 60-minute sessions for passive range of motion, techniques for tone reduction to include rocking and prone lying, tilt table, kneeling and prone lying for weight bearing activities, and sensory stimulation to increase environmental awareness. She is showing no active, functional movement. All active movement has been reflexive . . . We have seen no significant change in her cognitive status although she is awake during the sessions at this time."

A few weeks later, there was another report. "Terri has been seen five times a week for individual therapy sessions focusing on eliciting localized responses, following commands and yes/no communication development. Sensory stimulation has been presented. . . . No functional changes have been noted with her responses elicited from sensory stimulation. Responses to verbal and written commands continue to be very limited . . . and yes/no has not been established due to her lack of response to commands/volitional movements."

Psychology services filed a detailed report, concluding, "Overall her general responsiveness score increased slightly from 19 to 23, but she remains at a Rancho Level II. These scores indicate a need for sensory stimulation programming and this is being developed."

The therapeutic recreation department reported seeing Terri five times a week for thirty-minute one-on-one sessions. She also was taken to a quadriplegic rugby match and to the beach, but she didn't cognitively react at either outing.

A month later, following evaluation of the mid-March to mid-April summary, I attended a conference to review Terri's treatment plan with the heads of each of the disciplines at Mediplex. There I was, sitting at a long conference table in a small room, feeling as though I was the only one on Terri's side. They'd prepared a printed summary of her latest evaluations. The treatment focus was not encouraging: "Reduce

level of therapy as appropriate, continue scheduled stimulator program, monitor/evaluate any functional/cognitive gains for increase
in therapy regimen." More ominous was the brief comment under
"Length of Stay." It said, "pending family meeting with administration."

Dr. Eugene Alcazaren, the director of Physical Medicine and Rehabilitation Services, opened the session by reporting on a conversation with Dr. Charles Yingling in San Francisco about the implanted
stimulation unit and the belief that it had produced no changes in
Terri's brain activity.

With respect to the Mediplex regimen, Alcazaren said that "If a
patient doesn't progress in ninety days then we recommend step-
down care, continued nursing care, and look at long term options, i.e.:
extended care or home. We have not established a consistent pattern
of awareness."

I didn't like what I was hearing, and asked, "What are we saying
here?" I was very angry. I wanted them to do more, but was getting
the sense that they were just giving up on her. I didn't want that to
happen. I wanted them to keep her there, even if they had to put her
in the Medicare wing.

According to the minutes of the meeting, Dr. Alcazaren responded,
"Due to no functional improvements, three hours of therapy is not
appropriate and it is time to decrease therapy time."

At which point, Dr. Peter Kaplan, the staff psychologist—who I'd
actually been seeing privately—asked me, "What is your idea of what
active therapy does for a patient?"

I had a one-word answer: Improvement.

Dr. Kaplan came back with his explanation: "There's no rule to say
when we say 'no more therapy'—also no evidence that not giving therapy decreases the possibility of recovery. Spontaneous evidence of an
improvement would lead to increasing her therapy to potentiate it."

Dr. Alcazaren responded, "If we'd started this rehab two to three
months post injury and not a year later, we would be less pessimistic at
this time."

None of this was what I wanted to hear. I'd put my hope and faith in Mediplex's reputation and ability to help heal patients like Terri. Now they sounded as though they were ready to dump her overboard. I said, "I don't want her to tighten up. Nursing can keep her loosened, work on her range of motion. Terri is my wife."

And Dr. Alcazaren came back, "We understand this and your need to fight for her. We can't feel your feelings, but we have to do what we must. There's no saying she won't improve. Now she needs good care."

Then the rep from physical therapy summarized Terri's condition: "All movement seen is reflexive versus active movement," and occupational therapy piled on, "No local response or purposeful movement." It continued this way through each of the other departments, finally coming back to the boss, Dr. Alcazaren, who said, "She needs good nursing care, closer to home maybe. Now we need to look at turning over care more to nursing. . . . Her length of stay is between you and the administration."

I managed to delay Terri's removal from Mediplex until July 19. Three days earlier, her discharge summary was prepared. It wasn't encouraging:

"Despite a full post coma therapy regimen and daily application of the stimulator, there has been little change noted cognitively or functionally. Terri does make an occasional sound but this appears to be random. She does have a regular sleep-wake cycle and will open her eyes when her name is called and appears to momentarily focus. It would appear that she turns to sound. She startles to loud noise and despite all efforts, no communication system has been established. Terri is best described as a Rancho II–III at this time but does not, even inconsistently, respond to commands.

"There is an ongoing need for family counseling to assist them in their adjustment to the implications of Terri's devastating incident upon her, as well as their, lives." And that was that at Mediplex.

The final meeting ended very abruptly. I'd managed to stay in my chair, because I'd learned from experience that some people see a very loud, pissed-off six-foot-six-inch guy as threatening. Mrs. Schindler hadn't said anything at all during the session, but as it ended I remember her telling me to be calm. Dr. Kaplan remained after the others left and I probably took some of my anger out on him, even though he's the one person who I was sure really wanted to help me deal with all this. All that was going through my mind was, *Don't sit there and tell me you can't do something better for my wife!*

I include this technical detail about Terri's time at Mediplex because I want you to have the raw truth. Why? Because twelve years later Sara Mele, a speech pathologist at the Rehabilitation Institute of Chicago, who was supportive of the Schindlers, would claim to use these same Mediplex records to swear in an affidavit that, "Based on my experience and my observations, Mrs. Schiavo is clearly aware of her environment and interacts with it, albeit inconsistently. She is able to comprehend spoken language, and can, at least inconsistently, follow simple one-step commands. This is documented . . . in the Mediplex records. . . ." *Comprehend spoken language? My wife Terri?*

The closest this licensed medical professional got to Terri's room in Florida was Chicago's Near North Side. Mele was one among several other long-distance diagnosticians who later would play a significant role in this case.

The Mediplex people were good people who could see things that I couldn't or wouldn't see. They saw the truth at the end; I didn't see it yet. Yes, in their initial evaluation of Terri they thought they saw potential; they really did. But as time went on, as they worked extensively with Terri, they knew.

While I was fighting like crazy for Terri, I was also fighting my own demons. I was depressed, angry, and lonely. I missed Terri. What it came down to was that I didn't like my life and I wanted to die. That's why it was a good thing that I'd accepted the offer to see the staff psychologist, Dr. Kaplan. I'd never felt this way before in my entire life. If you had asked me back then whether I was suicidal, I might have said yes.

I guess I was in bad enough shape during the Mediplex months that

Dr. Kaplan became concerned about me. He kept asking me all the time if I was going to hurt myself and I kept telling him, "No, I don't want to hurt myself; I just don't want to be here." There's a big difference. You just don't want to be in this world; you don't want to be in this situation. I'd rather just be dead—but that didn't mean I wanted to kill myself.

Depression is a scary thing. I've had bouts with it for fifteen years, ever since Terri collapsed. I honestly don't think I'd be normal if I weren't depressed under these circumstances, but I was never as depressed as I was when Terri was being shoved out of Mediplex. I felt like I was in this big black hole, and it just kept getting deeper and deeper and deeper. I didn't know how to handle it.

The records at Mediplex acknowledge that Mary Schindler and I were regular visitors for the six months Terri was there. There's one reference in those records to Suzanne, Terri's sister, but nowhere is there any mention of either Bob Schindler, Sr., or Bobby, Jr., ever making an appearance, attending an evaluation, or participating in a staff/family conference in the six and a half months between her admission at the end of January to her discharge in the middle of July. Of course this was well before television cameras were posed outside a medical facility to record the comings and goings of the Schindler family.

While Terri was at Mediplex, my attorneys continued their research into whether Terri's condition could have been prevented by the doctors who had been seeing her prior to the collapse, or whether they'd committed malpractice. In late April, a Washington, D.C., specialist in reproductive medicine evaluated Terri's outpatient records, the emergency department records, some inpatient records as well as the appropriate literature, and concluded that the care provided to my wife had been substandard.

He wrote, "Basically, Mrs. Schiavo had developed unusual and probably non-nutritious eating habits stemming from her desire to control her teenage obesity. During the course of her HMO care, she developed two symptom complexes that should have prompted evaluation of her nutritional and fluid and electrolyte status. Namely, she complained of lightheadedness and 'near-fainting' to her family practice doctor and she complained of irregularity of her menstrual cycle and involuntary sterility to her gynecologist.

"I feel very strongly that standard care would have discovered the chronic nutritional imbalance long before her devastating cardiac arrhythmia and brain injury."

I'm not a lawyer, but when I read that, I thought, "Finally, someone will be held accountable. This should not have happened to Terri." What I didn't know at the time was that the doctor who wrote that letter allegedly had less than a pristine reputation when it came to providing testimony upon which a case could be based. Despite the fact that the letter sounds like good news, it played right into the anger and depression I was experiencing at that time.

The HMO was supposed to have assembled a list of qualified medical doctors in a variety of specialties, any of whom should have been able to provide care that at least met a standard of practice. Terri chose her doctors from the list the HMO provided; she wasn't supposed to research their backgrounds and qualifications, the HMO was. The HMO gave the doctors its seal of approval. It was much later that I learned that the ob-gyn she'd chosen from the HMO list went to medical school in Spain because he wasn't accepted by any U.S. medical school, and he'd tried and failed twice to pass the exams that would make him a board-certified obstetrician and gynecologist. Other than that, no problem.

What that consulting doctor's letter said to me was that if I expected Terri to recover, it was my job to question every medical decision that was made. It was my job to educate myself so that I could evaluate the answers that I got. It had probably been floating around in my head for some time that I wanted to get into the medical field as a career because I felt it would help me help Terri. It wasn't long after I read the letter that I decided to take the first step and get trained as an EMT—an emergency medical technician—and ultimately become a registered nurse.

On July 19, 1991, we transferred Terri to the Sabal Palms Health Care Center in Largo, which was considerably closer to where we lived. I wasn't going to give up on her, and I felt that even though it wasn't a certified rehabilitation facility like Mediplex, Sabal Palms was equipped to continue aggressive therapy aimed at helping me get Terri back.

While all this sounds as though I was dealing with Terri as if I were a medical technician on autopilot, the truth was it was tearing me up inside. I couldn't get past the anguish I felt; I didn't feel it was right to try to live the normal life of a guy in his late twenties while the woman I loved was bedridden in an institution that was filled almost entirely with old people at the end of their days. It had been a year and a half since her collapse, and I had done nothing but try and care for her. And I missed everything about her. I missed the way she smelled; I missed the back scratches; I missed the way she would sit with the cats; I missed slipping into bed with her when I came home from work late and just spooning. I just missed her whole being, and it felt as though there was a hole in my soul because she was gone.

I'd gotten some help from the psychologist at Mediplex but didn't consider continuing with therapy. I thought that I should be able to deal with things by myself. So when I wasn't with Terri, I'd sit in my bedroom alone, knowing that however bad I felt, Terri felt worse.

If you've ever visited a nursing home, odds are you've seen lots of patients spending most of their waking hours in bed. That's not what I wanted for Terri. My instructions were that she was to be up, out of bed, dressed nicely, with her hair done. I'd learned by then how to apply the makeup she used, and I'd gone shopping at The Limited for her clothes. In short, she was to be treated with dignity like a sentient human being, not as though she was unaware of herself and her surroundings.

Let me say a word about what, admittedly, seems a bit strange. Why would I want a patient in Terri's condition to wear makeup, perfume, and the same kind of clothes she wore before her collapse? One of her doctors had told me that it can sometimes help for patients to be maintained in circumstances as close as possible to the way they lived before their illness. In our case, we couldn't properly take care of Terri at home, but I thought that having her dressed the way she used to dress might help. I was willing to try anything. Maybe just the smell of perfume could have triggered a response. It was worth the extra effort that it took. There was also another reason. If Terri came out of it one day, I wanted her to see that I'd made sure she was taken care of, that she hadn't been abandoned. The makeup and clothes were a part of that.

What made it possible for her to be out of bed and sitting in a chair was the weeks of work they'd done at Mediplex to get her legs to bend at the knee. They call it "breaking the contractures" that occur because the muscles shorten and atrophy after lengthy periods of nonuse.

In the first few weeks at Sabal Palms I hired a special aide named Diane Gomes to help take care of Terri five days a week. She would take Terri on outings—to art galleries, museums, and parks. What I wanted was to keep my wife in environments that would stimulate her; my hope was that one day, she'd suddenly react.

It was just a few weeks after Terri's move to Sabal Palms that I was questioned for the first time by the attorneys defending Doctors Prawer and Igel in the malpractice suit. The ninety-minute session was polite, no tension, no hostility, and, frankly, not very interesting. Naturally, the attorneys focused on Terri's concern about her weight. At one point they asked me if her eating habits had changed during our marriage, and I realized that they had. I knew she wasn't eating breakfast during the week, because I was still home when she went to work each day. And several of her friends at work told me that they would go out at lunchtime and couldn't get Terri to eat anything. One of the lawyers also asked me about Terri's ingestion of liquids. I had told the lawyers that she drank an enormous amount of iced tea, water, and soda.

The move to Sabal Palms from Mediplex seemed like a fresh start, not just for Terri, but for me and Mary Schindler, who spent a lot of time with me caring for her daughter. Mary and I had a conversation about the possibility that Terri might be able to take food orally. We talked with her internist, Dr. Patrick Mulroy, and asked him about it. We understood that Terri's primary nutrition would have to continue through the PEG tube, but if she could take something by mouth it would be an encouraging sign. Before he was willing to try it, Terri would have to have a swallowing test.

On August 13, she was taken to the Largo Medical Center, where she was evaluated by Nancy C. Freeman, a speech-language pathologist. In years to come the Schindlers and their supporters, including long-distance diagnosticians, would make a big deal about swallowing tests. I'm going to describe this one in detail.

Freeman noted that "the patient was unable to cooperate for any of the oral exam. Dentition is present. She has a bite reflex to oral stimulation. She also has a sucking reflex to stimulation of the lips. Tapping of the lips resulted in strong lip closure. She has continual drooing and occasional gagging on secretions."

The speech pathologist noted that Terri produced no vocalizations at any time during the procedure. She noted, "Patient was not able to open her mouth to receive a bolus when food was presented. A small amount of liquid barium was presented in the left buccal cavity via a 3cc syringe. There was no oral control of the bolus or recognition of the bolus. The small bolus immediately fell into the pharynx."

The next step is where it gets scary. "There was immediate aspiration of the liquid into the trachea. The patient responded with gagging but not coughing. Much of the bolus had been left in the oral cavity and was then expelled with secretions. Since the patient habitually fell forward, the secretions drained from the mouth without her active propulsion."

Other strategies were attempted to get Terri to accept food, but none worked. The speech pathologist concluded that Terri "is not ready to attempt PO [oral] feeding of any type. She could be worked with to try to inhibit some of the primitive reflexes she demonstrates and to establish some appropriate reflex to oral stimulation. Since she has just finished a strong rehab program without improvement in this area, it is suggested that she be evaluated and that her family be taught some techniques that they can use with her over a period of several weeks and that she can then be re-evaluated by the speech pathologist. This young woman should be seen for another video-esophagram when she has shown significant change in the oral function." It wasn't the result we were hoping for, but, in truth, it's the one that I had expected.

I wanted Terri to have the best care possible, and I wasn't shy about complaining when I thought she wasn't getting it. A patient who spends many hours a day in bed is likely to develop serious skin problems, such as bedsores, if she's not turned regularly. Because of Terri's condition, it took two people to turn her, and that often meant pulling someone on the floor from another patient's room in order to get the job done. Similarly, just getting her from the bed into a chair was a major procedure, and I demanded that it be done every day.

As a result of my demands, I'd gotten a terrible reputation with many of the staff. There was one nursing assistant, however, with whom I hit it off immediately. Gloria Covino worked the eleven-to-seven shift, and seemed to enjoy taking care of Terri because she was the only young patient in the facility.

Gloria was different from most of the other staff because, as she put it recently, "Everybody else focused on Mike and what he was doing, and I focused more on why he was doing it." I introduced her to Hawaiian pizza—ham and pineapple—and the two of us would sit with Terri and just talk and eat.

You might be wondering how it is that I'm still in touch with a woman who was one of Terri's caretakers through the mid-nineties. Well, it's not that we stayed in touch over all that time. A few years ago, Gloria began dating a guy who came to work at Sabal Palms. And then she married him. His name is John Centonze, and by coincidence he is the brother of the woman I'm now married to, who is the mother of our two children. So Gloria is now my sister-in-law.

I introduced Gloria to my co-author, and I left so he could ask her what I was really like back then. Here's the unvarnished truth. "I think Michael was lost. I don't think he really knew how to act—nobody teaches you that. You don't go to class and say, 'Well, all of a sudden your wife is in this state that she's in; this is what you do, this is how you act.' There are no classes for that. He was acting the way that he did because he didn't know how else to handle it.

"I'm not sure if this makes sense, but Mike never treated Terri as though she was sick. She was, and he knew she was. It was just his attitude. He also never talked about leaving her, or anything like that. He was a young guy who lost his wife, more or less, from this freak thing that happened, and I think he was realistic and unrealistic at the same time. Every time their anniversary came around, there was always a card and roses.

"More than once he said to me, 'This would kill her if she could see herself this way.' "

So that's one positive voice from our years at Sabal Palms. Gloria's thoughts do not, however, reflect the way that the majority of the staff felt about me. Sabal Palms is the place where I would become known as a nursing home administrator's worst nightmare.

4 | The Malpractice Trial

I spent time almost every day with Terri, making certain the staff at Sabal Palms was giving her the kind of care that I'd specified and usually helping out myself. I still believed that one day a medical miracle was going to happen and Terri would come back. Substandard care might have prevented that miracle, and I wasn't going to tolerate it.

But there were times when I was alone with Terri in her room that I would ask her the questions that haunted me. "Why couldn't you just tell somebody if you had problems? Why couldn't you have just told me? We told each other everything, we shared everything. But this? Why did you do this to us? What about our dreams and plans?"

It wasn't fair, I know. And it was not because I was blaming her. I never blamed her. I seem to recall people giving me advice about getting some help, some counseling, but as I've said before and I'll probably say again, I'm not really good at taking that kind of help.

Since early 1991, I'd been getting myself emotionally prepared for the malpractice trial against the two physicians whom I thought could and should have diagnosed Terri's eating disorder and done something about it. My attorneys had been researching the case, evaluating the evidence, and planning our strategy.

On February 4, 1992, Glenn Woodworth asked Mary Schindler and me to come to his office in St. Petersburg. What he had to tell us was not what I wanted to hear. In short, he said that after completing all the steps necessary to prepare for the filing of the complaint, he'd decided that he couldn't go ahead with it. I was devastated.

Cases like this are handled on a contingency basis. The attorney pays all the costs associated with the case up front, in the belief that he will prevail at trial and win a large judgment, out of which he receives 40 percent for his work and that of his co-counsel and staff, plus reimbursement of their out-of-pocket expenses.

What Glenn told us was that he'd spent well over a year and more than $8,500 to build our case. He'd consulted with experts in internal medicine, obstetrics and gynecology, psychiatry, and nutrition. He'd also brought in an attorney from a Miami law firm, Gary D. Fox, who specialized in medical mismanagement cases. As Glenn told us in a follow-up letter to the February 4 meeting, Fox's firm "had expressed a willingness to associate in the handling of this lawsuit on certain conditions, namely that we were prepared to present direct testimony of Theresa's eating disorder, and direct testimony that, had it been reported to her physicians, in all likelihood, she would have changed her eating habits. Obviously, such testimony is required in order to establish a connection between the failure of the physicians to inquire of such matters and her low potassium levels. If, indeed, such testimony is not available, the defense will surely prevail because they will be able to take the position that their failure to properly manage Theresa did not make any difference in the outcome."

Glenn went on to tell us that this kind of testimony is impossible to obtain from any source. He added, "The obvious result, therefore, is that, despite our hopes and our preparations, I do not believe that the venture is sufficiently promising to proceed."

Glenn's decision crushed me. I was looking for justice for Terri, for money that would allow her to be taken care of properly for the rest of her life, and he was telling me that the fact that she'd been improperly treated by her doctors wasn't enough to get us to trial, much less to victory. Frankly, I was very angry that this doctor was getting away with something.

Glenn recalls that I said to him, "Look, I don't care about how long the shot is. I want an opportunity to have enough money to take care of Theresa. That's all I'm interested in. And if it takes a long shot to see if we can do that—I want her to be taken care of in a first-rate way."

Fortunately, Glenn's meeting with us and his letter indicating that he wouldn't file the case proved to be premature. Gary Fox had been trying cases like this for nearly sixteen years, but he'd never had one involving an eating disorder. He'd been researching bulimia, and then had talked with a number of Terri's friends as well as medical experts. A day or so after Glenn said they couldn't go forward, Gary changed his mind. He said, "The more we looked into the case and the more people we talked to, the more convinced I became that she did, indeed, have the eating disorder. Proving it was going to be something else."

It was welcome news that took me from the depths of depression up to, let's say, the basement. A short while later, Gary came to Clearwater to meet with me. It might be stretching a bit to say that I felt a little as though I was under a microscope, but he told me that if he were to go forward with the case, he had to have a plaintiff that was both believable and likable. I guess I passed his test.

He'd made it clear that there were a lot of hurdles to jump between where we were and a winning verdict. Fox was convinced that we could prove that Terri had bulimia, but proving malpractice was a whole separate issue because none of her medical records referred to any type of eating disorder. There were quotes from Mary Schindler in at least two of Terri's records, but nothing from a doctor confirming it. There were no references to any nutritional problem and none of her friends could testify that they'd actually seen her go to the bathroom and purge. A lot of people could talk about her bingeing—remembering huge Sunday omelets that were even too big for me to finish—but no one came forward to say they'd seen her deliberately vomit. Without witnesses, how could we prove that she had the disease, and how could we prove that the doctors were negligent in their care and treatment of her? That's the way Gary presented it to me.

There was one other element that seemed even more difficult to Fox. He asked, "How could we prove that had they diagnosed it the outcome would have been different? I have never had a case that had this degree of difficulty at every level. But I decided this was a winnable case and that Michael deserved his day in court and we were willing to run the risk of going forward with it."

When Gary talked about the risk, he wasn't kidding. By the time it was over, the case cost roughly a quarter of a million dollars to prosecute—expert witnesses and mock juries don't come cheap—not even counting the thousands of man-hours spent in preparation and trial. Gary also knew that losing a case like this would take an emotional toll on him—because he'd feel as though he failed both Terri and me.

What I now know is that the malpractice trial is what drove The Schiavo Case. If we hadn't sued and won a substantial judgment, it's my belief, and Gary Fox's belief, that no one outside the family would have ever heard the name Terri Schiavo.

Because this trial was critical to everything that would follow—it dealt with what happened to Terri the night of her collapse, with whether or not the collapse was caused by bulimia, with the quality of care she'd been receiving—it's important to understand how the trial was handled.

Explaining the legal steps that had to be taken is complicated. Years after the trial, Gary Fox explained the intricacies. "The first problem was trying to prove that Dr. Igel, Terri's ob-gyn, was negligent under Florida law—that he violated the standard of care. And our position there was that Terri came to see him because she had menstrual irregularities, and the thing that I think helped to make our case is that she didn't just go to him once. When she continued to have the problems, she went back to him again and again.

"The reason that was important was because the defense to the case is that most of these women who have bulimia are very secretive—they don't want help, and therefore the defense in this case was that, number one, he wasn't negligent. Igel had no reason to believe that Terri had an eating disorder because she was what they call a 'normal weight bulimic.' She didn't have that Karen Carpenter look about her—she looked normal and she was attractive, and therefore there was no reason, according to the defense, for the physician to believe that she was bulimic. Therefore, there was no need for him to ask her questions about diet and nutrition.

"According to the defense, he had figured out that her problem was that she was lacking certain hormones and the proof of that was when he prescribed hormones for her, her cycles became regular and her menstrual problems disappeared.

"Of course my position was that's not the end of the inquiry—you have to figure out why she has these hormonal problems. One of the things that can cause it is bad nutrition, and therefore you have to take a careful dietary history.

"The problem there is that many bulimics will lie about their condition."

Fox continued, "Most bulimics are embarrassed about their condition—think about it: When you talk about vomiting, that's a horrible, painful, disgusting thing for a human to do, and for these women who do it to themselves voluntarily, two or three times a day, that's not something they want to disclose to anybody.

"We took Igel's deposition, and to me, the whole case hinged around what he was going to say in response to my questions about whether or not he took a nutritional history. Some defendants in malpractice cases have zero compunction about looking you in the eye and lying through their teeth. We had looked through the records and there was clearly no evidence of any history concerning nutrition in either Igel's or [Terri's] primary care physician, Dr. Prawer's, charts.

"I asked the question in deposition and he admitted he did not take a nutritional history from her, and that became the linchpin of the case. That was the evidence we were looking for and I think he told the truth, and as I recall, he said the reason he didn't do it was because he was satisfied that he had the answer to why she was not menstruating regularly.

"Our expert witness said that with this kind of patient, what a doctor has to do is sit down and take the time to develop a careful history, which brings us back to the supposition that all bulimics lie. Our expert admitted that it was true, a lot of bulimics didn't tell the truth, but some of them did. Some of them wanted to get better, and what our expert witness said is that Terri was one of those patients who, had the questions been asked, probably would have told him the truth. Why? Because she was trying to get pregnant. She wanted to get better. She wasn't one of these patients who just went to a doctor once for a problem and disappeared, and never returned."

Gary Fox told me that the opposing attorneys would be a top-notch defense team; he said that malpractice insurers only hire the best. One of the things they did was thoroughly investigate me, paying particular attention to the morning that Terri collapsed. Had I taken even the slightest improper action, they would have nailed me with it during the trial. The fact is—the truth is—they never even mentioned it during the trial because no matter how hard they tried to find something, I'd done nothing wrong. Too bad Jeb Bush wasn't paying attention.

In May 1992, I got my own apartment and moved out of the home I had rented and lived in with the Schindlers, whom I still called Mom and Dad. They had been urging me to begin dating, telling me that I should be getting on with my life.

While I was working with the lawyers in the year that they prepared for the malpractice trial, I had started going out with a young woman named Cindy Brashers, whom I'd met in a human anatomy class at St. Petersburg Junior College, where I was studying to become an emergency medical technician. She was a very petite, very pretty brunette who lived in Bradenton. Her parents were divorced and Cindy told me her family life was difficult. I think Cindy was looking for someone to take her away from that but I wasn't the guy.

At one point, I actually brought Cindy home to meet the Schindlers. There was nothing strange about that to me, because my relationship with Cindy wasn't romantic, and the Schindlers were very nice to her.

Frankly, I thought they were just looking out for my well-being; only much later did I suspect that there might be another reason they wanted me to date.

Once Cindy and I began going out, we'd see each other a lot and talk on the phone while she was at work. Very late in our friendship, we both worked in different departments at the same hospital.

Now this gets into a kiss-and-tell aspect of the story, but if it weren't going to be documented in depositions years down the road, I wouldn't mention it at all. In the beginning, we were dating. We had some moments, but I felt as though I was betraying Terri, and even though later, under oath, I answered yes when asked if our relationship was "intimate," no one ever defined that term. The truth is that I just couldn't do it. I knew that Cindy was looking for more than I could give at that time, so eventually, we just stopped seeing each other. The whole thing lasted about six months, ending around the time that the malpractice trial began.

In May 1992, Terri's primary care physician, Dr. Joel S. Prawer, and his insurance company settled with us for $250,000, the policy limit under the Physicians' Protective Trust Fund.

In order to understand what happened next, you have to understand a peculiarity that existed in Florida law with respect to malpractice verdicts. Let's say that a doctor carries a maximum liability limit of $250,000 in his malpractice coverage. If the patient sues for ten million dollars and wins, what most often happens is the insurance company pays the $250,000, and since it's the rare doctor who can write a check for the remaining $9,750,000, the doctor declares bankruptcy and the patient collects nothing more.

However, under Florida law in 1991, if the patient sues and offers to settle for the limits of the doctor's policy, and the insurance company unreasonably refuses to settle and basically says, "screw you, we're not paying a penny," the case can go to trial, and if the patient wins, the insurance company is obligated to pay the full amount of the verdict—no matter what the limit was on the malpractice policy.

So it's a gamble for both sides: The patient filing suit can take a chance and make the offer to settle for the policy's limits, running the risk that the insurance company will say, "Hell yes," and thus be denied the opportunity to collect the millions that the case might really be worth; on the other hand, the insurance company might believe that the case isn't even deserving of a ten-dollar settlement, but it agrees to pay the full limit of its policy because that prevents the patient from going to court and, perhaps, winning millions.

It's a chess game, except that it's not a game and the consequences of losing are extraordinarily high. My attorneys first offered a settlement agreement to Dr. Prawer. That left us with one other defendant, Dr. G. Stephen Igel, who was Terri's obstetrician and gynecologist.

By the time Prawer settled, Gary Fox had done enough research to believe that we had a case worth many millions of dollars. But in order to put ourselves in a position where Igel's insurance carrier would be obligated to pay a huge settlement if we won, we had to gamble and offer him and his insurer the opportunity to settle for a quarter of a million.

On May 28, 1992, Gary sent a letter to Igel's attorney that spelled out the damages that might be awarded by a jury. The estimates were arrived at by two specialists whose job it was to evaluate cases and come up with reasonable expectations.

In his letter to Igel's lawyer, Kenneth C. Deacon, Jr., Fox warned Igel and his attorneys that a jury verdict in favor of Terri and me could easily reach $15,000,000.

A few days later, on June 2, Gary Fox took Dr. Igel's deposition. From my attorney's point of view, Igel had put himself in deep trouble. The next day, Fox wrote to Igel's attorney again, giving him one last chance to settle. "The long and short of Dr. Igel's testimony is that Terri Schiavo was showing signs and symptoms of an easily diagnosable condition. He did not diagnose or treat her problem and, as a result, Terri Schiavo suffered a heart attack [sic] and will remain in a coma [sic] for the rest of her life." (For the sake of accuracy, Terri didn't suffer a heart attack as the term is commonly used; her heart went into ventricular fibrillation, which led to cardiac arrest—her heart just stopped beating. And she wasn't in a coma, she was in a persistent vegetative state.)

Fox continued, "The most incredible part of Dr. Igel's testimony is that, even though he recognized that irregular periods can be caused by low potassium, he did not even *consider* low potassium as a cause of Terri's condition. He admitted that irregular bleeding can be caused by eating disorders and nutritional deficiencies yet, amazingly, took neither an eating history or a nutritional history."

My attorney continued, "All of this is made particularly tragic by the fact that, had Dr. Igel only taken an adequate history, Terri's eating disorders, which produced the low potassium, which Dr. Igel acknowledges she had, would have been diagnosed and treated."

Fox went on to indicate that Igel would not be able to "escape responsibility for his negligence by attempting to blame the emergency medical personnel for allegedly improperly intubating Terri" following her collapse. "Had Dr. Igel done his job, Terri would never have had a heart attack."

He concluded, "If there was any doubt as to his [Igel's] liability for Terri's injuries before his deposition, those doubts have now been eliminated."

Dr. Igel's insurance company was insufficiently moved by the letter to settle for the mandated liability limit of $250,000. Their attorneys were also incredibly arrogant. They said that if we went to trial, we would surely lose. And when that happened, they would sue Terri's guardianship to recover the costs for their defense. The only money in the guardianship was the $250,000 that had been paid by Dr. Prawer's insurance company. Under their scenario, they'd take most of it, leaving Terri with next to nothing.

Gary discussed all of this with me. He told me what we were risking by going to trial and left the decision up to me. Two weeks later, we withdrew our offer to settle, and we began preparing for a jury trial. That doesn't mean that I didn't second-guess my decision a few dozen times, but I wasn't going to change my mind.

Civil cases in Florida are tried in front of a six-person jury, and the verdict must be unanimous. Clearwater was not known as a large-verdict town. But the bigger problem was that the jury pool would most likely have a very large number of elderly people, living on fixed incomes, and dependent on the care of their doctors. That simple fact makes them less likely to return a verdict *against* physicians. Gary told me that we needed a jury of people who were reasonably intelligent, because he was convinced that if the jurors understood the medicine, we would win the case.

The preparation that Gary and Glenn did for the trial was extensive and instructive. They ran a mock trial in front of a focus group of people selected to mirror the Clearwater jury pool, and we lost. They changed their arguments, tried it with another focus group mock jury, and lost again.

It turned out, Gary explained, that the jurors weren't buying the argument that this was all Dr. Igel's fault; that if only he had recognized the disease and Terri had been treated for it, she would never have collapsed. The mock jurors told my lawyers that much of this was Terri's own fault, and that unless we admitted that, they wouldn't find the doctor even partially responsible. I still couldn't bring myself to admit to others that Terri had brought this on herself.

Glenn Woodworth had been losing sleep over that problem from the first time I discussed the case with him. He felt I was sincere, that I wasn't making things up. And he admired the character I showed by taking care of Terri the way I did and not walking away like he thought most men my age would probably do.

Yes, people with lung cancer have won judgments against tobacco companies, but they're tough cases because jurors know that no one forced the smoker to light up. Seagrams didn't demand that the alcoholic pickle his own liver in gin. The drinker has to bear some responsibility for drinking. Terri made a choice—not an altogether rational one—to lose weight in the unhealthiest way imaginable. So she had some responsibility for her actions.

That problem required a radical rethinking of our case, because all along, the plan had been to fight to keep the jury from hearing anything that might place the blame for Terri's bulimia on Terri herself. But Glenn and Gary worked out a new strategy, and spent the money, somewhere in the neighborhood of $25,000, to hold another mock trial in front of a third focus group. This time, the verdict went our way.

In early November, the malpractice trial against Dr. Igel began in Courtroom B of the Pinellas County Courthouse in Clearwater, with Circuit Judge Philip A. Federico presiding. What I wanted from the trial, aside from the money that would enable us to care for Terri, was to learn why the doctors didn't properly treat her. Why didn't they recognize that her amenorrhea was being caused by *something*, and look for the cause?

I still held onto the belief that I was going to bring Terri home and we would pick up right where we had left off building a life together. I wasn't willing to be told that my wife is in this condition for the rest of her life—even though my attorney appeared to believe that.

Our trial plan called for Glenn Woodworth to examine me, and Gary Fox to examine Dr. Igel. Early in his examination of the doctor, Gary asked if the fact that Terri wasn't ovulating and having periods was caused by an eating disorder or nutritional problems. The doctor said that he did not think so, adding that Terri "did have a nutritional type of assessment done. She did have her urine checked which gives . . . me an idea of her nutritional status. The urinalysis checks the glucose and ketones to see whether the body is absorbing food . . . we also check the weight and the weight was stable. Also looking at her and talking to her, she did not look like a person with an eating disorder."

Gary came back at the doctor, "You didn't even consider the possibility that nutritional problems were causing her condition?"

And Igel responded, "In Terri's case, no."

Fox established as fact that Dr. Igel had never taken a complete history of Terri, certainly not the type of history that was called for in a medical text introduced into evidence: that he had prescribed progesterone, which seemed to help bring on her periods. Nevertheless, he said she came back to him at least three times because of amenorrhea, and he still never looked for the actual cause of the problem. On none of these visits did the doctor order any blood work done. At the same time, he was prescribing hormone pills for Terri.

The following are transcripts of Gary Fox questioning Dr. Igel:

Q. On none of these visits, doctor, did you notice any loose or excess skin on Terri's arms or legs?

A. No, sir, I did not.

Q. Would that have been of any significance to you had you noticed that?

A. It may have been, yes.

Q. What would you have done had you noticed that?

A. Assuming she had—had it been there or had it been noticed, then I may have—I would have proceeded further as far as asking questions of weight loss, weight gain possibly.

Q. Doctor, this eating disorder that Terri had when you treated her, I think we've already agreed that she had an eating disorder when you were treating her, correct?

A. Yes, sir.

Q. That would be related, her eating disorder to her amenorrhea, wouldn't it?

A. No, sir, not in her particular case.

What Dr. Igel had just done was a complete flip-flop from what he'd said at his deposition. He'd said that Terri's amenorrhea would be related to her eating disorder, and at the trial, he'd denied that they were related.

Gary had to drive the point home by reading from Igel's deposition:

Q. [Fox] I want your medical opinion as to whether it was more likely than not that Terri's eating disorder, which she had at the time that you were treating her, was related to the secondary amenorrhea which you diagnosed. Answer: It would be related.

And then, in front of the jury, the doctor flip-flopped again. It's about as close as you can come to a Perry Mason moment:

A. It could be.

Q. No, sir, doctor, it says it would be, doesn't it?

A. If you've got it there.

Q. It says it would be related, doesn't it?

A. Yes, sir.

Q. And that is just the opposite of what your lawyer told this jury in his opening statement, wasn't it? You were in the courtroom yesterday when he said the amenorrhea was unrelated to an eating disorder. You heard that, didn't you?

A. I think so.

Q. Certainly not your opinion. Your opinion is that her eating disorder was related to her amenorrhea? I'm sorry?

A. No, sir.

Q. That was the under-oath testimony in any event that you gave just four or five months ago.

A. I understand that. I see that.

Q. You were sworn to tell the truth?

A. Just as I am now.

MR. FOX: Your honor, may I have a moment?

THE COURT: Surely.

At the deposition Igel had said "would," and had now switched to "could." Just in case the jury missed it, he gave them a little time to think about it, then:

MR. FOX: Your honor, I have no further questions of this witness.

Because of the dispute that would later erupt between the Schindlers and me, it's important that I quote for you a few lines from Mary Schindler's testimony at the malpractice trial. They're the lines that State Attorney McCabe would also quote in his report to Governor Bush. Asked about me, Mrs. Schindler said, "He's there every day. She [Terri] does not want for anything. He is loving, caring. I don't know of any young boy that would be as attentive. He is—he's just unbelievable, and I know without him there is no way I would have survived this."

Perhaps you're wondering why my attorneys called Mrs. Schindler to testify, but not Terri's father. In a recent conversation, Glenn explained:

"My first impression of him was that he was a very angry negatively minded person. Secondly, it was my conclusion that for whatever reason he simply did not find it necessary or within him to visit his daughter in the nursing home. In speaking with Mrs. Schindler about that, she said something to the effect that 'He just can't bring himself to do it.' I didn't pursue that. But I said to myself, 'Well, what happens when he gets up there on the witness stand and testifies as to what a wonderful daughter she was, and how vibrant she was, how perfect she was, and how much he loved her, and then this lawyer on the other side says, "Tell me how many times you've been to see her," and unlike Mrs. Schindler, unlike Michael—they say at least every day, and sometimes more than once a day—and he says, "I just can't bring myself to visit with her."' I didn't think that would sit very well."

But there was more. Bobby Schindler told one of the members of my legal team a disturbing story about Mr. Schindler and Terri. The lawyer recounted it like this:

"There was a time when Terri was in her adolescence or late adolescence when she was very, very heavy. When they were in a busy shopping center near where they lived, there was a young black gentleman walking with a rather obese, obviously overweight, white young lady, and it was reported to me that Terri's father said to her, 'Terri, you see there, if you don't lose weight, you're going to end up just like that girl with a guy just like that'—or words less politically correct to that effect . . . actually, he used the 'N' word."

After hearing the story, my lawyers decided it was enough to keep Mr. Schindler off the witness stand.

There was concern that some of the jurors might wonder why my attorneys called Terri's mom to the stand but didn't bring her father up to testify. However, when compelled to choose between not satis-fying the curiosity of jurors who might wonder about that, and taking the risk that the defendant's lawyers had heard the mall story and knew that Bob Schindler had often been heard using the offensive term, the safer choice was the former. Call it the Mark Fuhrman rule of trial strategy.

It wouldn't have taken much for investigators to turn up credible witnesses who could testify under oath that Mr. Schindler used the word "nigger" often enough that no one was shocked anymore when he said it. I'd heard him use it dozens of times; so had my brothers. So the idea that he'd tell Terri that if she didn't lose weight, "only a nigger would marry you" isn't surprising. It rings true.

And that's why Terri's loving, concerned, distraught father wasn't given an opportunity to tell the jurors how the loss of his daughter had affected his life.

———

A few days later, at nine in the morning, it was my turn on the stand as the last witness for our side. We'd called doctors as expert witnesses, nurses who'd taken care of Terri, her friends, an economist or two who could explain the cost of caring for her, and even the hairstylist who saw her the night before she collapsed. While I was a nervous wreck—this was the first time I'd ever been to a trial, let alone been involved in a lawsuit—I wasn't terribly concerned about the questions Glenn Woodworth was going to ask me. They'd actually taken me to an empty courtroom one day, put me in the witness box, and both of my lawyers threw questions at me. I think the main purpose was to help me prove to myself that I was capable of answering anything I was asked. The practice sessions definitely built my confidence, but I still wasn't looking forward to being cross-examined.

Gary Fox recalled, "I remember [Mike] being very upset. Here you had this confrontational legal proceeding where he himself wasn't be-ing accused of wrongdoing, but his lawyers were being accused of making up this whole thing. Because I was his lawyer, I think that he felt like there was an indirect accusation at him.

"He was our last witness, and I know he was very concerned that he was going to do something or say something that would screw up this case for Terri."

Gary had no idea how terrified I was. When I'm nervous I get butterflies. I always take it out on my stomach. I was sitting there, and I knew my name was about to be called, and my hands were starting to sweat. When I took them off the table, I could see the perspiration on the polished wood. But I went up there, took the oath, took a deep breath, remembered that this was for Terri, and, suddenly, I was okay. Once I got the feel of the room, once it started, I was fine.

Glenn began by asking me about Terri's attitude toward life. He established that she'd lost a lot of weight and was probably down to 110 or 115 pounds.

A. [Schiavo] Terri felt very happy with herself. She was content. She was very excited with herself.

Q. Did you notice anything unusual about her eating?

A. I noticed some peculiar eating habits, especially on Sunday which was my day off, and she'd make breakfast and she would make a huge omelet. I'm not talking Bob Evans omelet, I'm talking huge omelet, and sit there and eat all of it, or we'd order a pizza and she'd eat practically all of it.

Q. Did you have any indication that Terri had any kind of a psychological problem or an eating disorder as we've heard about during this trial?

A. None whatsoever.

Q. Tell our jury about her habits of drinking fluids. Did you notice anything unusual about that?

A. I noticed she would consume a large amount of iced tea. She would consume close to a gallon of it in one day.

Then Woodworth began asking me about Terri's appearance.

Q. Did there come a time when you got concerned about the fact that Terri was getting skinnier than you wanted her to be and did you talk to her about it?

A. I mentioned it a couple of times to her and it got to the point where a couple times when she took off her blouse or something at night, I could see her bones, collarbones and shoulder bones would stick out, and I'd mention, "Terri, enough is enough, let's gain a little weight now," and that was that.

Q. Did Terri ever go to Dr. Igel thinking she might be pregnant?

A. Yes.

Q. What was her reaction when she found out on those occasions that she wasn't pregnant?

A. We were both devastated.

At one point in preparing for the trial, some consideration had been given to bringing Terri to the courtroom. Ultimately, we decided it would be more useful to show the jury a videotape of a day in Terri's life at Sabal Palms.

The videotape ran for an hour and twenty minutes, and Glenn asked me to explain anything unusual that we were seeing; for example, at one point I talked about getting Terri dressed and I said, "I'm drying out her hands there. You have to keep the inside of the hands—since she's contracted—you have to keep them dry because infection can set in, and I usually do a little bit of range of motion [therapy] on her."

The tape went on, showing the speech pathologist working with Terri; it showed her being placed on the tilt table that brings her to a standing position; and it showed me connecting the bottle of liquid nutrients to the feeding tube that went directly into her stomach through an opening in her abdomen. After that, I could be seen changing the dressing around the stoma—the opening.

Once the tape finished, Glenn introduced a board that had a variety of pictures of Terri mounted on it; photos taken within a few years of her collapse. I hadn't seen the display until that moment, and it shocked me. There was a picture of her holding a stuffed lion and you could see that her cheekbones were sticking out, as well as her shoulder bones. It was awful. I think it was the first time I was truly seeing Terri.

Being with her every day I guess I didn't notice the changes, but seeing the pictures on the board was devastating.

I was asked why I'd enrolled in school to become a nurse, and told the court that I enjoyed the work and wanted to learn more about taking care of Terri.

Q. [Woodworth] You're a young man. Your life is ahead of you. Your future is beyond you. Up the road, when you look up the road, what do you see for yourself?

A. I see myself hopefully finishing school and taking care of my wife.

Q. Where do you want to take care of your wife?

A. I want to bring my wife home.

Q. If you had the resources available to you, if you had the equipment and the people, would you do that?

A. Yes, I would. In a heartbeat.

Q. How do you feel about being married to Terri now?

A. I feel wonderful. She's my life and I wouldn't trade her for the world. I believe in my wedding vows.

At that moment, it all got to me. Where we were, what we were fighting for, my belief that Terri would get better. And I started to crumble. Glenn asked if I wanted to take a minute to collect myself, which I did. A few minutes later, he resumed questioning me.

Q. You said you believe in your wedding vows. What do you mean by that?

A. I believe in the vows that I took with my wife: through sickness, in health, for richer or poorer. I married my wife because I love her and I want to spend the rest of my life with her. I'm going to do that.

With that, Dr. Igel's attorney, Kenneth C. Deacon, Jr., began his cross-examination. Not wanting to appear like an ogre in front of the jury, he began by asking how I was doing, if I was okay. Assured that I was, he started asking about the state of my marriage to Terri.

Q. [Deacon] Up to this incident happening, been married very long?

A. We'd been married five years.

Q. Up to this time that that had happened, that this incident happened to her, your marriage was a happy one, was it not?

A. It was very happy.

Q. Since this incident happened, and it happened on February 25, 1990, has her condition, in your observation, from your observation, changed appreciably?

A. No. She opens her eyes.

Q. She opens her eyes and she's off the ventilator?

A. Uh-huh.

I really couldn't figure out where he was going with those questions, but my attorney did. It was in their interest to show that Terri wasn't getting better and wouldn't get better. In fact, Gary felt the opposition would try to demonstrate that Terri would fall victim to any of several infections that often result in the death of patients in a vegetative state. If they could get the jury to believe that Terri's life would be relatively short, then if the jury brought back a money verdict for us, it would be considerably smaller than if the jury believed Terri could or would live a long life.

There were several more minutes of questioning, some redirect from Glenn Woodworth, and I was finished.

Five days later, Gary made his closing argument. Sitting in the courtroom were my father and mother, my brother Brian, as well as Bob and Mary Schindler, along with Bobby and Suzanne.

I remember my father telling me that my attorney's closing argument was brilliant, but I have to tell you, I only remember one thing that he said. The way it worked was, Gary gave his closing; then the opposing attorney presented his argument, and Gary came back with his rebuttal. Just before the rebuttal, I'd casually mentioned to Gary that it was strange that the last day of the trial happened to be our wedding anniversary.

Gary got up there, said a couple of things, and concluded, "On this, the eighth wedding anniversary of Michael Schiavo and Terri Schiavo, come back with a verdict for Terri."

At 2:16 P.M., the jury began deliberations. At 4:29, they had one question for the judge. I asked Gary what that meant and he told me that the question was favorable to us, but that I shouldn't read anything into it, nothing good, nothing bad.

At 5:02, after deliberating for only two hours and forty-six minutes, the jury signaled that they'd reached a verdict.

The two-page verdict form required the jurors to answer seven questions. The clerk read the first one. "Was there negligence on the part of Stephen Igel, M.D., which was a legal cause of injury to Theresa Schiavo? Yes."

I was thinking about Terri the whole time. She was just running through my mind.

"Was there negligence on the part of Theresa Schiavo which was a legal cause of her injuries? Yes."

That's when I closed my eyes, waiting to hear what she'd read next.

"State the percentage of negligence attributable to Stephen Igel, M.D. Thirty percent. To Theresa Schiavo. Seventy percent."

Now I really squeezed my eyes shut. What was Dr. Igel's 30 percent responsibility going to mean?

The clerk continued reading. "What is the amount of Theresa Schiavo's damages sustained for medical expenses and lost earnings or earning ability in the past? $480,271."

It sounded like a strange number, but I guessed that it came from the testimony that the economics experts had given.

She continued, "What is the amount of Theresa Schiavo's future damages for medical expenses and lost earning ability to be sustained in future years? Total damages over future years: $9,400,000. The number of years over which those future damages are intended to provide compensation? Seventeen. What is the present value of those future damages? $4,300,000."

The jury decided that Terri would live for another seventeen years in her current condition, and that it would cost $9.4 million dollars to maintain her over that period of time. Then they calculated the amount of money that would have to be invested today, to amount to $9.4 million over seventeen years, and came up with $4.3 million.

"What is the amount of Theresa Schiavo's damages for pain and suffering, disability, physical impairment, disfigurement, mental anguish, inconvenience, and loss of capacity for the enjoyment of life? In the past? Zero. In the future? Zero."

And she continued with the final item: "What is the amount of damages sustained by Michael Schiavo for the loss of Theresa Schiavo's services, comfort, society, and attentions: In the past? $100,000. In the future? Two million dollars."

I sat there stunned, and very close to tears as I listened to the judge calculate what the 70/30 split actually meant in real dollars, and that was it. Both Gary and Glenn gave me big hugs. My parents and Mrs. Schindler seemed to be thrilled with the award, but Bob Schindler, who had written down all the numbers on an envelope as the clerk read them off, was upset. He was convinced that the judge had made an error in announcing the 70/30 split.

Since it was close to six o'clock and everyone was hungry, my parents and in-laws decided they'd go to a local restaurant, Leverock's, for dinner. I opted out, saying that I hadn't seen Terri enough while the trial was under way, and wanted to go to Sabal Palms to be with her. Nothing that had been said by witnesses at the trial had changed my mind about Terri's prognosis. I was still convinced that someday I'd bring her home. I sat next to her, on her bed, and told her how the jury had punished her doctor.

I found out later that dinner at Leverock's was not exactly a celebration. My father related the story to my brother Brian that Bob Schindler was so obsessed with the judge's math that he wouldn't eat dinner. Dad said Mr. Schindler was consumed with anger that the judge had made a mistake and that Terri wasn't getting her proper amount. He kept scratching numbers on the back of the envelope he'd written the verdict award on, until finally Mrs. Schindler said, "Bob, would you knock it off?" He didn't, and according to Dad, Terri's mom said something no one had ever heard her say to her husband: "Bob, you need to shut up about it!"

The next day, my dad was outside cutting the grass when my mom came out and waved him down. "Mary Schindler's on the phone. Can you come talk to her?" So my dad went inside and talked to Mary, who asked him to talk to Bob. Terri's father had taken a job as a draftsman, and Mary said that he couldn't go to work that day because he was so obsessed about the money.

Dad told us that Mr. Schindler just couldn't let it go, even after he'd explained the math to him over and over again. Terri's father wanted to call Judge Federico and argue with him about it. And he wanted my father to tell me to call my attorney and tell him that the numbers were not working and Terri wasn't getting her fair share.

When we were preparing for the trial, Mr. and Mrs. Schindler also wanted to sue the doctors. They both went to see Glenn Woodworth about it and were not thrilled when he told them they weren't entitled to do that. "She's over eighteen, she's married, and even if she wasn't married and eighteen, you still couldn't sue in her behalf." That enraged my father-in-law. He said, "I should be able to sue them because she's my daughter." That was his big thing throughout our ordeal. "She's my daughter. I have the right." That was, if I recall correctly, the first time that Mr. Schindler talked about money. I hoped that his post-trial rantings would be the last. How foolish could I have been?

When I had a chance to talk about the verdict with Gary Fox, he offered me some explanations as to why the jury did what they did.

First, declaring that Terri was 70 percent responsible for her condition just goes to show that what my attorneys learned from the mock juries was right on target. The jury wanted to do the right thing, they wanted to say that Terri was responsible—but once they did that and satisfied that need, they also assigned blame to Dr. Igel.

The award to me for loss of Terri's companionship really shocked all the lawyers. Fox said, "Two-point-one-million dollars is one helluva verdict for loss of consortium. No spouse I've represented—and we've tried a lot of cases—has ever gotten that kind of consortium award. And I think the jury granted it because after watching the video, they appreciated the sacrifices that Michael had made and was continuing to make for Terri."

But the most interesting thing that appeared on the verdict form, according to Gary, was the fact that the jury gave Terri zero dollars for pain and suffering. "The significance of that," he told me when I was working on this book, was that, "contrary to everything that's gone on over the last three, four, five years about her state of cognition, and her feeling of pain, the jury looked at all the facts in a lot more depth and a lot more detail than any of us have since the trial, and concluded that zero was the correct figure.

"What they meant was, they were convinced that she was not feeling any pain or suffering; that she had no cognition, and that she was truly in a deep, vegetative state from which she would never recover. Even the mainstream media never picked up on it. This issue was thoroughly analyzed, litigated, contested. We argued to the contrary, that she was feeling things, or at least we couldn't be sure she wasn't, and the jury decided no."

Terri had no cognition; she was truly in a persistent vegetative state from which she would never recover. She could feel no pain. And the jury said it on November 10, 1992, the date of our eighth wedding anniversary.

When all was said and done and the attorneys for both sides had finished negotiating to forestall an appeal, on January 20, 1993, Physicians' Protective Trust Fund wrote a check in the amount of two million dollars payable to Barnett Bank as Guardian of the property of Theresa Schiavo, Michael Schiavo, Individually, and their attorney, Glenn Woodworth. After attorneys' fees and costs were deducted, $725,000 was deposited into Terri's guardianship account and I received $300,000.

And now for the denouement of the malpractice trial. It happened close to the time my attorneys were expecting the check from the insurance company. I never knew this until Glenn Woodworth told it to me in late 2005, while we were writing this book. In his own words:

"Mrs. Schindler found her way to my office. Now whether Mr. Schindler was with her or not, I do not recall. Whether any of the siblings were with her or not, I do not recall. But here is the substance of the conversation.

" 'Now, how long is it going to take for us to get the money?' Mrs. Schindler asked.

" 'You don't understand. I don't represent you. You do not have under the law in the state of Florida any claim. I thought that had been made clear to you. Michael has a claim. And his wife has a claim. He ultimately will be appointed the guardian of her property even though the bank is the guardian now, and that money will be devoted to her, so all of the money that's available is hers, and Michael's, for their separate claims. Florida does not give the parents a claim.'

"And Mrs. Schindler said, 'Are you tellin' me after all we've been through, after all I have been through, that not one single dollar of that money will be turned over to us? Or to me?'

" 'That's exactly what I'm telling you, Mrs. Schindler.'

" 'Well, that is just totally wrong.' And at that point she demonstrated to me two things: number one, great surprise—and why, I don't know—and number two, great frustration, for reasons that are obvious.

"At that point, in my opinion, her adoration of Michael ceased. And I don't know for a fact, but I will bet you that at some point after my conversation with her, shortly after that case settled, she had a similar kind of conversation with Michael."

Glenn Woodworth got it almost right—but not quite. It wasn't Mrs. Schindler that had the similar conversation with me; it was her husband.

5 | The Fight

All over America on Valentine's Day, 1993, husbands were treating their wives to flowers, cards, gifts, and the ritual of the special Sunday brunch. In fact, my parents and Bob and Mary Schindler were planning on going out to a late-morning brunch together.

The third anniversary of Terri's collapse was less than two weeks away, and there didn't appear to be any change for the better in her condition. I planned on spending that Sunday the way I spent most days—sitting with Terri for as many hours as possible. At the time, I was taking classes at St. Petersburg Junior College in order to get my emergency medical technician certification, and that morning I was concentrating on my anatomy textbook.

I had my books spread out on the bedside table in the small but pleasant room. On the table were a dozen red roses in a vase that I'd brought her for Valentine's Day. Terri was sitting in her chair, dressed in clothes I'd bought her. Her hair was neatly done, though not as short as she'd gotten it cut the night before she collapsed. She'd slowly gone back to her natural brown, from the blonde she'd become on her last healthy day three years earlier. She was wearing makeup, carefully applied by one of the CNAs. I was still sure that one day Terri would snap out of it, and I wanted her to see that I'd taken care of her;

I wasn't going to allow her to become another faceless patient in a shapeless, colorless hospital gown.

I was surprised when the door opened and Bob and Mary came in. They both said hello, and then Mrs. Schindler added, "I didn't see your car out there."

They didn't know that I'd traded in the tiny royal blue Toyota Celica we'd bought for Terri for an end-of-the-model-year Acura Legend. Since I was six-feet-six, the Toyota was less than an ideal vehicle for me. Even though I was still close to the Schindlers, I hadn't told them about my new car, so all I said was, "It's out there," nodding toward the parking lot, which we could see through the window.

Both of them went over to Terri and said their ritual hello while I continued studying. Then, out of nowhere, her father asked, "Well, when's the money coming?"

Knowing how he'd driven everyone crazy with his calculations of the malpractice settlement, it made sense not to get into it with him. So all I said was, "Any time now."

I suppose I shouldn't have been surprised by what came next, but I was. He came around in front of the chair I was sitting in and asked, "How much am I going to get?"

I'm fairly certain that he still didn't understand how much money had actually been awarded to me for loss of consortium. Yes, the judge had announced a jury verdict of 2.1 million dollars, but it was reduced to $300,000 because the jury decided that Terri's bulimia was 70 percent her fault, and only 30 percent the fault of her doctor, and by attorneys' fees and expenses. Again, I was in no mood to get dragged into an argument, so I just kind of played it off. "I don't know how much anybody's getting yet."

He wasn't deterred. Here's a man who was disappointed beyond belief when he learned that he and Terri's mom had no standing to file their own malpractice suit against Terri's doctors. I could never be certain whether he was more interested in punishing the doctors, or in getting money to help bail him out of the desperate financial condition they were in as a result of his futon business going bust and their subsequent bankruptcy in 1989.

I decided that this wasn't the time or the place to get into it. But he kept pushing and pushing and pushing. A couple of times I glanced over at Mary, hoping that she'd intervene and get him to back off. It would have been totally out of character for her to do something like that, but I could hope. Finally, I had to respond.

"Y'know something? I'm just gonna give it all to Terri."

His head swiveled from my face to Terri's. He stood up straight, pulled his shoulders back, pointed at his daughter, who was sitting in the chair staring off into space, and said, "Well, how much is she gonna give me?" He didn't say "us," meaning Mary and him. He said "me," as though he and he alone was entitled to be compensated.

That's when it started to get heated. "Well, y'know something?" he said, mimicking me. "You might want to go out and get yourself a lawyer." The implication was that he would sue me for either Terri's guardianship money, or the money I'd received for loss of consortium. But neither he nor Mary had any legal claim, and I was certain that he couldn't grasp the fact that the bank and a trustee controlled the guardianship money—not me. I was also certain that he didn't want the legal responsibility of taking care of Terri.

I'd had enough of his crap. I said, "You go ahead and get a lawyer, and then find out how much she's going to give you."

His voice went up a few dozen decibels. "This isn't right. This is my daughter. I deserve money."

I just couldn't believe what I was hearing. He didn't say anything about having money to pay for Terri's medical care. He didn't ask for money to hire an extra private-duty nurse so that she'd have one for more than the eight hours a day I had already contracted for. He didn't say anything about getting nicer clothes for Terri, or having a hairstylist come into the nursing home for her, or anything that would benefit Terri. I don't know what he wanted the money for— except that it was definitely not going to be used to do anything for his oldest child.

I looked over and I could tell that Mrs. Schindler was getting upset. She knew me really well, and knew that I had a slow fuse, but when it burned down and I exploded, things could get ugly. She'd seen me cut loose on nursing home managers when they were making excuses about not giving Terri the care to which she was entitled. The old man was beginning to pace back and forth in the room. "I deserve money. This is my daughter," he said, in a raised voice.

I responded, my voice level up a couple of notches, too. "I don't know what anybody's going to get, yet."

Then Mrs. Schindler said, "You know, Michael, that's true. She's our daughter."

The next thing I knew, he was getting red-faced and furious. "You're going to give me money." He had moved closer to where I was sitting. Considering my height, even when I'm seated, it was not easy for him to tower over me. He's only about five-eight. But he was pointing a finger and jabbing it in my direction, and I was fighting to remain calm. I said, "You go get your damned lawyer and find out how much money you're going to get."

He shouted back at me, "I'm going to take over this guardianship; you'll see!"

That's the point at which it became clear that he'd already been thinking about how to get control of Terri's money. Before he left his business in Pennsylvania, he'd been one of the bosses. He was used to being in control, and I knew from the first time I met him that he liked being in control. I say this because I find it hard to believe that, greedy as he was, he really didn't believe that if he controlled Terri's guardianship, he could tell the bank to write him a check any time he felt like it. Bob Schindler, Sr., might not be the sharpest knife in the drawer, but he wasn't stupid. This was all about control.

I shouted at him, "Get a lawyer and find out. Go get a lawyer and take it over. We'll see who'll win that battle." As I write this, it just struck me that with all the noise and commotion in the room, Terri never reacted. She never shifted her gaze to where the noise was coming from. She never responded vocally. She never gave any indication that a fight between her husband and her parents was disturbing her.

He headed toward the door, but now he was screaming at me. "C'mon. Out in the hall, you fucking jerkoff." Now I was getting out of control. I could see him balling up his fists. I'd had it. I pushed my books aside, then jumped up, pushing the table away hard enough that the books went flying all over the room. Next thing I knew I was following him toward the hallway, shouting, "All right!" I was mad and Mrs. Schindler knew it. She jumped between us and slammed the door, saying, "Don't you dare go out there. Michael, this is not right."

"What's not right?" I shouted back at her. "I just got done telling you I don't know who's getting what, and he wants money?" A few more words were exchanged between us, and she opened the door wide enough to squeeze through, and I could hear her say, "C'mon, Bob, c'mon, c'mon, let's go."

If I could have looked in a mirror at that moment, the face looking back at me would have been an ugly one, filled with anger, even hatred. But what I saw on the face of Terri's father was worse. Because what I saw that day was greed. Red-faced anger and greed. I yanked the door to Terri's room open, and yelled, "Here I am."

I figured he'd be intimidated, but he shouted at me, "I'm going to get this guardianship; you watch!"

The amazing thing is that no one—not a visitor or a staffer—popped a head out of a room to see what the commotion was. We were screaming at each other walking down the hall. Schindler was screaming that he's going to get a lawyer, he's going to take this guardianship from me, and I'm shouting, "Go ahead! Get it! Go!"

He'd turn a bit to look at me, and then turn back. All the while, Mary was pulling him along, pleading, "C'mon, Bob, c'mon."

Before we got to the lobby, I stopped and they kept going. They turned to the right to exit through the lobby doors, and I went straight to the front desk to use the phone. I called my parents and my mother answered the phone. I said, "Do not go to this brunch. We just had a knock-down, drag-out fight." She asked me what happened, and I tried to tell her, but I'm not sure how much sense I was making. I did say, "Don't ever speak to these people again."

From the things he said and did, I could only reach one conclusion: Schindler was all about the money and this wasn't about Terri. When he began asking how much money he was going to get, he never said, "How much money am I going to get so we can build a place to take care of Terri at home?" Before the malpractice trial, we'd fantasized that if money were no object, wouldn't it be great if we could build a house with a special wing for Terri and her nurses. But that was a fantasy that the malpractice settlement would never pay for. Don't forget that the jury said the doctors were only 30 percent responsible for her problem. One of the doctors had settled before trial for a quarter million dollars. But when attorneys' fees and costs were taken off of everything, and a $100,000 bill from Mediplex was paid, we were left with less than seven hundred thousand dollars. Even Prudential went after a piece of the settlement in order to get back money it had grudgingly paid for Terri's care. While they were never able to collect, attorneys' fees to fight them took a chunk.

The Schindlers had never, ever criticized the way I was taking care of their daughter. Until the day of the fight, Mary had been a regular visitor to Sabal Palms, and she could see firsthand the demands I made for Terri's care. The truth is that Terri was being so well taken care of that the nursing home management said they'd gotten complaints from the relatives of other patients who were saying that because I was demanding such perfection in Terri's care, the other patients were being short-changed. Frankly, that argument didn't move me, because my concern was my wife. The other patients weren't my problem. Was I being selfish? Actually, no. If the other patients had relatives who were as concerned about them as I was about the care Terri was getting, maybe they would have received more attention. Stop by a nursing home and ask them how many patients they have whose relatives never check up on the care being given to their supposed loved one. You might be shocked by the answer.

Was I the "nursing home administrator's worst nightmare"? It's what the Sabal Palms administration called me when they sought a restraining order to keep me from visiting Terri. Maybe I was. I just wasn't willing to compromise on the care I wanted Terri to have. I guess I was right, because the judge laughed their request for a restraining order right out of court.

That's when I came to believe that Mr. Schindler cared more about money than about his daughter. It would take years for it all to begin to make sense—the Schindlers encouraging me to date other women well before I was emotionally ready to do so, them trying to get control of Terri's guardianship. I wanted Terri to get better. I'm convinced he wanted the money.

That's when the Schindler v. Schiavo battle actually began.

6 | Reality Strikes

One good clue that I needed to get a life was that when I had spare time, I'd hang out in the office of an orthodontist I'd become friends with, Alan Shoopak. Alan and his wife had been regulars at Agostino's, and he was very supportive of me. His entire office staff was female, and I'm now convinced that there is something genetic that makes it impossible for groups of women to resist the urge to match unattached women—even ones who profess not to be looking—with any reasonably available male. Everyone in the office knew my circumstances; Terri's collapse had been more than three years earlier, and I had stopped seeing Cindy Brashers. That put me in the target category: reasonably available. Shoopak, of course, was on board with all of this.

One day in July 1993, I was visiting Shoopak and a couple of his assistants told me that there was a patient in the waiting room that I'd really like. Her name was Jodi, she was in her late twenties, and like high-school girls trying to fix up a friend for prom, they almost pushed me through the door to the waiting room so that I could see for myself.

I walked out and took a look around a room that was filled with young moms and their kids, trying to figure out which one wasn't there with a child. Unable to sort it out by myself, I decided on the direct approach.

"Is Jodi here?" I asked.

"Here," came the rather shy reply. I walked over to her, stuck out my hand, and introduced myself.

"I just want you to know that Dr. Shoopak will be right with you." Just at that moment, one of the co-conspirators stuck her head out the door and called, "Jodi Centonze."

Jodi mumbled that she had to go, and I tried hard not to stare as she walked back to the treatment room. She had long, beautiful legs. I'm thinking *Gorgeous girl*. She was dressed in a business suit. Later I learned that she was an agent with a large insurance agency. I followed her into the back, enduring the giggling from the small pack of dental assistants who were witnesses to this encounter. Jodi had been divorced since '89 after a three-year marriage, and had recently ended a relationship with her high-school sweetheart, which to the gigglers meant she was available.

I started asking her questions, and she was a good sport, trying to give me answers, which was a difficult thing to do with her mouth open and filled with assorted hands, instruments, and suction devices. When Alan had finished with her, I followed her to the appointment desk and then out to her car. I happened to glance back at the building and could see Shoopak's staff failing miserably at being discreet as they watched us through the blinds. I asked Jodi if we could get together for dinner or whatever. "Whatever" is a guy thing; it provides an immediate alternative if the target female isn't free for the specific suggested event. Her answer was disappointing. She said, "I don't date or anything like that." I had to assume that "anything like that" was a girl thing, the female defense against the male all-purpose "whatever."

She followed up with some explanation about not being available because her five-year-old niece and eleven-year-old nephew were coming to town and she'd be tied up for the next several weeks. In Jodi's own words:

"I wasn't interested. It's hard to explain. I had a complicated child-hood. I was in a car accident in 1986 and had neck injuries from that, and then about eight months later I was in a hit-and-run car accident and was re-injured. In 1988 my parents were in a devastating crash on the Interstate where a car lost control, crossed over the entire median, and came into oncoming traffic, which happened to be the car carry-ing my parents and younger brother. My father ended up dying a cou-ple of weeks later. He was only fifty-four. My mother was a widow at fifty. She had some permanent injuries, and my brother was also hurt.

"A lot of traumatic things happened in one year's time, and I was freaked out by them. Life was short, and I had gotten married very young—I was twenty-one and he was twenty. And I just decided I wanted a divorce. I suffered a lot of anxiety attacks after that that kept me from a lot of social outings. I wasn't shy the way they describe Terri, but I wasn't very outgoing.

"When I met Mike, it was an exciting thing, because someone was interested. But I really did have plans with the kids. A few weeks later, he called me at my office and asked if I wanted to get together for 'din-ner or whatever.' I said, 'I don't do dinners,' and he said, 'Well, you must eat sometime.'

"That's when I told him—again—that I really don't date. But I told him we could meet for lunch, so he came to the office to pick me up and we went to Leverock's in Pinellas Park. It was nice; nothing spec-tacular. But we just kind of hit it off, and I agreed to see him again.

"I think we were just two hurt, lost souls who kind of needed some-one to talk to—not a sexual thing or an in-love thing, just someone to have dinner with or pick up the phone and talk to each other about whatever.

"I never paid much attention to the fact that Mike was the poster boy for Guys with Baggage; it wasn't as though I'm thinking that I'm madly in love with this guy, and he's got a wife. We'd get together and we would talk. The first time we went out on something like a real date was on a weekend, and the following Monday a dozen roses were delivered to my office with a note saying that he'd had a really nice time, and thank you.

"He was just so easy to talk to. I could tell him things that most people didn't know about me. I felt comfortable with him because I knew he had a wife, and he wasn't going to be someone trying to get me into bed right away. He was just looking for company, and that's all I wanted. What I had was a growing friendship, not a lover. It wasn't a boyfriend-girlfriend thing. It wasn't kissing. It was just comfortable."

That's Jodi. We were just so comfortable together. We went out several times, and talked on the phone a lot before I even kissed her. And it was just a simple kiss good-bye at the door when I dropped her off at her house. There were no lightning bolts. No skyrockets. Jodi had a good handle on me. She knew that I wasn't capable of getting into any kind of serious relationship. For me, this was as intimate as it got.

Meantime, I was getting tired of hearing doctors say about Terri, "Mike, there's nothing we can do." It kept echoing. *Nothing we can do nothing we can do nothing we can do . . .*

I refused to hear it. "Yes there is," I said. *Yes there is yes there is yes there is.* Because there *must* be. And I was going to bring her home. I needed to speak with someone who knew Terri, someone who had treated her for a while. Not just a specialist who blew in, read the chart, did some mumbo jumbo in the room, and declared, "nothing we can do." The malpractice settlement gave us the money to buy the best treatment possible for Terri, and I was frustrated that her condition wasn't improving.

The person I turned to was Terri's internist, Dr. Patrick Mulroy. I set up an appointment, and even though there was no need to bring Terri along, I couldn't imagine discussing the case without her sitting in the room with us. Maybe I was thinking that if she were there—if he could see her as we talked—it might make him try harder to find a way to heal her enough so that I could bring her home.

Taking her with me was a major operation. I had to get Terri to his office, about a twenty-minute ride from Sabal Palms to Largo off of East Bay Drive. So on the appointed day, we got her dressed, the private nurse I'd hired and I did her makeup, did her hair, and then put her in the special wheelchair I had gotten made for her. The nursing desk would call the wheelchair-transport company and they'd come and take Terri. Sometimes, on these off-campus trips to various doctors, I'd follow in my car, while other times I'd ride with her. I honestly don't remember which I did this time.

Dr. Mulroy wasn't Terri's physician from the start, but he saw her not too long after she was discharged from Humana Northside and sent to a nursing facility. I liked the way he dealt with both of us, so we stayed with him. I was confident he knew what he was doing. Mulroy had testified at the malpractice trial, and at that time, he had suggested that Terri could live for years in her current condition.

We got to his office and waited to see him. Eventually, we went inside. Terri was sitting in her chair and I was sitting on the exam table. When he came in, we shook hands, and I said, "This is really just a visit for you and me." He acknowledged that he understood, so I went on, "What do you think is going to happen to Terri?" I don't do subtle very well, and I have a hard time beating around the bush. I just opened up with the only thing that was on my mind; the only thing that had been on my mind since the early morning of February 25, 1990.

And Dr. Mulroy answered the question about as directly as I'd asked it. "Well, this is the way Terri is going to be the rest of her life." Just like that.

I wanted an honest answer, I wanted him to be real with me. But deep down inside I wasn't ready to hear that from him. I reacted to it the same way I reacted to every other doctor who said, "This is the way she's going to be"—with doubt. But there was something different this time, a feeling in the pit of my stomach. I sensed that I was less in doubt than I used to be. In the beginning, I was always thinking, *I'm bringing her home.* That was me—then.

But now it started to sink in. We talked for a little while. I'm not sure if I was stalling or if he was. Finally he said to me, "Why don't you let her go?" There was a long pause before either of us spoke another word. He seemed to lower his voice, sort of putting his arm around me without actually doing it, and said, "Have you thought about letting her go?"

And I said, "I know that Terri doesn't want to be like this." Almost every time I saw Terri I'd think how she'd hate being this way, how she'd never want to be this helpless, this dependent. But until this moment, I never said it out loud to anyone. Dr. Mulroy didn't give me much time to think about what he'd said before he explained further. "Why don't you think about stopping her feeding?" I had a tough time with that at the beginning. *Oh, God. Stop her feeding?* I felt that was harsh.

I said, "I don't know about that."

He told me that nature would take its course. It would be painless. Her organs would gradually shut down. But then he presented an alternative to stopping her tube-feeding. "What we can do, next infection—we can just not treat it." Terri was always prone to urinary tract infections. I knew it was just a matter of time before she had another one. "We won't treat it, and what'll happen is, things will just shut down slowly. She'll get sepsis, and it'll be very painless, and she'll just drift off." I didn't question what *painless* meant. To me it was self-explanatory; there wasn't really any question I could ask about it at that point.

My mind was still reeling from Dr. Mulroy's suggestion as we left the office. There were people outside and traffic going by, but I felt empty and alone. I was trying to reconcile how I felt going in the door with how I felt coming out. How do I come to grips with this? How do I do this? Can I do this? We had to wait for the wheelchair transport; sometimes they'd be there right on time, sometimes we'd sit there for an hour before they'd show up. I'm not sure how long we waited that day, but however long it actually was, it seemed five times longer.

The trip was always difficult because Terri was wearing a diaper and had no control of her bowels, and I had nowhere to change her. It was awful, just awful, knowing that she was sitting there in her soiled diaper.

Then there was her drooling. It would just pour out of her mouth. She'd gag, and I didn't have a suction machine with me. Her mouth would open up and all this drool would come out. I carried lots of towels with me and would keep wiping her face. Don't misunderstand me: I wasn't embarrassed that this was happening in public; I just felt horrible for Terri, because it would have humiliated her if she'd known.

In the beginning, when I first took her places in her wheelchair, I'd carry on these one-sided conversations with her. I'd hold her hand and say, "All right, Terri, we're here now. We're going to sit here and wait for the van, you know how it goes. When we get back, I'll get you in bed, get you cleaned up, and you can take a rest." I used to tell her everything that we were going to do. I'd tell her not to worry, that I would be with her, I'd stay with her. But that day, I didn't talk to her. I couldn't.

On July 29, 1993, Bob Schindler made good on his Valentine's Day threat to try to take the guardianship of Terri away from me. He and Mary filed suit in the probate division of the Pinellas County Circuit Court. It marked the first of what would be an almost uncountable number of times that *Schindler v. Schiavo*—and vice versa—would appear on a legal document. Debbie Bushnell, the attorney who had handled Terri's trust, suggested that I hire a litigator named Steven G. Nilsson of Clearwater to handle the case, and I now had to divide my attention between Terri's care and preparing for a legal battle.

Before the first depositions were to be taken, Nilsson followed up a phone call to the Schindlers' attorney, James A. Sheehan, with a letter to him addressing the issue they purported was all they really cared about—Terri's care. It said, in part:

I have represented to you that I am willing to start working immediately toward a stipulation between Michael Schiavo and Mr. and

Mrs. Schindler for the appointment of an independent guardian of the person which would provide that Mr. Schiavo and Mr. and Mrs. Schindler all have the ability to see medical records, be informed of medical decisions and have input into the care of Theresa Marie Schiavo . . . Please feel free to have Mr. and Mrs. Schindler visit Theresa Marie. There are no orders issued by Michael to prohibit the Schindlers from seeing their daughter.

I was offering to share decision-making for Terri's health care. There was no response.

On the afternoon of August 31, Steve and I met at the office of a court reporting company in Clearwater. Mary Schindler's deposition was going to be taken, and I had told my lawyer that I wanted a ring-side seat. I was surprised to discover that the event had drawn a small crowd. In addition to my attorney, there were two other lawyers: Sheehan, representing the Schindlers, and Gyneth S. Stanley, representing South Trust Bank, which handled Terri's trust fund. South Trust had also sent along one of their trust officers. The other person present, besides the court reporter, was my father-in-law, Bob Schindler, who I had last seen on Valentine's Day with his dukes up, looking for a fight. *This is going to be interesting*, I thought.

The session began at 1:22 P.M., and the BS began shortly thereafter. Mrs. Schindler said she couldn't describe the relationship I'd had with Terri up to the time of her collapse. She couldn't say whether she believed Terri loved me.

A few minutes later, Steve asked a relatively simple question: "As you sit here right now, ma'am, can you recall any incidents that occurred prior to the time Terri went into a coma that caused you to believe that she didn't love Mike as her husband?"

Instead of answering, Mary turned to her lawyer and said, "Mmm, excuse me, could I see you?"

Nilsson objected, saying the question "requires a factual answer. I don't think she's entitled to confer with counsel in order to give me a factual answer to a factual question."

At a deposition, there's no judge present to rule on objections. The lawyers just sort of try to out-bully each other to get what they want on the record in the short term, knowing that if the matter gets to a courtroom, the judge can then rule on objections and admissibility of statements made in depositions.

So Sheehan ignored my attorney and just got up and took my mother-in-law out of the room. When they returned a few minutes later, the court reporter read back the question. This time, Mary's memory appeared to have miraculously recovered.

A. There wasn't any one specific incident. She just told me that she didn't love him anymore.

Q. How many times did she tell you that she didn't love Mike?

A. A few times.

I couldn't believe what I was hearing. Mary Schindler knew we had been trying to get pregnant when Terri collapsed. Steve then asked if Terri gave her any reasons for what she'd said about not loving me.

A. She just said they were having some problems that she would work out, but she didn't think she loved him any more.

Q. Did she ever tell you that she was going to divorce him?

A. Yes.

When I heard Mary's testimony, I thought these people were willing to say anything to win. The same thought would occur to me often for the next dozen years. The notion that Terri would be trying to have a baby when she was thinking of divorcing me is about six miles beyond preposterous.

There's something I'd like to point out now, even though it only comes into play much, much later in this saga. The Schindlers were going to be painting Terri as a devout Catholic girl who regularly went to Mass and who would never consider doing anything to end a life prematurely. But this deposition was being taken years before it would help their cause for Terri to be extremely religious. And on this date, Terri's mother said her daughter had been considering divorce.

The Schindlers were contesting my guardianship of Terri, telling the court not just that they could do a better job than me in caring for their daughter, but that I was doing a lousy job. Recall that the fight in Terri's hospital room had taken place on February 14, 1993, and this deposition was being taken six and a half months later, on August 31. My attorney asked Mary about the frequency of her visits to Terri. She began by saying that whenever I went to see Terri, she was right there with me. But she wasn't. By the time my attorney finished with her, she admitted to visiting her daughter "seven, eight, or nine times—I'm not sure exactly," between February 14 and August 31. At best, that's once every three weeks, but she was "not sure exactly," so it might have been only once a month.

Now, let's look at Mary Schindler's answers to questions about money. She told my lawyer that she never anticipating receiving any of the money that Terri or I had been awarded.

Q. Okay. Did your husband ever indicate to you in any way that he thought you and your husband might receive money as a result of the lawsuit?
A. No.

Just file that response away for future reference.

———

When Steve Nilsson began preparing me for the depositions, he pointed out that the fact that I was seeing another woman—Jodi— while guardianship of my wife was being challenged would probably be used against me by the Schindlers. He wasn't making a moral judgment, just preparing me for the fact that it could become an issue. Because the Schindlers' Petition for Removal of Guardian and Appointment of Guardian claimed that "Since his appointment as guardian, the husband has been engaged in a relationship with a person other than his wife," Steve felt he might as well take the bullshit by the horns with Mrs. Schindler in the hot seat. He got her to acknowledge that she thought I had a relationship with Cindy Brashers, that I'd brought Cindy home to met her and Mr. Schindler, and that they'd never objected to my seeing Cindy:

Q. Are you aware of your husband ever saying anything to Mike like, "No, you can't go out with her," or, "We'll object, you are married, you can't do that"?
A. I don't know if he did . . .
Q. And you never did anything like that?
A. No.

Then my attorney went back to the money issue. It turns out that even though Mary Schindler had just said, under oath, that she had no information that anyone had ever told her or Bob that they might receive money as a result of the lawsuit, a letter signed "Mary and Bob Schindler" and now marked "Deposition Exhibit 2" had been sent to me in July, just six weeks before this deposition, which began, "Long before and during the malpractice trial, you made a number of commitments to Mary and myself. One of your commitments was that award money was to be used to enhance Terri's medical and neurological care.

"You also committed that the award proceeds would be used to provide a home for Terri so that Mary and I could live with her, and as her parents, we could provide the love and care she deserves on a long term basis."

The letter that both Bob and Mary Schindler had signed contradicted the statement she'd just made—under oath. I had reached the point where the contradictions no longer shocked me.

Then it was time to get into the care that I was giving Terri.

Q. Now, in the next sentence of the letter it says, "One of your commitments was that award money was to be used to enhance Terri's medical and neurological care" . . . As you sit here right now, do you believe that Mike carried through with that?
A. No . . .
Q. You say she's not been looked at since this happened?

A. Not neurologically.

Q. Okay, since she went into the coma?

A. Yes . . .

Terri spent forty-five days in intensive care at Humana Northside Hospital for a brain injury, and my mother-in-law had just testified, under oath, that since my wife went into a coma, she'd never been examined neurologically. And I guess the guys in the scrub suits wearing masks who implanted electrodes deep in my wife's brain, and who then spent months following up in the hope that Terri's brain could be stimulated into recovery, must have been what? Trick-or-treaters?

That deposition took just over three and a half hours. When it was over, Steve Nilsson told me he thought it had gone quite well. Clearly, he was accustomed to seeing the truth bent like a pretzel at these sessions. I was shocked, but it was still relatively early in my education about adversary proceedings.

Shortly after the session with Mary Schindler, Terri came down with a bladder infection. It was the first one since our visit with Dr. Mulroy. As you can imagine, what he'd said to me had been weighing on my mind. I'd thought long and hard about the times Terri had said, in one way or another, that she wouldn't want to be kept alive by extraordinary means, and while I couldn't bring myself to order her feeding tube removed, I'd reached a decision about letting her go. It was Mulroy who'd told me that if I was unable to give the order to remove the tube, I should consider not treating Terri if she developed an infection that someone in her condition almost routinely contracts. To the medical professionals, this was an equally acceptable way of "letting her go."

As a result, I issued an order to the staff at Sabal Palms that her UTI (urinary tract infection) wasn't to be treated, and had entered a DNR—do not resuscitate—order on her charts. By the time I did this, I had not won any gold stars for my behavior with the management of Sabal Palms. They had a thick folder with grievance forms that I'd filed and saw me as a royal pain in the ass. That was their problem, not mine—or so I thought.

I was sitting with Terri when one of the Sabal Palm administrators came in to tell me that by law, they were not allowed to withhold treatment. I said, "What do you mean you can't do this by law? Patients have the right to refuse medication and treatment."

And she said, "Well, we can't do it here," adding that they would not enforce my DNR order because it violated Florida law. I had no idea at the time that this wasn't so. I tried to tell her that they had to back off, that this was a decision between my wife, me, and her doctor. They disputed that, and chose to make things more complicated by informing the Schindlers' attorney about my order. Since we were already in the middle of litigation, my attorneys suggested that, for the time being, we rescind the DNR and have Terri's bladder infection treated.

On Wednesday, November 17, ten weeks after Mary Schindler's deposition, it was Bob Schindler's turn to be deposed. The same cast of characters was present as had been at Mary's session. Steve Nilsson was purposeful as he got Schindler to acknowledge that he knew Terri and I were trying to have a baby.

Q. Who told you that your daughter was trying to get pregnant?
A. I don't recall. Maybe my wife.

The same wife who said Terri told her she wanted to divorce me. Now I was beginning to understand how these deposition things worked.

Q. Did you ever have a question of why she wanted to become pregnant by Mike?
A. As opposed to Robert Redford or somebody else?
Q. As to her being dissatisfied with him in some way as a husband, so why does she want to become pregnant?
A. No.

Nilsson didn't follow up, but immediately went on to the money issue, which was what I thought this whole battle was really about.

Q. Did that upset you that you weren't able to sue to recover money on behalf of the injury that was done to your daughter?

A. No, because Michael agreed he was going to share the money with us.

I never could keep their stories straight. First I was going to give them money, then I wasn't, now I was. Mr. Schindler said during his deposition, "I do know that I fully expected to share in whatever was received other than what was given to Terri." And when Nilsson pressed him on what the meaning of "share" was, he said, "I expected half of the money."

My attorney asked Schindler if he would have still filed the petition to remove me as Terri's guardian if I'd paid him the money. His answer was barely intelligible. "If Terri would have been handled the same way she is now, yes . . . it's my daughter and I have some—just grave concerns."

Q. What is it about the way she's being handled now that is a problem for you?

A. I don't know how she's being handled. She's being maintained. That's all I know.

Q. Are you aware of any information that Mike is not doing a good job in terms of maintaining Terri?

After an objection by Schindler's attorney, who tried admirably to save his client from stepping in it, Terri's father responded, "Am I aware of that? I'm not aware that he's maintaining her. The nursing home, I think, is maintaining her."

Perhaps if he had shown up at the nursing home on a regular basis, he'd have been more aware. That's assuming he would have spent more than the usual ten or fifteen minutes per visit when he did bother to show up—most of it out in the hallway. The frequency of his visits to his daughter was best described by my attorney as "random."

Then it was time for Schindler to weigh in on what he erroneously presumed was my very active sex life. He acknowledged that I'd brought Cindy Brashers home to meet him and Mary.

A. I thought that was the step in a direction that he was really working toward, what our end plan was with Terri.

Q. Which was what?

A. That Mary and I would be taking care of her. I anticipated that he would eventually go off on his way.

Q. Get divorced?

A. Whatever.

Q. Did you anticipate that Mike would divorce Terri and remarry and start a new life with another woman?

A. I would hope that he would do that.

And he also acknowledged condoning it. A few moments later, Nilsson got to his real point, that Schindler believed that if I was in a relationship with Cindy, I would be unable to take care of Terri because, in Schindler's words, it would "be a hell of a conflict." However, he was forced to admit that the first time he ever raised this as an issue was when they filed the petition to remove me as guardian.

Toward the end of Schindler's deposition, he suggested that because I stood to inherit from Terri's estate, I had a built-in conflict in trying to care for Terri. It was apparently lost on both Schindler, his attorney, and ultimately on their legion of supporters that in a vast majority of cases in this country, the heirs are usually the ones taking care of the individual who is ill. When my attorney turned the question around and asked why it would be a conflict for me when it wouldn't be a conflict for her parents to simultaneously be her guardian and her heirs, Schindler dissembled. So Steve Nilsson changed the subject, and after getting my father-in-law to acknowledge that he had socialized with both of my parents and with my older brother, Brian, he popped this one:

Q. Did you tell Mr. and Mrs. Schiavo, Mike's parents, that the best thing for Michael was to see other women?

A. I may have.

Q. Did you tell Brian Schiavo while you were sitting at Tierra Verde Tiki Hut that Michael needed to get laid?

A. I might have. I said a lot of people need that. Both male and female.

Sure they do. But do you say it to a guy—much less think it—when his sister-in-law, who happens to be your daughter, collapsed just two weeks earlier and she was still in intensive care, in a coma, with a tube in her throat?

The deposition ended in late afternoon with an agreement that we would all meet in two days, on November 19, in Steve Nilsson's office, where the Schindlers' lawyer would have an opportunity to question me. Since my "don't treat"/DNR order hadn't come up in any of Mr. Schindler's responses to questions about how I was caring for Terri, I could be certain that the subject would arise on Friday.

The next morning, however, I had too much to do to worry about my upcoming deposition. I went to Sabal Palms early to get Terri ready for a trip to see a neurologist, Dr. Thomas Harrison. She'd been having trouble with her hip—it was starting to turn out—and the physiatrist who'd been treating her suggested that she be taken off an antiseizure medication called Tegretol. In order to do that, we had to rule out any continuing seizure activity. That meant she had to have an electroencephalogram (EEG) done, which prompted the appointment with Harrison at his office in Largo.

After an uneventful trip in the wheelchair van, I helped the technician move Terri to the reclining exam chair, and watched as she attached fifteen or twenty flat metal electrodes to her scalp. The theory of how the EEG machine works is simple: Brain cells communicate by producing tiny electrical impulses. Each electrode picks up those impulses from a specific area of the brain and transmits them to a recording device that allows the neurologist to view the patterns of electrical activity and to detect whether any abnormalities exist.

After the test, the technician left the room and Terri and I waited for Dr. Harrison. In a few moments he came back in and spent some time quietly looking at the results on the paper printout. I remember him concentrating on the EEG graph, glancing over at Terri, and then looking up at me with this very calm but questioning look on his face. And then he smacked me with the medical equivalent of a two-by-four: "Why do you let her live? She died three years ago."

I didn't have anything to say. I think my mouth may have dropped open, and I just sat there. "I'm looking at her EEG," Dr. Harrison explained, "and it's flat. There are portions where there's some electrical activity, but there's nothing cortically. Nothing, no cortical, top functioning."

How do you absorb something like that? I was thirty years old. I met Terri when she was twenty and I was twenty-one. We thought we'd be together for the rest of our lives—and that meant a long, long time. Twenty-year-olds don't expect to be dead in ten years. A lifetime means forever, and forever doesn't have an expiration date on it. Now I'm sitting in a doctor's office and he's asking me, *Why do I let my wife live?* Can you imagine how it feels to get asked that question? It says you have the power of life and death over the person who is closest to you in the whole world. It says you can legitimately play Roman emperor, and give a thumbs-up or thumbs-down.

I was just stunned. No doctor had ever said anything just like that to me—not even Mulroy had put it in terms that stark. Dr. Harrison must have seen the look on my face—how could he miss it?—and tried to explain what he meant. He said, "Her top functioning, her knowing, her feeling, her awareness of who she is and who's around her—all of that is gone."

Dr. Harrison and I talked for a few more minutes while he tried to help me understand Terri's condition. Then he said, "I notice you've taken her to Largo Medical Center for treatment. The next time she gets an infection, you could consider not treating it." That was the same thing that Dr. Mulroy had said to me, and I'd tried it, only to be told by Sabal Palms administration that it was against the law. Now, however, I knew that it wasn't; that it was a viable option. But Dr. Harrison wasn't finished. "You could also remove her feeding tube," he said. Now I'd heard it from two doctors who knew Terri and knew me.

He wasn't pushing me to do it. He was presenting it as a legitimate option for a patient in Terri's condition. As much difficulty as I had with the "don't treat" plan, I couldn't even fathom the idea of removing Terri's feeding tube. But now I had two doctors who'd reached the same conclusion about my wife's condition, and had made the same suggestion: Let her go.

That evening I spoke with Jodi and she asked me how things had gone. She recalled, "I remember him being not cold, but kind of matter-of-fact and shut down. He said they'd gone into the doctor's office and he sat him down and said, 'You realize that your wife died three years ago.' I think it was so bluntly laid out there for him that, in my opinion, it kind of really hit home for Mike. I think part of him must have known, or he wouldn't have been seeing me, but the other part didn't know or didn't want to accept it, so he was kind of leading two lives. It's as though he's thinking, 'I have Terri and she's coming back and I'm leading that life, and I'm dating Jodi because Terri's not coming back and I'm leading that life.' I just think he traveled a very fine road of confusion, because I think half of him accepted it and half of him didn't."

The next afternoon, I showed up at Steve Nilsson's office for what I now expected to be a grueling afternoon of questions from Schindler's attorney, Jim Sheehan. I was surprised when Bob Schindler showed up without Mary, and I kept glancing at the door, thinking she might be waiting to come in at the last second so she wouldn't have to spend several uncomfortable minutes facing me across the table with nothing going on in the room. But by 1:20, when Sheehan asked me to state my name and address for the record, she hadn't shown up. I had been wondering where he was going to start, and his choice shouldn't have taken me by surprise, but it did. Steve had warned me.

Sheehan asked me if I was involved "in a romantic relationship with anyone." When I said that I was, he wanted her name, and Steve Nilsson objected. He would allow me to say that we met about three months earlier, that we saw each other on weekends and once or twice during the week, that I occasionally slept over at her place, and that at the moment, I had no idea whether I anticipated a future with her.

Next he asked about my relationship with Cindy, and I told him that it had lasted about eight months, that we didn't live together, and when he asked me if it was intimate, I said it was. The fact is, nobody defined "intimate." Everyone made the assumption that I'd been sleeping with Cindy, and then with Jodi. But I wasn't. That's not to say I didn't want to, but I was so conflicted about things that I couldn't. Was my relationship with Jodi *intimate*? Absolutely. And that's how I answered Sheehan.

I was trying to figure out where he was going with this line of questioning, when he asked, "Do you anticipate that if the relationship continues that you may eventually want to divorce Terri and remarry?" I said no.

Then he got into the order I'd given not to treat Terri's urinary tract infection, and that Dr. Mulroy told me that the consequence of that decision meant Terri would develop sepsis, and die.

Q. So when you made the decision not to treat Terri's bladder infection you, in effect, were making a decision to allow her to pass on?

A. I was making a decision on what Terri would want.

There it was. The gauntlet was thrown down for all to see. It was the first time I'd declared in a legal proceeding that I knew what Terri's wishes were, and that she would not want to go on living in her current condition.

Moments later, Sheehan got into my visit with Dr. Harrison the day before, and I went on the record that the neurologist had asked me why I let Terri live, adding that he'd suggested not treating her infections and that I consider removing her feeding tube.

Next, the Schindlers' attorney began to explore why I believed Terri would not want to live in her present condition.

A. She was my wife. I lived with her. We shared things. We shared a bed. We shared our thoughts.

I told him about Terri and me coming by train from Philadelphia to Florida and talking about her uncle Fred, who'd lost his wife and child in a train wreck. He was so distraught that he got drunk and wrapped his car around a telephone pole, ending up in a coma. Terri told me he was never the same again. He was unable to walk or do things for himself; his kids had to handle all his legal affairs. That's when Terri said, "I would never want to live like that. I would want to just die."

At that point, Sheehan went back to questions that led to the argument over whether or not I'd promised the Schindlers money from the malpractice settlement. Yet again, I denied that I'd ever made any statement indicating that I'd share the money with them. I acknowledged that when the lawyers had mentioned that our malpractice case could be worth upward of fifteen million dollars, there had been talk of renting or buying a house where Terri would be able to live with the family. But that morphed into my father-in-law wanting a house with a separate apartment for Terri, and a separate entrance for her nurses to use. Sheehan asked me what I thought about Terri living at home with her mother and father.

I told him that we'd tried it and it didn't work. My mother-in-law got upset trying to help care for Terri at home, and my father-in-law never lifted one finger to help out. I was the one who got up in the middle of the night, every night, to check on Terri. I was the one who slept in her room. Terri's care was complicated; I concluded that we needed to have professionals looking after her.

Before the deposition ended, the Schindlers' attorney lobbed one other very offensive question at me. He attempted to get me to admit that it was my fault—and mine alone—that I didn't recognize the fact that Terri had an eating disorder long before her collapse. I feel badly enough that I didn't spot the symptoms, that I wasn't knowledgeable enough to have figured it out. But neither did the entire Schindler family. If they were all so close to Terri that she was telling them supposed dark secrets about her marriage, why didn't they spot the eating disorder?

Here's the bottom line. Here's where I saw the bitterness coming from. Bob and Mary Schindler were living in a small condo because that's what they could afford, and they were used to living better than that. He wanted a big house. I supposed he figured if we got a huge settlement in the malpractice case, I could build them a house where he and Mary could live. And he must have hoped that there'd be a separate wing for Terri, with its own outside entrance so her nurses could come and go without bothering them. And the worst part is that I believe it was also so that he didn't have to see Terri any more than he did when she was in a nursing home, which was best described by my attorney as "random." So, to me, this let's-build-a-house idea wasn't about taking care of Terri. It was a welfare plan for Bob and Mary Schindler.

7 | Life Gets Really Complicated

To say that my life had gotten complicated is a bit like saying hurricanes can be a bother in Florida. It grossly understates the case.

Toward the end of 1993, I was locked in a court battle over Terri's guardianship; I was conflicted about the suggestions made by two doctors, both of whom said that I should let Terri go; I was working as a nursing assistant in the Alzheimer's unit at Freedom Square Nursing Home while going to St. Petersburg Junior College to become an emergency medical technician (EMT); I was on the brink of having Sabal Palms Nursing Home take legal action against me for harassing its staff about the care being given to Terri; and I was falling in love with Jodi.

It hadn't taken long for Jodi and me to become good friends. We could talk to each other. At the time, I was living with my parents, and while I was close to them, it was more difficult to be open about what was on my mind.

The friends that Terri and I had made seemed to have drifted away as I got more and more involved with taking care of her, and I was really feeling alone when Jodi came along. She made a great confidante and sounding board.

Jodi recalled that we talked about Terri a lot. Usually I'd call her when I was leaving the nursing home and, often, I'd be upset about something that had happened. She listened to me. And the truth was, I had a lot to be upset about. In my opinion, Sabal Palms was just not giving Terri quality, around-the-clock care. I'd walked in on some appalling situations and had gotten into some loud battles with their nursing staff. Instead of fixing the problems, their response was to threaten to get an injunction that would keep me from visiting my wife and checking on her care.

Since Terri had been moved to Sabal Palms, I'd been documenting problems on their own grievance forms, which required them to respond within five working days. Unfortunately, the responses were very often defensive, rather than solution-oriented. By the fall of 1993, I had a stack that was an inch thick and growing. Here's a sampling from her stay at the place:

- Upon visiting this morning I found that Terri was not showered. The CNA (certified nursing assistant) on duty replied, "I didn't know she gets one."
- Came to visit Terri at 6:30 P.M. Found Terri sitting in the hall. Noticed another patient sitting in front of Terri. She was picking at Terri's bandages on her foot.
- Was informed . . . that Terri had a problem with diarrhea and had to be changed frequently. She also told me that Terri started to cry and moan in pain, quite loudly. The CNA had to ask the nurse a few times to do something for Terri. The CNA said the nurse would not get off the phone. The nurse finally told the CNA to go and get the nurse [from another unit] to do something for Terri. I will not hear that Terri was screaming out in pain and nobody will help her.
- Diane Gomes [the private nursing aide I'd hired] left two diapers on top of a new bag [of diapers] at 6 P.M. on 1/5/94. I came in at 9:45 A.M. on 1/6/94. Found that only two diapers were used for fifteen hours. Theresa was soaked.
- Came to visit my wife. Upon opening her door I came upon Terri sitting in a shower chair along with the CNA, Gwen. Gwen was very upset because she could not get any help in lifting Terri.

- Terri was completely soaked with urine. This is a complete lack of care in that nobody noticed that she has not turned for six hours.
- Called last night as usual to see if Terri was OK. Phone was answered by agency CNA. She proceeded to tell me Terri was doing OK. After about ten minutes conversation, the CNA told me she was giving her a whirlpool. She left Terri unattended in the whirlpool while she spoke to me on the phone.
- I was told that the physical therapy department put up a big argument about Theresa's order from the doctor. This is not the first time they have done this. If they don't want to follow a direct order from a physician, then it will be put into other people's hands.
- Found Terri without a diaper. She was soaked all the way up to her breasts. Gown was wet.

In October, the Sabal Palms' attorney wrote to my lawyer, Steve Nilsson, saying, "I realize this is a difficult situation for your client and perhaps due to this difficulty some of the anger he projects to the nursing staff at Sabal Palms Health Care Center is a result of his frustration."

The attorney, Lisa Augspurger, went on to say, "Basically, from the Sabal Palms Health Care Center perspective, Mr. Schiavo causes distress to the staff due to screaming at the staff for what he feels is delayed care for Mrs. Schiavo's needs. As I am sure you are aware, Sabal Palms is an excellent skilled nursing facility."

I have a confession to make. It comes because I'm writing this as a maturing forty-two-year-old man, not an overwhelmed thirty-year-old. It comes because I've now worked for many years as a nurse, and have a profound, personal understanding of what goes on in emergency rooms, hospitals, and nursing homes. There were times at Sabal Palms when my behavior was over the top, when I thought I was justified to yell and scream and even swear at people in both high and low places in order to get Terri the care that I wanted her to have—and quite honestly, the care that was being paid for. But I now realize that some of my demands—while legitimate—may have resulted in other residents of the facility getting less care, so that Terri could get more. And while this comes too many years too late, I'd like to offer my apologies to those residents, and to their families. I'd also like to apologize to those nursing home workers who were trying hard to do their best, but who were often working shorthanded and were unable to devote adequate time to each of their patients.

In the fall of 1993, Jodi's sister-in-law and her two young children were living with her. Around Halloween I took them to buy pumpkins, and then came home and carved them with the kids. It felt good; a temporary escape from pain and conflict. Spending time with Jodi made me feel normal.

On October 28, I had my attorney send a letter to the Schindlers' lawyer asking if they'd like to have Terri visit with them in their home on Thanksgiving. They declined, saying they already had another commitment.

Next, I took a big step and asked Jodi to come up to Philadelphia and spend Thanksgiving with my family. She agreed, but was nervous. We stayed with my brother Steve, his wife, Pam, and their two kids, and slept in separate bedrooms. The whole experience was kind of awkward. Jodi wasn't comfortable with our relationship yet, and since my rather large extended family hadn't yet met her, there were a lot of well-intentioned but disconcerting comparisons to Terri. In fact, every so often someone would slip and call her Terri—something I'd actually done a few times, too.

It hurt Jodi's feelings when one of my sisters-in-law said she could understand why I liked her because she was so much like Terri. Jodi said, "The interesting thing is that as much as it was uncomfortable, I was comfortable with his family. It's difficult to explain. They took me in and accepted me and made me feel welcome—even with the references to Terri or the occasional slipup when someone called me Terri."

We went back to Florida after Thanksgiving and continued our relationship. But Jodi sensed that even as she and I were growing closer, I was conflicted. She's a smart woman and doesn't mince words—even now. "Mike couldn't handle it. His heart belonged to somebody else, and having a relationship with another woman was just not something he could deal with. And as our friendship progressed to more—once it kind of reached that threshold, he was gone."

Our first breakup was just before the holidays in December 1993. I could feel it coming, but more important, so could Jodi. She says it was as though I couldn't allow myself to enjoy life with her at Christmastime because it reminded me of the good times I'd had with Terri and both the Schindler and Schiavo families. So I just did a disappearing act.

Jodi recalled, "A couple of the girls that worked at my company didn't like Mike anymore. They felt he was hurting me—which he was—and that made them angry. But my mother used to tell me to just stick with him. She'd say, 'Jodi, he needs a friend, and he's just consumed with guilt because he's living and she's not. Trust me, I know.' My mom and dad had been in a car accident. She survived, my dad didn't, and she's suffered from survivor guilt ever since. She kept telling me that God sent me to Michael, and just to hang in there with him."

In January 1994, Terri had emergency gallbladder surgery. A week later, we got an indignant letter from the Schindlers' attorney, complaining that neither he nor the Schindlers had been notified about it.

Steve Nilsson responded in kind. "If the Schindlers visited their daughter on a daily rather than a rare basis, they would have learned of the surgery sooner than they did." He also said, "We previously offered in good faith a resolution of this matter by appointment of an independent guardian. Your clients have refused that proposal and have insisted on litigation." Steve was a lot nicer than I would have been. The Schindlers wanted sole control of Terri's guardianship, which would give them ultimate control of her money. They weren't interested in seeing an independent guardian have that control, something I had no problem with.

As things turned out, it was Judge Thomas Pennick in the Pinellas County Probate Court who decided that the way to resolve the issue was not with dueling depositions, but by appointing a guardian *ad litem* to conduct an investigation into whether I was fit to remain as Terri's guardian, or whether, as the Schindlers requested, I was unfit and should be removed.

The man he appointed was an attorney in nearby Largo, John H. Pecarek, who had appeared before Judge Pennick in several cases, and who the judge obviously trusted to do a credible job. Pecarek conducted his investigation by interviewing me, the Schindlers, and employees and management at Sabal Palms, and by reviewing the depositions that had been previously taken. Steve Nilsson pointed out, in a letter, that we had made an offer of settlement to the Schindlers in August 1993. Nilsson wrote, "I believe this proposal to the Schindlers absolutely reflected Mike's good faith and would have remedied all complaints the Schindlers made against Mike without the additional litigation expense that now is being incurred. Quite frankly, I believe it is Mr. and Mrs. Schindler and not Mike who are failing to proceed in good faith. Although Mike subsequently withdrew his settlement proposal on January 26, 1994, I do not believe it was unreasonable for Mike to do so when after the offer was on the table for five months, it becomes obvious that Mr. and Mrs. Schindler had no intention of accepting it and stopping the wasteful litigation."

Steve also sent Pecarek an affidavit from one of Terri's doctors who commented on the care that I was providing my wife.

About a month or so after I broke it off with Jodi, I went back to her. It was the start of a pattern that would go on for almost a year. At first, I just called to tell her about things that were happening at the nursing home with Terri. We would talk, and then it would grow again into something more. And I'd break up with her again. Jodi knew what was going on with me: I just couldn't handle the guilt that grew inside of me for having strong feelings for two women. I hadn't yet figured out that it was possible to have that kind of love for two women at the same time. Or maybe that's not quite correct. I think it's possible that I'd figured it out—but I couldn't bring myself to accept it. So it should come as no surprise to anyone when I tell you that our next breakup was in mid-February, around Valentine's Day. I sent red roses to Terri's room at Sabal Palms, went to visit her, and sat and cried.

On Tuesday, March 1, Judge Pennick held a hearing on the Schindlers' challenge to my guardianship of Terri at which the guardian *ad litem* orally presented his report. In the courtroom, Pecarek said that while I was "a nursing home administrator's worst nightmare," the result of my behavior was that Terri got better care than other patients in the same facility. His bottom line was very precise: I had acted "appropriately and attentively" toward Terri, and there was no cause to remove me as her guardian.

Shortly after the guardianship case was settled, we moved Terri out of Sabal Palms, to Palm Garden of Largo.

My Valentine's Day split from Jodi lasted a bit more than a month. By late March, we were back together. I'd moved out of my parents' home and into my own apartment, and I'd bought a Jeep, so I'd had some things to talk about and an excuse to call Jodi. We lasted a lot longer this time.

On April 3, Jodi went with me to my parents' home to celebrate my birthday. At the party I introduced her to a friend of mine named Russ, whose wife had terminal cancer. They had two small kids, and it was tough watching Russ deal with losing his wife. I'm not sure why, but for some reason Russ felt that it would be okay to set me up with a friend of his. Jodi and I had rented some movies and we were watching them, when this girl called. I spoke to her for a few minutes, then said, "I have company now. Can I call you back later?"

Jodi got upset, and said something like, "Clearly, you don't relay to your friends what you feel about me, because my friends would never give the number of another guy to me." One thing led to another, and suddenly Jodi was packing the movies she'd brought and heading down the stairs.

I'm screaming, "Don't leave," and she's saying, "You have ripped my heart out for the last time!" It was raining, and she was crying as she got in her car and drove home.

This is painful to remember. As Jodi describes the time, "I was thinking, *I've been through this up and down, up and down, and I'm done with it*. A few minutes later, there was a knock on my door, and I was all excited thinking that he had chased me down to apologize. Nope. He was angry, too, and had come to my house to pick up all his stuff. All I could say was, 'Here, take it and get out of my house'—which really meant get out of my *life*. That was our longest split. I was absolutely devastated.

"Months went by, and then one day he called to tell me that Russ's wife had died. I could tell he was having a tough time with it, so we got to talking. From there, we started back into the friendship thing—just phone calls, no get-togethers or dinners, and gradually, it just grew.

"I got the feeling then—it was early October 1994—that he was a little more emotionally available, but still with such a cluttered head. He was trying to lead two separate lives, and it was a challenge.

"One afternoon, I was on my hands and knees in my front yard. I'd just had a sprinkler system put in, and I was laying several pallets of sod. I'm a very independent woman, always have been—and I always will be. I didn't need a man. But Mike had come over to help me, and we were all grimy, and he asked me to marry him, someday.

"My response was something like, 'whatever.'

"He said, 'I knew you wouldn't believe me,' and then he reached into his pocket and took out this engagement ring. I'm not sure what kind of reaction Mike was expecting, but our situation was so different from most couples who get engaged. It wasn't, 'Oh, I got a ring! We're going to get married!' That wasn't even the intention of Mike when he gave it to me. I guess it really wasn't like an engagement ring. It was more like a promise—a pretty *big* promise. Michael gave it to me to show his sincerity. Maybe it was an apology for the entire year and a half, the ups and downs, I'm here, I'm not here. There was just so much hurt behind those eyes.

"Let me tell you something. When you first meet him, you could almost not like him if you were a guy. My brother didn't like him at all because he came across cocky. But he wasn't. It was just a cover, I believe, for all the hurt and pain. So, for me, the ring was more like he wanted to prove to me that whenever it would be, he would be there for me. He knew he couldn't marry me tomorrow or next year or whenever—it really didn't matter. He felt that I wouldn't believe him unless he produced something. That was his way of letting me know, 'I really did buy you a ring, and I can't promise you when or whatever, but I'm sincere.'

"For the longest time, I didn't even wear it. Didn't tell any of my girlfriends. I didn't want to tell people about it because it's so hard to explain. And that sucked all the joy right out of it. You know the glow that a girl has when she gets a ring? There was no glow. It was just different for us. I knew there was Terri, and I knew that she was his first priority, that he had a lot to do with her. Finally, when I started showing people the ring and they'd ask, 'When?' I'd say '2000,' because it was so far away."

———

The next three years were relatively quiet in terms of litigation. In 1995, Jodi and I built a house in Oldsmar. I had money from the malpractice award, and Jodi sold her house and the rental properties she owned. We put the new house in her name. No contracts between us, nothing. It was the best gesture I could have made. I was getting started in my career as a registered nurse, and Jodi was being regularly promoted at the insurance agency where she continued to work. We lived our lives like normal people. A couple of times a week I'd go visit Terri at Palm Garden. On Sundays, my parents would visit Terri, pick up her laundry, and my mom would do it and bring it back the following week. Don't forget that Terri's own parents lived in the area, closer to the nursing home than my folks or I did at the time. They rarely visited—and they certainly didn't do her laundry.

Living together was an adjustment for us, just as it's an adjustment for every committed couple that does it. We had our hopes and dreams, but I felt they were on indefinite hold because I also had Terri. Jodi loved me enough that she was willing to accept it. Talk about unconditional love. How many women do you know who'd do that for a man?

In 1996, my mom, Claire, was diagnosed with cancer of the gall-bladder. It's a rare form of the disease that occurs most often in women, and it's often diagnosed too late for effective treatment. Jodi and I were over there every day, helping and taking care of her. We reached a point, however, where none of the therapies being tried was working. One of my sisters-in-law in Philadelphia is a nurse, and she was able to get Mom into the care of some doctors up there. We explained this to Mom, and she made the decision to move up north.

Unfortunately, it didn't help. When I took my parents to the airport, my dad got out of the van to get a wheelchair and my mother asked, "Am I coming home?" Imagine that. And I lied to her. I said, "Yes, you're going to come home." That ripped my heart out for years, knowing that I had to say that to my mother when I didn't really know the answer, but I didn't want to say no.

They did a lot of tests, and after a few months, they did surgery—opened her up and closed her right back up. She had adenocarcinoma. It grows like a sheath, wrapped around everything, and couldn't be picked up on a CT scan. Mom was only sixty-five, and it was incredibly hard for all of us to deal with the fact that she wasn't going to make it.

She wasn't able to eat by mouth, and the doctors wanted to know if they could feed her through a tube. It was my dad who went in to talk it over with her. They'd been together more than forty years. They were like buddies—people said they even looked alike. He told her what the doctors suggested, and that it would give her a few more weeks. And she said, "No, no. Just leave it alone." When he came out of her room, he was in tears, and we all were, too. I told him it would be okay, and then I hugged my dad. It was the first time in a long time that he'd hugged me. I said, "It'll be all right, Dad, we'll all get through this."

After Mom was transferred to a nursing home because there were no hospice beds available, Jodi flew up to see her. Jodi remembers walking into Mom's room, and being shocked at how sick she looked. Jodi said, "She knew she was dying. She looked at me, and said, 'I knew you would come.' I sat there and clipped and filed her nails, and we just talked. After a few days, I said good-bye, and flew back home."

My mom slept most of the time. A few days before the end, I was sitting next to her bed just holding her hand, when she woke up. She looked at me and said, "You know something? It's okay." Then she went back to sleep. I knew what she was talking about. I knew she was telling me that it was okay to die, and to stop being selfish. Right then is when I made my decision with Terri. I couldn't be selfish anymore. I couldn't keep Terri alive for me.

It's as though she answered for Terri. There's not a day that goes by that I don't think about that. Not a day. My mother gave me the strength to get through all this. She told me it was okay; just those few little words made it feel so right. I had a long conversation with a woman from the hospice, talking about my mom, talking about Terri, and I realized that the hospice had a lot to offer people in our situation. I think it was that woman who described the realization mom had given me as a gift.

In June 1997, Mom died. My dad had placed an obituary in the local newspapers in Philadelphia, and it said Jodi Centonze was my fiancée. Someone must have sent it to the Schindlers in Florida. It was the first time they'd seen her name.

When I returned home to Florida, Jodi and I took the time to talk about what I'd experienced with my mom's death, and it clarified some of the things I'd discussed with the hospice woman in Philadelphia. When I talk about not carrying out Terri's wishes because I was selfish, I mean that I'm the one who had a tough time dealing with the removal of her feeding tube. I didn't want to put *myself* through the emotional pain of doing it; it really didn't have anything to do with Terri.

The lesson I took from the experience of watching my mom face death was that I should stop putting off the decision for Terri.

Jodi watched me wrestle with this change in attitude. She saw it happening, step by step. And she was probably a lot clearer about what was going on than I was. Jodi said, "It wasn't that Mike suddenly remembered what Terri wanted; it was just a psychological thing for him. Now that he'd walked through it with his mom, he felt it was okay to walk through it with Terri. Claire had made him see that it was okay. She gave him the courage and strength to finally do what he needed to do for Terri."

I went to see Debbie Bushnell, my guardianship attorney, in Dunedin, a small, historic village about fifteen minutes from where we lived. We talked for a while, and she put me in touch with George Felos, the litigator who would be with me on this case all the way to the end.

At my first meeting with George, I told him that I wanted to carry out Terri's wishes. I think Debbie had already given him a heads-up on the antagonism between the Schindlers and me. I explained the entire story to him, from Terri's collapse, what went through my head, the malpractice case, and the guardianship battle. I took him all the way through my mother dying and how her telling me that it was okay to die finally showed me the right course to follow with Terri.

George asked me to tell him all the times that Terri had, in various ways, expressed her desire not to live the way she was being kept alive, and I went through each of them. He told me to track down everyone who might be able to testify to Terri's wishes, even though he explained that it was possible that just my testimony would be enough for the judge to conclude that there was clear and convincing evidence that Terri would not have wanted to live this way.

"Clear and convincing" was the standard that was established by the Florida Supreme Court in 1990, when it decided the case of Estelle Browning. It was a case that George Felos handled, a case that made him, in the minds of some, a "right-to-die" attorney.

Estelle Browning was an eighty-six-year-old woman who had suffered a stroke that had left her brain-damaged. Because she was unable to swallow, she was being fed and hydrated by a tube that went through her abdomen and directly into her stomach. Technically, her condition wasn't terminal, but she had no hope of recovery. The court ruled in *Browning* that there was a right to die if clear and convincing evidence

existed that the patient had expressed such a desire in writing, in conversation, or by designating someone to make the decision.

George said that it would take eight months to a year to develop a
legal plan that would result in me having the backing of the court to
withdraw Terri's feeding tube. In the meantime, a month after my
mom died I had received my license as a registered respiratory therapist (RRT), and in yet another almost bizarre twist in this saga, I found
myself assisting other families in carrying out the end-of-life wishes of
their loved ones.

An RRT is the person who intubates patients who are unable to
breathe on their own. To do that, we insert an instrument called a la-
ryngoscope through the vocal cords and into the trachea so that oxygen can be delivered to the lungs through a tube going through either
the mouth or the nose. There are a number of other procedures we
do, as well, but for the sake of this discussion, I'll just talk about intu-
bation and ventilators.

The ventilator is a machine that is actually breathing for a patient
who is unable to do it on his or her own. It pumps in oxygenated air
under pressure, and removes carbon dioxide, causing the chest to rise
and fall. Terri was on a ventilator for several days after her cardiac arrest, but even though she was in a coma, and then in a persistent vegetative state, she regained the ability to breathe on her own and the
ventilator was removed.

Most of the patients I was working with at Mease Dunedin Hospital were elderly, and had conditions that were clearly terminal. Were it
not for the ventilator breathing for them, they would have died. So it
was a regular occurrence for me to be there when a family and their
physician made the decision to remove life support.

The procedure itself is relatively simple. Some families stay throughout it, others leave the room and return when it's all over. What I
would do is turn off the ventilator, then disconnect it from the patient's mouth, and carefully pull the tube out. All that remains to do is
to push the machine back and help the nurse clean the patient and
disconnect IVs.

Depending on the patient's condition, some expire very quickly, some live a little while, perhaps ten minutes. Their heart is still beating, but they're not breathing. Having a chance to work with patients for a while, to talk with their families, and to understand that they were working through the decision was the nice part of the job. They know their loved one isn't going to suffer anymore. My first patient was an elderly woman whose heart had failed. I was able to stay with the family after I'd removed the ventilator—stay with them until it was over, and even cry with them. And when it is over, they're often overwhelmed, suddenly missing their mom or dad or wife or husband. I've hugged a lot of people as an RRT and, later, as a nurse.

That said, you may find it strange when I say that I also hated when the families came in. I loved taking care of people and helping families. I stood there with them, held them, and cried with them. But it was the part that I hated the most because I knew they were hurting. I knew the person who just died wasn't hurting anymore. They were peaceful; they were with God. But their family was hurting, and I knew what it was like because I'd lost grandparents, and at that point in time I'd lost my mother. It hurts and it's very sad.

I always thought about Terri when I was in a situation like that. Sometimes, when a priest would come in to administer last rites, I'd watch him putting the sign of the cross on their forehead, and I'd flash back to that room at Humana Northside with Terri. But I always knew that Terri would go the same way as these people I'd helped. Very peacefully.

While George was preparing to file the court papers, I continued working as an RRT and went to school to become a registered nurse. Jodi was now a vice president with the insurance agency, and we were living in the house we'd built in the Eastlake section of Oldsmar.

I thought that the first Christmas after my mom died would be the saddest of my life, but something happened that made it one of the happiest in recent years. Jodi and I had been talking about getting a dog. Every Christmas eve since we'd gotten serious, we'd exchange some silly little present. In '97, she gave me a golden retriever calendar.

We always had Christmas at our house. It was always a family mob scene, with twenty-five or thirty people. But on that Christmas, Jodi was acting very strange. She kept running in and out of the garage, and when I asked her what she was doing, she said, "Oh, just getting things ready for dinner."

Well, I was sitting on the patio, and the next thing I knew Jodi's mother comes barreling through with, "Merry Christmas, Merry Christmas," and she comes right to me, not stopping to say hello to anyone else. I thought, *This is strange*. But her mom stood there and kept talking to me, and Jodi disappeared into the garage again.

"Where's Jodi?" I asked, and her mom said she'd gone out to help her brother Steve. Next thing I knew, I was standing there with my back to the garage, talking with Jodi's mom, Ellie, and I heard an un-expected noise behind me—sort of a little cry. I turned around and there was Jodi with this tiny golden retriever puppy in her arms.

I said, "Oh, my God, what's this?"

Jodi said, "This is your Christmas gift." And I started crying. It was the best gift I ever got in my life—along with my little red wagon, maybe. The puppy just sat there and licked me; I was crying; every-body was crying. My mother had just died, it wasn't going to be a very good Christmas, and then Jodi got me the puppy. She was per-fect. We called her Samantha, or Sam—or some more creative names when she's bad. It was the perfect end to an imperfect year.

8 | The First Petition

Under Florida law, there's no question that I, as Terri's guardian, had the sole right to decide if and when the feeding tube should be removed, or treatment should be withheld, or a DNR order should be placed.

The problem, as it was explained to me by a very patient George Felos, was that if I aggressively went ahead and issued those orders, we'd be overwhelmed by a blizzard of motions from the Schindlers, and a judge would likely prevent me from proceeding until the case was heard in court.

Felos felt it would be better to take the proactive step of asking a judge to issue an order for the removal of Terri's feeding tube, and in May 1998, that's what we did. The petition was filed in the probate division of the Pinellas County Circuit Court, and was randomly assigned to Judge George Greer.

The Petition for Authorization to Discontinue Artificial Life Support, and Suggestion for Appointment of Guardian Ad Litem, asked the court to do four very specific things. First, "Make a finding there is clear and convincing evidence of the Ward's intent to forego artificial provision of sustenance in her current condition." "Clear and convincing" is the standard that must be met under the *Browning* decision for the court to rule that even though the patient did not leave a written directive, there is enough other evidence that the court is convinced that the patient did not want to be sustained on artificial life support.

Then, "Enter an order authorizing Petitioner to proceed with the discontinuance of said artificial life support."

Next, "In the event this court does not find clear and convincing evidence of the Ward's intent, make a finding it is in the best interest of the Ward that artificial life support be discontinued, and thereupon, enter an order authorizing the guardian to proceed with the discontinuance of said life support."

Finally, "Appoint, should the court feel it appropriate and necessary, a guardian *ad litem* in this cause."

The petition succinctly laid out the facts as we saw them. It said, "since the date of this cardiorespiratory arrest, the Ward has been in an irreversible profoundly debilitated condition," and that "the Ward has lost the ability to intake fluid and nutrition naturally and her life can only be sustained by the artificial provision of nutrition and hydration."

It spelled out our belief that before her collapse, Terri "specifically expressed her desire not to remain alive should she be in an irreversible condition as described above, and not to have her life maintained by artificial means should she be in such condition," adding that Terri "is entitled to have artificial sustenance discontinued pursuant to Article I, Section 23 of the Florida Constitution, Chapter 765 of the Florida Statutes, the common law of the State of Florida, and the Fourteenth Amendment to the United States Constitution."

The petition also dealt with the notion of a financial conflict of interest, making clear that both the Schindlers and I hypothetically could "substantially gain financially by asserting their respective positions regarding discontinuance of the Ward's artificial life support." That's why we suggested to the court that the appointment of a guardian *ad litem* might be advisable in connection with the issue of discontinuance of artificial life support. Clearly, although the Schindlers and their lawyers did their best to make it appear as though they'd exposed this conflict of interest, we were the ones who raised the issue, not because we believed that the inheritance of Terri's estate would have any impact whatsoever on my decision to end artificial life support, but to call attention to it so that it could be dismissed as a meaningful issue.

On June 11, 1998, Judge Greer appointed a local attorney, Richard L. Pearse, Jr., as guardian *ad litem* (GAL) for Terri. The appointment order said that Pearse was appointed "for the purpose of reviewing the request for termination of life support," and that he "shall make such inquiry as is deemed necessary and shall file a written report and recommendations with the Court." The fee for his services was to be paid out of the guardianship assets.

George was not happy with the choice of Pearse. The two of them had an adversarial history, and he was concerned whether we were going to get a fair hearing. When I asked what the problem was, George explained that he'd cross-examined Pearse in a guardianship battle back in 1991 and that Pearse felt that Felos had gone on the attack without justification. During the cross-examination, it apparently became clear that Pearse was not aware of various aspects of the case, that he was not prepared to discuss it in as much detail as other expert witnesses, and that he'd spent only an hour reviewing the lengthy briefs that were submitted in the appellate court, compared to more than six hours for the attorney that Felos had called as an expert witness.

The contested issue had to do with setting the fee that George would be paid for his work on the case. Pearse testified that a reasonable appellate fee would range between $10,000 and $12,500. The court ultimately ordered that George should be paid $17,250.

It wasn't a life or death matter, but all we could do was wait and watch because Judge Greer stuck with Pearse.

We had one face-to-face conference with Pearse at which he asked me what my response was to what he referred to as a "settlement proposal" made by the Schindlers. We had been told by one of the Schindlers' lawyers that a private donor would be willing to give me $700,000 if I would just give Terri to her parents and walk away. Just the notion that Pearse would call an attempt to buy Terri from me a "settlement proposal" really ticked me off. Since this was never about the money for me, I was clear that no amount of money could make that happen. Debbie Bushnell conveyed that message to them, but they never seemed to get it. They kept upping the ante. We didn't know whether or not they were out there soliciting this ransom money, or whether the offers were being spontaneously made. Toward the end, one confidential offer was submitted to George Felos by an attorney in Boca Raton, Florida. The amount was several million dollars. We got another offer from a San Diego businessman of a million dollars. My answer never changed: No.

After telling Pearse that I rejected the Schindlers' cash offer, I said to him that as Terri's husband, I should be the one making the decision and following her wishes. There was more that I wanted to say, but didn't think I'd be able to stay calm while saying it, so on July 13, George sent Pearse a letter setting forth my position and the reasons for it.

"My client does not believe the Schindlers' proposal was made in good faith. He is certain the Schindlers realize that he would never accept the proposal, and therefore believes the Schindlers made the proposal just for purposes of posturing."

After briefly commenting on the dispute I had with Bob Schindler over his contention that I'd promised him money from the malpractice settlement, George added, "Mr. Schindler's animus towards my client is also evidenced in his deposition testimony about Theresa's eating disorder. He, in essence, blames Michael for contributing to Theresa's death because Michael didn't recognize the eating disorder. (This, notwithstanding the fact, that Mr. Schindler later admits that neither he nor Theresa's mother had any indication that she suffered from an eating disorder.)"

Debbie's take on the cash offers was that it was just another way for the Schindlers to keep the media focused on their side of the story. Think of TV news cameras as a nest of baby birds, mouths open, always needing to be fed. They're not fussy about what you feed them, just so it keeps coming. The Schindlers, with their well-financed PR campaign, were better able to tend to that kind of feeding than we were.

———

In September, while waiting for Pearse to deliver his report to Judge Greer, we arranged to have neurologist Jeffrey Karp examine Terri and study her complete medical history. The Schindlers had regularly complained that she hadn't been checked out by neurologists, and this was evidence that I hadn't been properly taking care of her. Evidently they didn't like the prognosis that every doctor who'd examined Terri had made, just like I didn't for the first three years, and they kept hoping that if we just shopped for the right doctor, we'd find one who felt that Terri would one day recover from her brain injury.

Dr. Karp's report began with a history of her case, and then he described in detail the examination he conducted at the Palm Garden Convalescent Center, where she'd been since 1994. Finally, he reported his impression, below, precisely as he presented it to us:

The patient has evidence of profound brain injury. She apparently had this as a result of anoxic cerebral damage, secondary to a cardiopulmonary arrest in 1990. There was some seizure activity initially, but this has not been present for many years and she has been off of Tegretol or other anticonvulsants for several years now. According to Dr. DeSousa's notes, her EEG did not show seizures but just showed slowing compatible with her encephalopathy. A CT scan showed significant atrophy of a generalized nature.

Her examination does indicate that she is in a chronic vegetative state. She does not meet the criteria of being brain dead, but according to the Florida Statue [sic] definitions provided to me by Mr. Felos, under Section 765-101, subset 15-B, the patient is in a persistent vegetative state. She has permanent and irreversible condition. Despite her eyes being open, she does not appear to be aware or responsive to her environment. There is an absence of voluntary activity or cognitive behavior, and inability to communicate or interact purposefully with her environment.

In the absence of good total and skilled nursing care, this patient would be unable to survive. She has a percutaneous feeding tube in place as her only source of nutrition. She is at high risk for recurrent infections, plus respiratory, secondary to aspiration, in her chronic vegetative state, as well as urinary infections and decubitus ulcer formation with subsequent infections.

Again, since this has been a long time since the incident, I feel that her chance of improvement to a functional level is essentially zero. She again meets the definitions by Florida Statute for chronic vegetative state.

Regretfully, there were no surprises in Dr. Karp's report. We provided the guardian *ad litem* with a copy, and waited to see what impact it would have.

Our first clue that Pearse wasn't doing what we thought he should be doing came when we discovered that while he interviewed a number of witnesses for the Schindlers, the only person on our side of the case that he spoke with was me.

Our second clue came about a month after we had given Pearse the results of Dr. Karp's exam, in a phone call on October 13 to my guardianship attorney, Debbie Bushnell. During the conversation, Pearse said he had a "problem" with my credibility because of the potential inheritance of Terri's trust funds, which at the time amounted to between $350,000 and $400,000. Pearse said this "problem" could be alleviated if I gave up the money. He suggested to Debbie that I should agree to donate to charity any inheritance I'd receive when Terri died.

In that same phone call, for no apparent reason other than making conversation, Debbie says Pearse brought up the incident when George Felos had cross-examined him in the 1991 case. At the time, Debbie didn't think it was a big deal, so when she told Felos about the inheritance issue, it didn't cross her mind to mention that Pearse was still annoyed with him because of what had happened between them seven years earlier.

The next day, Felos called Pearse to get some idea of when he would be issuing his report. During that conversation, Pearse said that from his personal and moral point of view, tube feeding was different from other life support, and that he generally had problems with the practice of discontinuing artificial feeding. In response, George reminded Pearse that under Florida law, artificial feeding is viewed as any other form of medical treatment, and thus can be refused or withdrawn as is legally done with other forms of medical treatment. The GAL said he was aware of the law, and that he could set aside his personal feelings and convictions and make his determination according to the law. I think that's the point at which alarm bells began sounding in George's Dunedin offices.

A week after Pearse's phone call to Debbie, Felos sent a letter to the Schindlers' attorney, Pamela Campbell, with a copy to the guardian *ad litem*, that attempted to deal with my alleged credibility problem. It reiterated my position that my effort to let Terri go was based on what I knew her wishes were.

Then George got into the money issue. "Unfortunately, the fact that the law makes Mr. Schiavo the recipient of his wife's estate, has been utilized to cast suspicion on his motives. My client has also repeated with frequency that Theresa's well-being is his only concern. As it appears that the issue of money may be impeding the release of Theresa from this lingering and extended death, my client makes the following offer to resolve this case:

"One. Mr. and Mrs. Schindler shall withdraw their objection to the termination of artificial provision of nutrition and hydration.

"Two. Mr. Schiavo, shall donate the net proceeds of Theresa's estate to a charity of his choice, so long as it is duly recognized by the Internal Revenue Service as a tax-exempt entity under Section 501 of the Internal Revenue Code."

George gave the Schindlers ten days to accept the offer, at which time it would be automatically withdrawn. On November 5, he sent a letter to Pearse informing him that the Schindlers had rejected our settlement proposal. All we could do then was sit back and wait to see what the GAL's report to Judge Greer was going to say.

On December 29, 1998, six months after he accepted the assignment, Pearse filed a fourteen-page report in which he recommended against the removal of Terri's feeding tube. As I studied it, I found myself getting angry. It was filled with misinformation, innuendo, and personal attacks on me. Or at least that's the way I read it; whether or not he intended it that way, only he can say.

Pearse got derailed at the bottom of the first page, and it went downhill from there. Referring to Terri as "the ward"—a phrase I never got used to—he wrote, "The ward was raised as a Roman Catholic, and according to the ward's parents, continued to practice her religion." Why didn't he ask me? I would have told him that Terri only attended church once or twice a year, never went to confession, never took holy communion, used birth control, and we both had agreed that if she were to get pregnant and the fetus suffered from a serious abnormality she would have had an abortion.

Allow me to share with you the highlights of my attorney's response, which was filed with the court on February 2, 1999. (Pearse's report can be viewed on the Web in the Schiavo Timeline at Miami. edu.)

For starters, the GAL failed to disclose to Judge Greer that I had offered to divest myself of my financial interest, "an offer which was orchestrated by the Guardian Ad Litem himself." Felos noted that the GAL "was not appointed to mediate or arbitrate this matter. His conduct in trying to effect a settlement . . . is highly questionable."

Next, George said that the GAL "chose to minimize the potential gain of Respondents," the Schindlers. The report said that if the petition is denied and Mr. and Mrs. Schindler become the ward's heirs, "there is no way to quantify the projected potential financial gain to the Ward's parents upon her eventual death because there is no reliable way of predicting how much of her estate will be left." Felos charged that "the Guardian Ad Litem fails to mention that if the Schindlers become heirs-at-law upon a denial of this petition, they could change their position, have the artificial life support removed and thus realize the same 'substantial and fairly immediate financial gain' the Guardian Ad Litem asserts the Petitioner [me] would receive."

I had thought, as I've said, that for Bob Schindler, the case is all about the money. Under "Relative Financial Need of the Parties," Felos wrote, "The Guardian Ad Litem omitted information regarding condition of the parties. Financial need is a relevant factor in determining whether a party is motivated by financial gain. Mr. Schiavo is financially stable. He received a $630,000 net verdict for loss of consortium in the medical malpractice litigation [which actually was reduced by attorneys' fees and costs], and is well employed at this time [I was working as a registered respiratory therapist at a local hospital]. By contrast, Mr. and Mrs. Schindler experienced financial pressures and a bankruptcy [that was established in the 1993 depositions when they attempted to take guardianship of Terri, a petition they later withdrew with prejudice]. According to Petitioner, Respondents have a significant financial need."

Next, Felos went after Pearse's suggestion that immediately after I received the settlement, I decided to let Terri die. It's a notion that would be used against me by the Schindlers' supporters for the next several years. Pearse's report concludes that "at or around the time the litigation was finally concluded, he has a change of heart concerning further treatment . . ."

Pearse falsely claimed that before February 1993, I was a regular visitor at Terri's bedside, but that after I got the money, he implies that I didn't visit her regularly and was not actively and closely involved in her care. "Not only is this implication false," Felos wrote, "it conveniently supports the Guardian Ad Litem's conclusion that receipt of litigation money affected the Petitioner's relationship or care for his wife."

George goes on to write, "From February, 1993, through 1996,

Petitioner visited the Ward three to five times per week with most visits lasting between five and seven hours. In 1997 and 1998, because Petitioner has been in school and is working, he has visited the Ward at least once or twice per week and calls the nursing home at least once or twice a week. He still retrieves his wife's clothes from the nursing home, does her laundry, and makes sure that all her medical needs are attended. By not reciting these facts in his report, the Guardian Ad Litem attempts to create an erroneous inference to support his opinion of adverse 'chronology.' "

Pearse's report recited the Schindlers' contention that our marriage "was in difficulty during months prior to the accident." The report also included Mrs. Schindler's statement that "the Ward told her that she was no longer in love with her husband and was considering ending their marriage." My attorney wrote, "Here again, the Guardian Ad Litem purposefully omits a crucial piece of information from the report. At the time of the Ward's accident, the Ward was seeking medical treatment to become pregnant. Why, as asserted by the Petitioner, would the Ward be taking extraordinary measures to have a child with him, if their marriage was in the condition characterized by Respondents?"

Ultimately, my attorney castigated Pearse for failing to include in his report two very important legal points: first, that Florida law holds that artificial feeding can be withdrawn from a permanently vegetative patient, even when there is no evidence of patient intent such as a written directive. Second, he failed to include the law that argues against his financial conflict of interest conclusions. George Felos was the attorney who argued the controlling case on this subject, known as *Browning*. In his petition to Judge Greer condemning Pearse for bias, George wrote, "The fact that a surrogate may receive some money or emotional relief upon the death of a loved one is not *necessarily* adverse to the surrogate's credibility. The Guardian Ad Litem, to be even-handed in his presentation, should have at least mentioned this countervailing policy in his report, and the societal ramifications of ignoring the policy."

Hindsight being 20/20, it's possible that we might not have gotten to the stage where Richard Pearse filed such a biased report if Debbie Bushnell had told George Felos that Pearse, himself, brought up the conflict he'd had with George years earlier. George stated in his brief that he didn't learn about the comment to Debbie until January 8, 1999, a week after Pearse released his report. He wrote, "Had the undersigned known of these comments of the Guardian Ad Litem made October 13, 1998, the undersigned would have filed a motion to remove the Guardian Ad Litem . . . (In defense of Attorney Bushnell, one is inclined not to think the worst of someone else.)"

So Felos asked, "Why did the Guardian Ad Litem omit crucial facts, recite half-truths, state outright inaccuracies, attempt to leave erroneous inferences, and fail to provide the Court with an even-handed statement of the law? Why did the Guardian Ad Litem produce a report which is biased? Petitioner cannot answer that question with absolute certainty. The Guardian Ad Litem cannot claim ignorance as he has been privy to those matters which he has omitted and misconstrued. The Guardian Ad Litem cannot claim the pressure of time since he took more than six months to issue his report." And then George went on to lay out what he called the "identifiable facts which reasonably explain the cause" of Pearse's bias.

Here's the short version: personal animus toward my attorney; a personal aversion to the removal of feeding tubes; and personal emotions that colored his judgment, including an attempt to extend his role beyond submitting this report and stay with the case throughout the litigation.

George Felos writes legal briefs with elegance. He was at the top of his game here when he concluded, "Theresa Schiavo's fate is at stake here. The Guardian Ad Litem's conclusions and recommendations could contribute towards Theresa Schiavo being maintained in a decrepit, degrading, humiliating and mortifying condition for decades. According to Petitioner, such a result would not only be inhumane, but would be against the express wishes of his wife. With so much at stake, Theresa Schiavo deserved more from the Guardian Ad Litem. She was entitled to his best. She was let down.

"It is not the final recommendation of the Guardian Ad Litem at issue here. Reasonable people may disagree in a case such as this, and in good faith reach different conclusions. But this Court can accept no less than the utmost in good faith, high-mindedness and fair dealing from the Guardian Ad Litem. Petitioner asserts that the Report of the Guardian Ad Litem is so tainted that it should be disregarded by the Court."

Judge Greer ultimately found that Pearse "did a good job," but as you'll see, rejected his key conclusions.

———

If it weren't for the fact that the trial was going to start in less than a week, Jodi and I would have been celebrating. On January 18, 2000, I received notice that I'd met all the qualifications for my registered nurse license. All the effort I'd put into attending school throughout the turmoil of the last ten years would now pay off. There was a high demand for R.N.s in Florida, and getting the license was a giant step toward our future financial security.

By January 23, the day before the trial was due to begin, there had been no response of any kind from Judge Greer to our petition regarding Pearse's report. That didn't seem to bother George. In truth, nothing seemed to bother George. He just maintained this calm exterior, not letting on whether or not events swirling around him were affecting his blood pressure. Eventually, it would come to bug me. I was given to emotional outbursts when I felt they were warranted, such as at Sabal Palms. But more often than not I went stoic and suppressed my feelings. I haven't yet mentioned that a few years earlier I'd been diagnosed with ulcerative colitis and was on medication for it. They'd come to believe that the disease was caused by a bacteria, but that its symptoms were aggravated by stress. Draw your own conclusions.

In the afternoon, I'd picked up my sister-in-law Joan, coming in on a flight from Philadelphia. That evening, my dad went to the airport to pick up my brother Scott, who was coming in from Indianapolis to testify.

We had a little reunion at the house and then George spoke with all of us as a group, and then met with each of us individually. It was all very low-key, with George just explaining court procedure, letting everyone know in what order they'd be called, and answering any questions. I wasn't concerned about Scott. He's rock solid and there was no way that the Schindlers' attorney would be able to push him around.

Joan was another matter. Frankly, I was somewhat amazed that she'd gotten on an airplane. She was deathly afraid of flying, and I'm guessing that the thing that got her on that aircraft was the fact that she was clearly Terri's best friend in the family and knew her testimony would matter.

I was a little concerned that Joan can be somewhat ditzy. Think Lucy Ricardo, but a lot shorter, with brown hair. The best family story about Joan is the time she and a girlfriend, Pat, went to St. Matthew's Church to serve as lunch mothers at the school. Usually, they carpooled, but on this one particular Friday, they drove separately. When lunch hour was over, the two women walked out of the school talking to each other and, out of habit, went to Pat's car, and drove home. When Joan got to her house, she looked around, realized her car was missing, and jumped to the immediate conclusion that it had been stolen. She called her husband, Bill. She called her father-in-law. And then she called the cops, who came out and took a report.

The next morning, Pat called her. She'd gone to church, and "found" Joan's gold Ford LTD in the school parking lot. Joan rushed right over to see how much damage had been done by the thieves, and was surprised to find that nothing was wrong—there was no evidence that the car had been hot-wired. Slowly, it began to dawn on her. They'd both driven to school on Friday; they hadn't carpooled, and of course, the car hadn't been stolen.

That's Joan—and we were counting on her testimony. But I knew that if she'd been brave enough to get on a plane and fly down here, she was ready for anything the Schindlers' lawyers would throw at her.

Scott went home with my dad; Joan spent the night with Jodi and me. I think they slept. I know that I didn't.

9 | The Trial Called *Schiavo I*

I wasn't looking forward to the trial for many reasons, not the least of which was that if we won, it meant that Terri would die. Yes, I was certain that it's what she would have wanted. Yes, I knew that her doctors had said that letting her go would be the best thing to do because there was absolutely no hope for any improvement in her condition. And yes, it meant that all of us who loved Terri could put the anger and hostility behind us and move on with our lives. That doesn't mean forgetting Terri.

As I walked into the old Pinellas County Courthouse building around 8:30 on the morning of January 24, 2000, I picked up a copy of the *St. Petersburg Times*. Even though the newspaper had run several stories about Terri since her collapse—most of them dealing with our attempts to raise funds for her treatment in San Francisco, the battle we fought with Prudential Insurance, and the malpractice trial—there was nothing about us on the front page or anywhere else in the paper the morning the trial began. The page one headlines reported "Eight Killed in Fiery Pileup in Kansas City"; "Atlanta Goes Dark in Cold and Icy Sheath"; "In Iowa Nominee Sprint Starts"; and "Golden Globes an Oscar Preview?" There was also mention of the St. Louis Rams defeating the Tampa Bay Bucs, 11–6.

The Schiavo Case was being ignored, and that was just fine with me. This was a private family matter being resolved in the courts be-cause it had turned ugly and there appeared to be no other way to re-solve it. I didn't want the news media all over it.

By nature I'm a worrier. If I had a buck for every time I'd asked George Felos a question starting with "what if" I'd be rich. I hadn't slept well the night before the trial. When I woke up, I was on pins and needles. Even though this was the second time I'd been involved in a trial, I had butterflies.

When I arrived in Judge Greer's second-floor courtroom, George was already at the petitioner's table with his wife, Constance—also an attorney—who was helping him try the case. I left them alone and killed time talking with my father, my brother Brian, and Jodi's mom. We'd agreed that much as I would have liked Jodi's support in the courtroom, it would be better if she stayed out of sight. The fact that we'd been living together and that I called her my fiancée had been made an issue in the past and it was bound to come up in this trial. There was no point in aggravating the situation.

At two minutes to nine, just before the judge was due to take the bench, my heart sank: A cameraman from Bay News Nine walked into the courtroom, followed by Anita Kumar, a reporter for the *St. Petersburg Times*. Years after the trial, I learned that she showed up because the paper had received an anonymous, handwritten letter saying that there might be a story in what was going on in Judge Greer's courtroom. I'd also assumed that Kumar was sympathetic to the Schindlers because she usually sat on what seemed to be their side of the courtroom. (In the early days, there were no special seats reserved for reporters.) During the writing of this book, Kumar was told of my assumption about her sympathies, and laughed. "I sat there because the Schindler people would talk to me—Michael wouldn't."

Half an hour after Kumar entered the courtroom, a second TV sta-tion showed up. I hadn't yet figured out that it was—or would become—part of the Schindlers' game plan to try and win the case with the help of the media. I believe the notion of inviting the press to cover the trial would have appalled Terri, who was at heart a very private person.

The first official order of business was to exclude from the courtroom those expected to be called as witnesses—except Mr. and Mrs. Schindler and myself. The judge's instructions were that potential witnesses were forbidden to discuss their testimony or the facts of the case with anyone other than the lawyers. My brother Scott, my sister-in-law Joan, and Dr. James Barnhill, a neurologist who would be testifying for us, were put in one room just down the corridor from Judge Greer's courtroom. Bobby and Suzanne Schindler were put in another room right next to our side's. The doors were left open, and a bailiff was assigned to keep an eye on things.

That piece of business taken care of, George Felos made his opening statement:

Your Honor, in this case there are no winners. Whatever the outcome of this case, everyone has lost. A little less than ten years ago, February 1990, a beautiful, vivacious young woman's heart stopped beating. Her brain was deprived of oxygen and since that time she's existed in a permanent vegetative state, whereas her parents have agreed in the proceedings, it's an irreversible, profoundly debilitating condition.

On that day close to ten years ago, my client, Mr. Schiavo, lost the wife he knew. Her parents lost their dreams and hopes of a full life with their daughter and her siblings, and friends lost a shining presence in their lives. So in this case, there is no final judgment order, decree, that can ever bring Theresa Schiavo back.

If this Court grants the petition and permits Theresa Schiavo's artificial life support to be removed, all the parties will have to suffer the agony of watching a beloved one die, even though it is my client's belief and wish that is what his wife wanted. If this Court does not grant the petition, Theresa Schiavo's body will be maintained in this condition, perhaps for decades, and there is no victory or win in that for anyone.

I found myself listening to George with tears in my eyes. I'd thought about the outcome of the trial often, and there were times when I didn't know which of the two alternatives he'd just pointed out was worse.

After recounting Theresa's youth, including the fact that through high school she was very heavy, detailing our marriage and telling the judge that she had been under a doctor's care for help in getting pregnant, and explaining that it was an apparent potassium imbalance that caused her heart to stop beating, my attorney promised evidence from physicians that would prove that Terri had no hope for recovery and that she was, indeed, in a permanent vegetative state. George then stated a fact that had been and would be ignored by our opposition. ". . . a patient does not starve to death. A patient quickly develops an electrolyte imbalance which causes death within a short time, and that death as a result of this process is not painful."

Then he got into the major disputed issues. First, with respect to whether or not Terri had cognition, George said that this is "really a nonissue in this case. The major issue . . . is what Terri's intent was."

He told the judge that he could expect to hear testimony that Terri had stated that she would not want to live dependent on the care of others, and that she would not want to be kept alive or maintained artificially. George spelled out the fact that "her wishes were not contingent upon being totally unconscious or vegetative."

George went on to preview the testimony he'd be presenting from experts, including an authoritative Roman Catholic priest who believed that our request to let Terri go was highly consistent with the teachings of the Catholic faith. And then my attorney previewed the most macabre evidence that would be presented:

You will hear testimony from Theresa's father that if Terri needed open heart surgery, he would choose to have open heart surgery performed on her rather than have her die. You will hear testimony from her father that if Theresa developed gangrene and limbs needed to be amputated, he would choose to have that for his daughter.

Once again, I found myself in the bizarre situation of hearing my wife of fifteen years referred to more as an object than as a person. I suppose I should have gotten used to it by then, but I hadn't.

While George was making his opening statement, I found myself thinking that my testimony was going to be extraneous. He'd said it all—and certainly said it better than I would. There was no jury here to impress with emotion or tears; just Judge Greer sitting on the bench dispassionately evaluating the evidence being presented. I was also concerned that since I'd been deposed for this trial, been deposed for the guardianship challenge, and had been deposed and testified at the malpractice trial, I'd answered the questions I was about to be asked so many times that my testimony might not be convincing. After all, I'm not an actor skilled at performing the same role on stage night after night.

Near the conclusion of his opening statement, George addressed the report of the guardian *ad litem*, Richard Pearse, and the notion that Pearse himself had said that his decision to recommend against removal of artificial life support was "a close call." Felos reminded the judge that we'd charged Pearse with bias, adding that "he believes patients should not have the right, although the Supreme Court of Florida has given the patient the right, to cease food and water."

Finally, my attorney said that, "We believe at the conclusion of the case the court will find clear and convincing evidence that Theresa Schiavo would not want to be kept alive in this condition and would want the feeding tube removed."

Then it was the Schindlers' attorney's turn. Pamela Campbell's opening was considerably shorter. "You will hear a lot of medical testimony concerning the persistent vegetative state that Theresa Schiavo currently exists in. We do not doubt she's in a permanent vegetative state. However, a lot goes to the cognitive activity and brain activity of

Theresa Schiavo. In reading through some of the medical records, you will hear testimony about her no recognition [sic]. However, you will hear testimony from our side there is recognition. She does recognize her mother."

To me, Campbell's statement was a signal that we were about to drown in doublespeak. Florida State Law 765.101(12) defines a persistent vegetative state:

(12) "Persistent vegetative state" means a permanent and irreversible condition of unconsciousness in which there is:
(a) The absence of voluntary action or cognitive behavior of any kind.
(b) An inability to communicate or interact purposefully with the environment.

To me, there doesn't seem to be a whole lot of wiggle room in the definition. If a patient is PVS, by definition she can't recognize her mother. And Campbell wasn't contesting the assertion that Terri was PVS.

But I didn't have long to dwell on the inconsistency. Campbell had one parting shot to take at me before I was called to testify. She called on the court "to review the conflict of interest of Michael Schiavo and the financial situation that would rest in the intestate estate." In English, she was implying that I wanted Terri to die so I could inherit what was left of her malpractice settlement money, but she was ignoring the fact that I'd formally offered to donate all of that money to charity.

As I sat there listening, I glanced down at the polished wood table and saw the imprint of my hands and forearms. As the bailiff called me to the stand to be sworn in, I would have given a few bucks for a towel.

I took the stand and George guided me through routine questions about my life with Terri, ultimately asking about her weight problem.

Q. To your knowledge, while living with Terri, did you know whether or not she ever had an eating disorder such as anorexia or bulimia?

A. I did not. No.

Q. Were you in love with your wife?

A. I was deeply in love with my wife and I still am.

Then George began working on the "clear and convincing" standard we had to meet in order to convince the judge that if Terri were able to, she would opt to refuse artificial nutrition and hydration rather than continue to live in her current condition. The testimony on this issue was crucial, because Terri had not left written instructions detailing her wishes. But Florida law was clear that the determination of an individual's wishes could be made by a judge based on spoken expression of wishes.

That's why George asked about what Terri said on our train trip from Philadelphia to Florida while her grandmother was in intensive care. She had been reading a book, but put it down to talk about what was obviously on her mind. "I'm concerned about my grandmother," Terri said. "What if she dies? Who is going to take care of my uncle?" And then she added, "If I ever have to be a burden to anybody, I don't want to live like that." I told her that I felt the same way. It was a serious subject for two young people in their mid-twenties, but I felt as though we had made a pact.

Next, George moved on to another incident that we hoped would illustrate Terri's belief that artificial life support had its limitations. He asked about conversations I'd had with Terri that were sparked by something we'd seen on television. I testified that we'd seen documentaries that showed adults and children being kept alive on ventilators, or being fed by tube with IVs going into both arms. On more than one occasion Terri said she would *never* want to be kept alive like that. Her exact words during one program were, "Don't ever keep me alive on anything artificial."

A bit later George turned to the matter of Terri's religious practices. Her parents were claiming that Terri was a practicing Catholic. It was a claim that would be presented all the way to the end of the entire saga and beyond. I testified that Terri would rarely go to Mass, perhaps once every few months, and that I accompanied her. She never received communion; she never went to confession.

Then George asked me a series of questions about Terri's current condition:

A. She's in a chronic vegetative state—anoxic encephalopathy due to cardiac arrest.

Q. For those of us who did not go to school in medicine—

A. Lack of oxygen because her heart was not pumping to her brain.

Q. Can Terri run?

A. No.

Q. Can Terri walk?

A. No.

Q. Can Terri stand on her own?

A. No. She can't.

Q. Sit on her own?

A. No. She can't.

Q. Can Terri turn over?

A. No. She can't.

Q. Does she talk?

A. No.

Q. Can she eat?

A. No.

Q. Can she drink?

A. No. She can't.

Q. Can she swallow?

A. No.

Q. Can she go to the bathroom?

A. No.

Q. Can she brush her teeth?

A. No.

Q. Can Terri clip her fingernails?

A. No.

Q. Comb her hair?

A. No.

Q. Can Terri dress herself?

A. No. She cannot.

My testimony continued, explaining how difficult it was for Terri to stay alive even though she had constant medical attention. I testified that Terri had actually been hospitalized more than twenty times, although some of those occasions were so-called twenty-four-hour admits, and I'd been with her every single day she was in the hospital. I'd also transported her to doctors' offices more than one hundred thirty times since her collapse.

She had repeated urinary tract infections, she was treated for kidney stones, had her gallbladder removed, suffered from vaginitis and pelvic inflammatory disease, and required two D and C procedures. She'd also been hospitalized for respiratory infections and suffered seizures. In addition, she'd had her left little toe removed because of osteomyelitis—a bone infection caused by a pressure sore that developed because of the special boots she wore on her feet. This was not what is commonly referred to as a bed sore, which she never had.

After testifying about her medical problems, George moved on to the subject of cognition:

Q. Michael, you have spent more time with Terri and have seen Terri more often than anyone since her incident. Have you ever seen any voluntary or volitional response on her part in all these years?

A. I have not.

Q. Does Terri emit any noises? Does her face move? Her head?

A. Terri will moan, but it's not to anything. I could be sitting next to her and she will start to moan. Her eyes will blink. Her head will kind of twitch. It will kind of move itself . . . her arms move to where it looks like it is tightening up and she is almost sitting in like a praying mantis position. I have never ever seen Terri have any voluntary movement or follow through with any commands.

I testified that Terri occasionally had tears, and while it may have looked as though she were emoting, they almost always followed her taking a big, deep breath. I said that I'd never seen Terri laugh or smile. She did make a moaning noise and her mouth would open—but it wasn't a laugh as we know it.

Unless by accident or mistake, litigators rarely ask questions to which they don't already know the answer. So a trial such as this one is all about who does a better job putting the desired facts before the judge in a manner designed to lead him down the path that ends where you want it to end. Judge Greer had a reputation as a fair and smart jurist. It would have been a mistake to attempt to fool him. What George Felos wanted to do was lay out the facts and let the judge make up his own mind. It almost didn't matter what our opposition was going to say.

We were reasonably certain that the Schindlers were going to tie my decision to end medical treatment for Terri to having won the malpractice judgment. As I've noted, in 1994, conversations with two of Terri's doctors led me to order the nursing home to not treat a urinary tract infection. The nursing home refused my order and informed the Schindlers, who amended their petition for guardianship of Terri with an accusation that not treating her constituted abuse. Ultimately, the Schindlers dropped the fight for guardianship.

Nevertheless, at the time, I didn't put in another do not treat and do not resuscitate order. And I didn't pursue removal of Terri's feeding tube, which both doctors had also suggested as a course of action. George wanted to make sure that incorrect inferences weren't drawn from my behavior in '94.

Q. At that time, why didn't you pursue removal of the feeding tube?

A. Because at that time my emotions were running. I couldn't—I was ready to do the natural thing [do not treat]. I was not ready to pull the feeding tube at that time.

Q. Even though you knew Terri wanted it?

A. Yes.

Q. Why were you not able?

A. It was—I was not ready for that yet.

What George was leading me to was an explanation of why I was now ready. He asked me about the death of my mother in July 1997, and I explained why I felt my mother had given me a gift when she was dying by telling me that it was okay to die. He asked me one final question—why I filed the petition to allow Terri to die. I said, "Because that is what Terri wanted, and it's my responsibility because I love her so much to follow out what she wanted." That was the truth.

And with that, the court took a short recess before my cross-examination by the Schindlers' attorney. I was trying to figure out where she would start. I knew that the only thing Judge Greer had to decide was whether there was clear and convincing evidence that Terri would not want artificial life support continued. Would Pam Campbell try to challenge directly my assertion that we were trying to do what Terri would have wanted? During preparation for the trial, we'd gone over everything they could be expected to throw at me—or at least I hoped we'd covered everything. So it was actually a relief when, right after a pleasant "Good morning," she took the low road—because we'd anticipated it—and asked about my relationship with Jodi. I said "We are boyfriend/girlfriend. We live together, and yes, I consider her my fiancée and we do own a house together."

And then she changed the subject—again and again and again. I'd been expecting to be cross-examined by a pit bull, not a pussycat, and I remember thinking that Pam Campbell seemed way too nice to be in this line of work. I don't recall how long her cross-examination took, but it runs only thirteen pages in the court transcript while my direct examination by George Felos is almost sixty pages.

It was at some point during my testimony that Scott and Joan noticed something very strange happening in the room where the Schindlers' witnesses were being held. It seems that on a regular basis, someone would leave the courtroom, walk past the open door where my witnesses were waiting, and go into the room next door. It seemed as though the person was always carrying sheets of paper into the room, and when they'd come back to the courtroom, there was no paper. At the time, Scott was under the impression that the Schindlers were keeping their witnesses informed of what was going on in the courtroom, but it didn't dawn on him immediately that what they were doing wasn't right. He wondered why he and Joan weren't getting similar updates, but didn't have a chance to say anything to me because he was called to testify as soon as I left the stand.

Scott was being called to tell the story of how he came to learn how Terri felt about being kept alive by artificial means. His testimony illustrates precisely why it never came out years earlier; why I was never told of the brief but poignant exchange:

"Mike spent years trying to save Terri's life. He tried to keep positive, and we would try to support him. Mike said, 'If I can have Terri back at fifty percent, I will be happy with that,' and basically he was killing himself trying to do this. She was everything in the world to him, and if that was what he wanted, that was going to be good enough for us—he could have her.

"The doctors would tell him, 'Mike, no more. There's nothing else you can do.' And he would just look beyond that and keep trying to find a way. There were several years of doctors basically pounding it into him that she's not coming back. We were talking about it one day and I said, 'Mike, she made that statement to me that she would never want to be kept alive like this.'

"He said, 'What do you mean?' and I told him the story."

Scott recounted what he told Judge Greer had happened back in February 1988:

"My father's mother, Helene Schiavo, had severe heart disease. She'd already had open heart surgery, and when she went back into the hospital she was very clear that she wanted a DNR order on her chart. She had taken a turn for the worse, and the people working at the hospital never respected it. And they ended up resuscitating her and putting her on a ventilator.

"Basically, she was gone, and we had to sit there for—it was a Friday, and it was almost two days that we sat there and watched this machine blow air into her and suck it out, until she passed away.

"Mike and Terri were not there at the time. They were down in Florida, and they came up for the funeral. We went to lunch afterward at a restaurant called The Buck Hotel. We were all sitting around this table—all the brothers and their wives and a couple of my cousins—and I made a statement how upset my grandmother would've been if she would have known that they did this to her, and how upsetting it was for the whole family.

"And Terri was sitting right to the left of me, and she turned around and looked me right in the eyes, and she said, 'Not me. I would never want to be left that way. Don't ever let them do that to me.'

"And that was just the statement. There's nothing to elaborate on. It was just those words, the way she looked me right in the eyes. Just point-blank, 'Not me. Don't ever let them do that to me.' "

Of course I asked Scott why he never told me that story years ago, and he said it was because I was so focused on trying to bring Terri back, that there was no point in telling it to me.

Following Scott's testimony, Felos called Dr. James Barnhill, the neurologist from the nearby community of Dunedin who had examined Terri. He affirmed that she was in a persistent vegetative state and that any movements or sounds she made were just reflexes. The doctor explained to the court that Terri's reflex actions, such as breathing and movement, merely demonstrated that her brain stem and spinal cord were intact; nothing more.

Two CT scans were offered as exhibits during Barnhill's testimony. One showed Terri's brain. The other, curiously enough, was of Dr. Barnhill's brain. Slowly and carefully, he explained what the CT scans showed, making the case that Terri's brain was permanently and catastrophically damaged.

As for her prognosis? "There's no treatment; no cure," the doctor testified. "Nothing known to science will help this woman."

10 | The Teachings of the Catholic Church

During a short recess in mid-afternoon, I was talking with my brother Brian, who told me about a strange encounter he'd had earlier in the day with Bob Schindler. He hadn't seen any of the Schindlers in years, so he was shocked when Terri's father came up to him as though they were long lost buddies and asked, "Brian, how are you?" Brian mumbled a meaningless response, figuring that Schindler would see that he really had no interest in a long conversation, but it didn't work. Schindler went on, "I'm sorry to hear about Claire," referring to our mom's passing away.

"I don't get it," Brian said to me. "On the one hand he's crucifying you, and then he comes over like nothing's going on. What is with him?"

As I turned to go back to my seat, who came up to meet me in the courtroom aisle but Bob Schindler. He stopped in front of me, looked up snarling, and said, "You're goin' down, boy," just like that. All I could do was shake my head, and brush past him.

At three in the afternoon, we called Father Gerard Murphy to the stand. I'd never met him before, and George had not taken his deposition. All I knew was that my attorney was excited about Father Murphy, telling me that he was "a good priest." The first time I saw him in the courtroom, I was surprised. My initial reaction was that he was a little old man, but I'd been told that he had recently turned fifty. Apparently, he'd had a congenital bone disease that had aged him, he had some difficulty walking, and with his white hair, he looked much older than he actually was.

Father Murphy had spent most of his career in the priesthood ministering to the sick and dying. It was a calling he discovered early in his career, and he'd become very good at it. He'd served as the Catholic chaplain at Sarasota Memorial Hospital where virtually all of his work involved bioethical consultations with families and physicians. He'd also been the director of pastoral care at St. Anthony's Hospital.

Father Murphy was recognized in the diocese of St. Petersburg as an authority on the Catholic Church's position on end-of-life care and treatment and clinical counseling on end-of-life care and treatment issues. In fact, he had written a series of pamphlets that the Church had distributed. He was a member of the diocese task force on assisted suicide, and was both the diocese chaplain and the statewide chaplain for the Catholic Medical Association.

In his initial comments upon taking the stand, he said, "I find that most people have no idea what the Catholic Church teaches. Even Catholics. And I think that gives rise to grave misunderstandings, and I have real fears about that."

George hadn't told me what he was going to ask Father Murphy, but I had a feeling that our side was about to hit a grand slam home run.

You'll notice that I've made the decision to give you much of Father Murphy's testimony verbatim, even though my editor tells me that readers tend to skim this sort of thing. I'm asking you not to do that. Please carefully read what Father Murphy told the court. It had far-reaching implications, all the way to the end of Terri's life, and beyond.

To begin, George asked about the statements made in 1953 by Pope Pius IV. Father Murphy testified that, after meeting with a group of physicians, the pontiff said that "Catholics are mortally bound to respect life and to care for life, but not at all costs." The priest explained that the pope "introduced the concept of extraordinary versus ordinary means," adding that "a Catholic is mortally bound to take advantage of ordinary, proportionate not disproportionate." Then, in response to further questioning by George, Father Murphy got to the heart of the matter, the reason that we found ourselves in this position with Terri, and why tens of thousands of other families have been confronted with the same situation, and the same difficult choices.

A. It is not as easy to die as it used to be. Nature would have taken care of a great many situations thirty or forty years ago. My belief in the health care system is that technology is a two-edged sword. The wonderful technology meant to heal and save people and get them back on the road can also interfere with nature.

Q. What factors does the Catholic Church take into consideration in determining whether a treatment is an ordinary action as opposed to extraordinary or proportionate as opposed to disproportionate?

A. It's not the procedure. It's the perception of the patient. Is the procedure, is it too emotionally draining? Is it too psychologically repugnant? It is too expensive? Does it offer no hope of treatment—of recovery or little or no hope? Based upon all those factors, then you make your moral decision based upon those issues.

Q. In some of the literature I've read, I come across the terms burdensome and useless. That is, a Catholic is not required to have a medical treatment if it is burdensome or useless. How do those concepts fit in with the ones you just mentioned?

A. Maybe if I gave an example it might be easier. You look like kind of a healthy guy. Say you caught pneumonia this flu season. You go to your doctor. He would prescribe a course of antibiotics for you. You would be better soon and back on the road.

But as a case I actually handled in Bayfront, St. Petersburg, many years ago, a woman in her late seventies was filled with cancer in the bronchial tree. She was dying. She came down with that pneumonia and the daughter insisted that the mother be treated for that pneumonia. I said why are you doing this? What do you hope to accomplish?

What you always have to do is weigh the proportion. What do you hope to accomplish against what it is going to take to get there. In that case, all she was doing was keeping the mother alive for an extra three or four weeks in order to die. So that was clearly a case of prolonging the inevitable as opposed to someone like you who comes down with that pneumonia.

Q. Does the Church then permit the consideration of whether or not the patient has any hope of recovery in whether the treatment may help the patient recover in considering whether it is ordinary or extraordinary?

A. Yes.

At this point, my attorney asked Father Murphy what materials he reviewed in order to prepare to testify. He said he'd seen the depositions of the Schindler family, he wasn't sure if he'd read my deposition, and he'd seen reports from the physicians taking care of Terri.

Q. I want you to assume, Father Murphy, for purposes of this question that Theresa Schiavo told her husband that if she were dependent on the care of others she would not want to live like that. And also Theresa Schiavo mentioned to her husband and to her brother- and sister-in-law that she would not want to be kept alive artificially. Assuming that information to be correct, Father, would the removal of Theresa Schiavo's feeding tube be consistent or inconsistent with the position of the Catholic Church?

A. After all that has transpired, I believe, yes, it would be consistent with the teaching of the Catholic Church.

Because the argument had been used by the Schindlers' attorneys—and would be used even more in the years to come—that Terri was a "practicing Catholic," my attorney asked Father Murphy how that phrase is defined:

A. Certainly. We have what we call Easter duty, which means sometime from Lent to Trinity Sunday, in that three or four month window, a Catholic is required to receive Holy Communion. If necessary, confession. Catholics are mortally bound to assist at Mass. Attend Mass every Sunday. Every holy day of obligation. Certainly those are all criteria for a practicing Catholic.

Q. If Theresa Schiavo had not taken communion over a two-year period before her medical incident and not participated in confession, would she be considered by the church to be a practicing Catholic?

A. Not according to the criteria. No. Practicing, no.

Next, George Felos asked whether it would be consistent with Church teachings for a loved one who has the best interests of the patient at heart to authorize removal of artificial life support. Father Murphy's answer made clear that the Church has no all-purpose answer to that question. It needs to be considered on a case-by-case basis, and it became clear that he'd studied Terri's situation.

A. I think in a case like this where so much time and effort has elapsed, I think, yes, it would be consistent. You have to remember, the Church will always uphold the ideal. One of the things they will do is hit the brakes, as it were, to make sure nobody is rushing into judgment. Trying to push the patient out of the picture. In view of the length and effort here, I would say yes. What you would hope for is somebody who cared about the best interest of the patient to make the decision for them.

Q. And such a decision by that—a decision to remove the feeding tube by such a person would be consistent with the Church teachings?

A. I believe so from my understanding of the Church teachings.

Q. Does the Catholic Church require, require someone to have all medical treatments and procedures to keep them alive?

A. No. In fact, Pope Pius said that in 1953. It was a direct quote. He said that kind of suffering may be admirable, but certainly not required.

Q. In fact, even if a patient is not vegetative, does the Catholic Church require all medical treatments to keep the patient alive?

A. No.

Q. There were also statements in the deposition also to the effect—and these are statements by the mother and the brother and sister—that if they were in that permanent unconscious state with no hope of recovery and had gangrene and their limbs had to be amputated, that they would choose that rather than to die. Do you recall reading that?

A. Yes.

Q. Does the Catholic Church require any such action—

A. No.

Q. —by a person like that?

A. No.

Q. In all your years of pastoral clinical counseling, Father Murphy, have you ever come across such extreme opinions?

A. With all due respect, no.

One reason Father Murphy's testimony was so important was that at the time he appeared in court, The Schiavo Case had not yet been politicized. He was answering George Felos's questions without regard for the impact that his responses might have on right-to-life groups, on his bishop, on politicians, and on media personalities. Once the case became front-page news, the answers being given by various Church authorities—official and self-proclaimed—to the same questions were not nearly as pure and untainted. Father Murphy had no ax to grind. He was responding based on his knowledge of evolving Church law and his experience providing end-of-life pastoral counseling to hundreds and hundreds of families. He was the perfect expert witness.

Since the reason we were sitting in a courtroom fighting this battle was that the Schindler family was bound and determined to do everything possible to keep Terri alive—seemingly forever, if they could—it became important to have Father Murphy evaluate the Schindlers' beliefs, starting with the fear of death.

Q. In the Catholic faith, is death something that a practicing Catholic need fear?

A. No. In fact, that is a fundamental part of the Catholic faith. We call ourselves a pilgrim people. Life here on earth is really seen as a temporary stay. Catholics believe that our destiny is heaven. Therefore, you can't do everything to prevent yourself from getting there. What is so hard to deal with in educating Catholics in these issues is that death is a part of life. It is a part of life. It's part of the process. No, Catholics should not fear death.

Q. There was a statement in Mrs. Schindler's deposition that, in addition to wanting every type of medical treatment to preserve herself in a permanent unconscious state should hypothetically she be in that state, that she would, if medical treatment impoverished her family, that she would still want that treatment. Is there any recognition in the Catholic faith in this area about the cost of treatment? Is the cost of treatment ever a factor?

A. That's one of the criteria in deciding whether it's proportionate or disproportionate. Excessive or ordinary. What you would hope is that somebody is helping the patient work through those issues.

Q. Now, in the deposition of Theresa's siblings, do you recall there was a discussion of God's will? I believe there were a number of statements. Well, Terri ought to remain alive because—she should be treated—she should have all type of medical treatment to keep her alive because it's God's will. If it was God's will that she die, she would be dead with medical treatment in place. Is such a position consistent with Catholic teaching?

A. No. I don't think so. I'll tell you why. When I mentioned the two-edged sword, God's will could have been easily done fifty years ago. I think this is a case where the wonderful technology, rather than being an act of health and recovery, has become the obstacle for nature taking its course.

Q. Father Murphy, there was a section in the depositions of Mr. and Mrs. Schindler read in court already. You may remember them. Mr. and Mrs. Schindler were basically asked, just hypothetically, assume these were Terri's wishes. That she did not want to be kept

alive if she were a burden to others. Would that change your position in this case? They both answered no. My question is, is disre-
garding the intent of the patient consistent at all with Catholic
teachings?

A. No. It is the perception of the patient that determines the mo-
rality of the action. Not the family, not the doctor, but the perception
of the patient.

Q. In Terri's sister's deposition, she made the statement that taking
away life support is murder. Is that the position of the Catholic
Church?

A. Absolutely not. Absolutely not true. Absolutely inconsistent
with Church teaching. All they do is allow nature to take its course.

Q. I believe the sister also made the statement in her deposition
that a patient may have medical treatment, even if it's against his or
her will, if it can keep the patient alive.

A. Absolutely not.

I'd been watching the Schindlers throughout Father Murphy's testimony. When I caught Mr. Schindler's eye, he'd given me his tough-
guy "Who cares" look.

Q. Do you recall in the deposition of Theresa's brother his testimony that he believes his parents or his parents believe, Mr. and Mrs.
Schindler, that Terri is aware of their presence, and he testified that
Terri's continued life is a joy to him? A joy to him and his family to
keep Terri alive in this condition. He was even asked if Terri needed a
respirator to keep her alive, would it still give you joy to have her alive
on a respirator? And he said yes. He was asked if her limb had to be
amputated would it give you joy to have her alive in this condition?
And he said yes.

My question is, Father, what are the teachings of the Catholic
Church regarding keeping a loved one alive for your own personal
pleasure or benefit?

A. I think that is contrary to the gospel. We all take pleasure in relationships with people, family. People who get married. I think, you

know, keeping someone around strictly for your own pleasure strikes me as very antigospel. Sounds more like using someone than loving someone.

With that, George thanked Father Murphy and turned him over to Pam Campbell for cross-examination. With her first question, she stepped in it.

Q. Good afternoon. My name is Pam Campbell. I represent Mr. and Mrs. Schindler. Have you had the opportunity to meet Mr. and Mrs. Schindler?
A. No. I regret that. I wish I were their pastor.

After a brief digression into questions about physician-assisted suicide—which the father said was wrong, later adding on redirect examination that people may be drawn to it because they fear that their end-of-life wishes will not be followed—the priest was asked if he felt, from reading the Schindler family's depositions, that "the people that were being deposed felt they were being backed into a corner?"

He didn't agree, explaining, "The sense that I felt more was great empathy. Not just because I'm a good pastor, but I watched my parents bury two of their own children. I know it destroyed them. My mother never got over it. My father did. They were an interesting case in grief.

"So my heart, without knowing them, my heart goes out to the Schindlers because this must be killing them. But you know it was awful for me to be a son and yet very good for me to be a son to my parents to help them work through it. I don't think most people have that. They have to rely on what they hear on radio or see on television."

Father Murphy was asked if he was familiar with the ethical and religious directives of Catholic Health Care Services published by the National Conference of Catholic Bishops. He said he was.

Campbell then read, "Number fifty-eight says there should be a presumption in favor of providing nutrition and hydration to all patients, including patients who require medically assisted nutrition and hydration, as long as this is of sufficient benefit that outweighs the burdens involved to the patient." Then she asked how he would square that directive with his earlier testimony about Terri Schiavo.

"As I think I said earlier, the Church will always take the high road. They will always uphold the ideal. They will always resist immediate action. I think they always want to slow down, take advantage of every possible opportunity, to make sure that the outcome is not promising.

"So even [Chicago's Joseph] Cardinal Bernardin, who taught us so much about how to die well, that one of his most forceful arguments is that artificial hydration and nutrition is not mandatory in every single case. You have to go back and evaluate the proportion. Where are you going? What do you hope to achieve against what is it going to take to get there? What is the outcome that you are looking for?"

Near the conclusion of Campbell's cross-examination, she asked Father Murphy about the possibility that God could work a miracle in the case of a terminally ill patient.

"I don't mean this as flip as it sounds," the priest responded. "If God is going to work a miracle, he does not need machinery or technology. I think he will just do it. So I have never been persuaded by the argument that we have to keep all the machinery going so God can work his miracle. I don't believe God needs that."

Then Campbell asked, "Do you think there is a timetable that God expects you to consider one way or the other?"

"No," replied Father Murphy. "I mean in terms of I don't think it's six months or a year or whatever. But I think that when it becomes a long, long time, I think a good pastor would have to sit down with the principals involved and say, maybe it's time to let go."

That ended her cross-examination of Father Murphy. She didn't bend him at all. On redirect examination, George asked whether the fact that Terri's mother derived joy from being with her daughter should negate Terri's wishes. The priest said, "No."

Q. As to Theresa and whether this continued life maintained artificially is burdensome, that was for Theresa to decide, not her mother; isn't that correct?

A. Yes.

After an hour and five minutes on the stand, Father Murphy was excused. I said to George, "I wish we were allowed to clap. I would have given him a one-person standing ovation." Jodi's mom, a truly devout Catholic and Eucharistic minister, who at the time was dying of cancer, told me afterward that she, too, wanted to stand and applaud.

If the Schindler family had been the church-going practicing Catholics that they claimed to be, they would have had a pastor to turn to, someone perhaps like Father Murphy, who could have given them comfort in their pain, and guided them into an acceptance of Terri's condition and inevitable death.

We'd been told by very reliable sources in Clearwater that Mr. Schindler went to Bishop Robert N. Lynch, and the bishop told him to consult with his own pastor at the parish where he belonged. Mr. Schindler had to tell the bishop that he had no pastor; they didn't belong to a parish.

And if you'll forgive me for jumping ahead in time a few weeks, to February 24, 2000, my attorney received a letter from Father Murphy, which said, in part, "The brother of Theresa Schiavo has written a letter to Bishop Robert N. Lynch, who, as you know, is my superior. This letter is highly critical of my testimony in the hearing which is of recent date."

Since it's no secret how this trial came out, it won't ruin the story for you if I tell you that the Schindlers were going to be asking for a new trial. That's why George Felos viewed Bobby Schindler's acts as witness tampering and was compelled to file an Emergency Petition for an Order Restraining Interference or Tampering with Witnesses. Our request said, "As a result, Father Murphy, who stands by his testimony, is now in a position of defending his testimony. This conduct of Robert Schindler, Jr., or Respondents through Robert Schindler, Jr., harasses a witness. Such conduct, with intent to hinder, delay, prevent, or dissuade subsequent testimony, constitutes witness tampering. At a minimum, this conduct interferes with the integrity of this court process. Respondents cannot ask for a new trial, and at the same time, seek to hinder Petitioner's witnesses from testifying."

After court ended on Monday, my family got together for dinner and Scott asked me, "How come nobody comes out to let *us* know what's going on?"

I asked him what he was talking about, and he said, "They've got people coming in and out of this courtroom bringing stuff to Bobby." I was shocked. Scott hadn't realized that the Schindlers appeared to be trying to get around Judge Greer's sequestration of witnesses, something the judge did so witnesses for either side wouldn't be tempted to adjust their testimony to deliberately support or attack what had already been presented by other witnesses. There was no indication that the Schindlers' lawyer was involved. I immediately called George Felos to tell him what was going on.

The next morning, I arrived at the courthouse with my brother Brian and was dismayed to see that Judge Greer's courtroom was packed with media and spectators. Apparently the coverage from day one had been enough to convince the assignment editors at the local TV stations that the circus was in town—Schiavo and Schindler instead of Barnum and Bailey. I was extremely grateful that George had put me on the stand first and that I didn't have to testify in front of a wall of cameras.

Shortly after nine o'clock, my oldest brother Bill's wife, Joan, took the stand. Both Scott and Joan had described to me the people who had been bringing notes to Bobby Schindler and his sister Suzanne in the witness room, and before George began his examination of Joan, I pointed out to him that one of the offenders, a young woman, was sitting in the rear of the courtroom with a notepad in her lap. George asked the judge for a sidebar in order to explain what had been going on. I hadn't seen Judge Greer's capacity for anger till that moment. Although he did not rule that his witness sequestration had been violated, he made it quite clear that the court would deal harshly with anyone taking notes for nefarious reasons. As I watched, the young woman in question slowly slid her notepad back into her purse and, as far as I can tell, it wasn't a problem for the remainder of the trial.

George spent the first few minutes asking Joan about her relationship with Terri, how it happened that the two of them had become such close friends, and how they were in daily contact with each other after Terri and I moved to Florida.

But he quickly got into the reason we'd asked Joan to come down and testify: what she knew about Terri's beliefs in regard to using extraordinary measures to keep someone alive.

Joan recounted her testimony, saying "Terri and I were watching a movie on television. I don't recall the name, but it was about a guy on a diving board who didn't do a good dive. He broke his neck and was brain dead as a result of the accident. The diver was being kept alive artificially, and Terri said, 'I would never put my husband through anything like that. If anything like that ever happened to me, I would hope to God that they would pull the plug, because I would never want to live like that.' "

Joan and my brother Bill had lost their first child, a little girl, who was born with the umbilical cord around her neck. In that same conversation with Terri about the patient in the movie, Joan began talking about their experience with the death of the baby, and it's a story she also told Judge Greer. "We were just sitting and talking about the baby. If she had stayed alive—because of the cord being wrapped around her neck—she probably would have been brain dead, and my husband and I would have to make that decision, if we were faced with it, if we wanted to keep her alive like that or not. And as we were talking, I said that as hard as it would be, it would be a decision where we'd probably pull the plug, because I couldn't stand to see her like that. 'Cause it wasn't a life for her, she's only a little baby. And Terri agreed with me."

Pam Campbell's cross-examination of Joan didn't rise to the level of *Law & Order* courtroom drama. She asked her how long Joan thought it took for the diver in the movie to die? Joan basically said, "How am I supposed to know? The movie was only an hour and a half." Then she tried to attack Joan's credibility by implying that she couldn't possibly have been as close to Terri as she claimed because she didn't come down here immediately after Terri's collapse. That really ticked Joan off.

"Back then," Joan recounted, "I had three young children; I had a brand-new home. We hardly were bringing that much money in. My husband was the only one working. I couldn't just run down to Florida. But I called every single day—I don't know how many times a day I called to find out what was going on."

Perhaps the most controversial witness George called to the stand was Beverly Tyler, the executive director of a group called Georgia Health Decisions. They did a study using thirty-six focus groups around the country to assess attitudes of people toward end-of-life decisions and advance care planning. You can read the summary report at http://www.critical-conditions.org/index/RelatedStud02.asp.

The reason George asked her to testify, however, was because of what the study revealed about the way young adults informally express their personal end-of-life wishes. In a conversation, Tyler said that for people of Terri's age, "When these conversations are had, it is sparked by some event—either something is on television, or something happens to a family member or a friend." The statement "generally doesn't go much further than, 'I never want that to happen to me' or 'If I'm in that kind of condition, please don't let that happen to me. Don't put me on feeding tubes; don't put me on respirators.' "

What Tyler described is precisely the way Terri expressed her end-of-life wishes. There's no question that saying, "Don't let that happen to me" isn't as specific as a five-page end-of-life directive that carefully considers all the gray areas, but what her study demonstrated to the court was that wishes expressed informally are just as sincere, just as meaningful, and just as valid. To disregard them would be a mistake.

Before George concluded our case, he had a few questions to ask of Richard Pearse, the guardian *ad litem* Judge Greer had appointed. Given what I would be accused of for the next five years—or longer—this brief exchange is important:

Q. What seems to bother you, as I understand it, is making an argument in a malpractice suit for damages based upon somebody's long life span, when somebody might believe that artificial life support will be removed and the life span in fact will be a short one? Is that the gist of your difficulty?

A. I think you captured the essence of the idea. Yeah.

Q. What I don't understand is, if you concluded that in the first three or four years Mr. Schiavo still had hope and still thought his wife was going to recover, there was a chance of recovery, and within that period filed the [malpractice] lawsuit, why—what is the difficulty or problem of claiming damages for a long life span when somebody still believes there is a chance of recovery and the person may live a long life span?

A. I don't think that particular isolated element of it is particularly problematic. I think the point you are trying to make—and I agree with you, that it is consistent.

When time came for Pam Campbell to put on her case, she called the entire Schindler family. There are only a few moments of testimony from Terri's father, Robert, and her brother, Bobby, that I want to reprint here, because after you read them it should become crystal clear why I refused to divorce Terri and let her parents take guardianship.

Q. Now, we discussed at your deposition what would happen if Terri developed gangrene and needed to have a limb amputated. I will ask you that question again and see if your opinion has changed. If Terri developed gangrene and a limb had to be amputated to save her life, would you be in favor of that?

A. [Robert Schindler] Before I made that decision, I would consult with the experts medically. Physicians that I would select. Get their opinions and be darn certain that I had all the facts on the table before I made that decision.

Q. In your deposition on page 68, line 25, I asked you, my question, if she developed gangrene and her leg needed to be amputated to save her life, would you be in favor of that?

A. Absolutely.

Q. Is there anything hypothetical about that?

A. The questions you were asking before that were all hypothetical. If you turn the page back a few, every question was hypothetical. I was giving you hypothetical answers.

Q. Sir, do you deny that you answered that question with the answer "absolutely"?

A. I said that, but it should have had in there "hypothetically."

Q. I asked you the question, if another leg had to be amputated? Answer. Yes. Question. And an arm? [Answer.] If necessary.

A. Hypothetically.

Can you imagine what it was like for me to hear him talking about cutting Terri's arms and legs off? I knew it was coming, but I still went white. I wanted to vomit right there. I was thinking, *Oh my God, do you realize what you're saying? How could you possibly consider cutting your daughter's arms and legs off, when she couldn't even think or communicate, just to keep her alive? Are you that horrible? That hateful?* It made me very ill just hearing it.

So there's no mistaking what I'm saying, I'm not talking about amputees like, for example, a lot of soldiers returning from Iraq after losing limbs. We all hope and pray that those brave men and women get the state-of-the-art prostheses and rehabilitation they deserve, and go on to live long and productive lives. There is a world of difference between their condition and Terri's.

At Bob Schindler's deposition he'd gone on record as saying that if all of Terri's limbs had to be amputated, and then she needed surgery, he would do it. At trial he fudged it. Maybe he changed his mind, or maybe he'd been given some heavy-duty coaching by his attorney. Personally, I don't think it helped. His attitude was clear. It was all about him; not about Terri. Both he and Mrs. Schindler testified that hypothetically, if Terri had told them of her desire to have artificial nutrition and hydration withdrawn, they wouldn't do it.

When Bobby Schindler took the stand, he opened wide the window on why the Schindlers would want to keep Terri alive, in a persistent vegetative state, even if all her limbs had to be amputated and open heart surgery had to be performed. Bobby said, "My parents and her were very, very close.

"It is not speculative to say if Terri knew that it was bringing my parents an ounce of joy in her [sic] life she would want to be like this."

I know the girl I married. I know that she valued her dignity. But I also know that she understood the concept of quality of life. We've already presented testimony from me, my brother Scott, and my sister-in-law Joan that Terri would not want to be kept alive by artificial means. If you accept that, can you imagine Terri saying to her parents, "If I'm in a vegetative state, and you need to lop off my arms and legs so I don't die of gangrene, and if keeping me alive in that condition will give you joy, then do it."

It's absurd. If they thought it was a demonstration of their love for Terri, it was a sick kind of love. And the fact that they were willing to say it, whether or not they believed it, was enough reason for me to never even consider giving them guardianship of my wife. Would you do that to the person you loved the most in the entire world?

Then there was Mrs. Schindler's testimony. She was emphatic in stating her belief that "where there's life there's hope." Unfortunately, it was a statement that rang hollow when George asked her why, if there's always hope, she had signed the papers to take her own mother off a ventilator and let her die. It was just one more example of the Schindlers' hypocrisy. They loved Terri, but after the first few years, rarely visited her. They later claimed to be devout Catholics, but didn't belong to a parish or regularly attend Mass. They claimed I wanted Terri to die so I could inherit her money, but didn't acknowledge that I'd offered to donate that money to charity. They faulted me for not knowing Terri had an eating disorder, but accepted no blame for not seeing it themselves. They encouraged me to date and get on with my life, and then called me an adulterer. And now, in court, Mary Schindler said, "where there's life, there's hope," but until it was dragged out of her by my lawyer, she failed to be forthcoming about pulling the plug on her own mother.

The trial lasted five days. Since there was no jury, there was no need for either side's attorney to get theatrical. George did a very strong summary of our case; Campbell followed.

Judge Greer said he'd have his order ready on Friday, February 11, less than two weeks' time. And with one last bang of his gavel, the trial was over. Everyone but me stood, and the media and spectators rushed out of the courtroom. I just sat there at our table, head in my hands, exhausted. So many years of history, so many years preparing for this moment. It was a big relief just to get it over, even though I didn't know whether we'd succeeded or not. So I sat there and cried.

Brian had taken over the task of dealing with the press for me, and he knew that there was no chance of getting out of the courthouse without answering their questions. But I didn't want to confront them all at once; I didn't want people screaming at me. So what Brian did was pull me out of the courtroom and take me to the witness waiting room. We closed the door, and he gave me a few more minutes to compose myself. Then I began seeing the media people, one on one.

I was still kind of emotional when I was being interviewed. That may make for better video, but it's not necessarily the best frame of mind to be in when people are going to hang on every word. The interviews were short, and the only thing I remember is focusing on the fact that here we have the Schindlers, whose attorney acknowledged that Terri was PVS, saying that they might even cut their daughter's arms and legs off and do surgery to keep her alive like that, because she gave them joy. *And they want me to give them custody of Terri?* I don't think so.

We went back to George's office in Dunedin and did interviews with *Dateline NBC* and *Inside Edition*. One of them wanted to turn the story into a viewer call-in game, and I wouldn't allow it. I told Brian to make it clear that if that was the way they were going to handle the story, there was not going to be any interview. I refused to turn Terri's life into a viewer's choice.

I also spoke with Anita Kumar for the first time. During the interview or shortly afterward, she asked if I would permit her to visit with Terri. Mrs. Schindler had actually suggested that she make the request. I thought about it for a second, and said yes. She said she'd like to go to the hospice immediately, and I said I'd make the arrangements to authorize it, which I did.

Kumar recalled her visit with Terri:

"I was surprised, first of all, that no one went with me. I was just shocked that I was allowed to go alone. So I drove over there. I was on the list. I talked to the nurses—they were all really, really nice. Took me into the room. Terri was by herself, and the nurse kind of showed me the room and said, 'Here she is,' and stood there for a couple of minutes, and then left me.

"Terri was in the bed, but she was propped up. It was very different than I thought [she would be]. That was the first thing that struck me. We had people on the stand in a courtroom testifying to coma or comatose, so to me, coma meant her eyes were closed and that she would be sleeplike. And so, even though near the end of the trial I had heard, 'Oh, no, no, no, her eyes are open,' I saw video, it still strikes you, because when you go into her room, it was just different than I thought. I didn't expect her to move as much or make as much noise or look like she did. Even though I thought I was prepared for it, it was different. Her room also struck me. She was definitely in a nice room. There was stuff everywhere: stuffed animals; things on her walls; photographs. It was very homey.

"She didn't react to me. I sat beside her bed on one side. I called her name, and I felt silly doing so, but I called her name. No reaction that I could see. And then, after a while, I sat on the other side and did the same thing. No reaction. I don't see her looking anywhere. I don't see her eyes focusing. I don't see her even pretending that she can hear me. Nothing."

When Kumar wrote her story in the *St. Petersburg Times* she reported what she'd experienced, "that there was no recognition that she could see or hear. I thought that was important. I came away thinking, 'Okay, there's no recognition and no acknowledgment that there's anyone in the room. That [Terri] didn't understand.' "

Kumar wondered if her experience with Terri affected her own evaluation of Mary Schindler. "It's hard for me," she said. "I don't have children, but I tried to think of both the Schindlers and Michael when I was there. I could think of how he would think, 'Okay, this is not the woman that she was before.' Clearly, she's not, and there's no recognition. But then I remembered the videotape, and I remembered the Schindlers, and I can see how they could think she makes noise, she moans. And I could see how they could think, desperately, 'This is my daughter. I want her to be alive. I want there to be something there.' I could see how they could make themselves think that because they were so desperate. Plus, it's just an eerie thing when her eyes aren't closed. You expect her to be what you see in the movies, you expect her eyes to be closed, you expect essentially an unconscious person. And she wasn't like that."

Conspiracy theorists would later try to say that I had time to change things in Terri's room, or to do something to Terri herself before Kumar's visit to the hospice. The reporter herself said that she went directly to the facility after making the request, and made a point of asking if what she was about to see had been changed in any way since they were notified that she was on the way. The answer, of course, was no.

That night George took us out to dinner at some trendy restaurant. I told him I was relieved that the trial was over, but that I was going to have a hard time waiting for Judge Greer's decision. That's when George said, "They could appeal his decision."

I'd never thought about that. Until then, I'd figured that once the judge made his decision that was it. Honestly, I'd never considered the possibility that if Greer went our way, it didn't necessarily mean that it was over.

The next day I went back to work at Countryside Hospital, where I was a respiratory therapist. It was a comfortable place to be, not only because I felt that I was doing something useful for people, but because everyone there was supportive. These were people who understood what it meant to have to make an end-of-life decision for a young person; they watched it being done every day, and helped families cope with it. They were good to me.

On Friday, February 11, I was still home when the phone rang shortly after noon. It was Jodi's brother, John, saying that he was sitting in a restaurant and Judge Greer's decision was being reported on television, and that it was in my favor.

I immediately called George, who answered the phone saying, "Mike, I'm reading the fax now."

"George," I said, "they're reporting that we won."

"Give me one second," he said, and I could actually hear him flipping through the pages. "Yes, we won."

I remember that I was standing in our kitchen when I heard those words, and I began running around shouting, "Jodi, it's back. We won. We won. We won." I was excited beyond belief for a few seconds, and then suddenly felt the cold chill of a dagger in my heart. The decision meant that Terri was going to die. That calmed me down very quickly, and I listened as George read the entire ten-page decision to me over the telephone.

The last paragraph seemed to twist that cold knife in my chest:

ORDERED AND ADJUDGED that the Petition for Authorization to Discontinue Artificial Life Support of Michael Schiavo, Guardian of the Person of Theresa Marie Schiavo, an incapacitated person, be and the same is hereby **GRANTED** and Petitioner/Guardian is hereby authorized to proceed with the discontinuance of said artificial life support for Theresa Marie Schiavo.

I'm not sure if it was in that phone call or a subsequent conversation that George told me that the judge would probably stay his decision, pending appeals. As I mentioned, I had never considered the appellate process and had no idea how it worked. George told me to expect another hearing, and then a possible appeal to the state Supreme Court. I thought, *This is going to take forever.* Who knew?

Judge Greer's written decision didn't just say that we'd met the standard of clear and convincing evidence of Terri's wishes, he made a point of acknowledging that Scott's and Joan's testimony was highly credible. On the flip side, he issued a stinging rebuke to the Schindlers.

The judge wrote, "The court also heard from witnesses who ran the gamut of credibility, from those clearly biased who slanted their testimony to those such as Father Murphy whom the court finds to have been completely candid."

Judge Greer continued, "The court also has concerns about the reliability of testimony which differed from prior deposition testimony. Vague and almost self-serving reasons were given for the changes including reflection, reviewed in another fashion, knowledge that this was a real issue, found a calendar, and so forth, to the extent that at trial recollections were sometimes significantly different and in one case were now 'vivid.'"

Judge Greer added, "Interestingly enough, there is little discrepancy in the testimony the court must rely upon in order to arrive at its decision in this case." He went on to say, "The court has reviewed the testimony of Scott Schiavo and Joan Schiavo and finds nothing contained therein to be unreliable. The court notes that neither of these witnesses appeared to have shaded his or her testimony or even attempt to exclude unfavorable comments or points regarding those discussions. They were not impeached on cross-examination."

With that statement, it was fairly clear which side the judge believed played fast and loose with the truth. One might have hoped that the Schindlers would take note of Judge Greer's comments about their credibility and learn a lesson or two for future reference.

If one harbored such hope, however, history would prove one to be a fool.

There's one more paragraph I'd like to quote here even though it may sound a bit self-serving. I figure it might help balance things out with those who may have believed the charges that have been leveled against me by the hysterical mob financed and encouraged by the religious right. Judge Greer wrote, "It has been suggested that Michael Schiavo has not acted in good faith by waiting eight plus years to file the Petition which is under consideration. That assertion hardly seems worthy of comment other than to say that he should not be faulted for having done what those opposed to him want to be continued. It is also interesting to note that Mr. Schiavo continues to be the most regular visitor to his wife even though he is criticized for wanting to remove her life support. Dr. Victor Gambone even noted that close attention to detail has resulted in her excellent physical condition and that Petitioner is very involved."

Not long after the trial, the chaplain at Woodside Hospice had conversations with the Schindlers, saying, "If you need anything, if you want to come and talk to us, we're here all the time." They gave the Schindler family direct phone numbers. The Schindlers always turned them down. A hospice employee told me the Schindlers said, "We don't need that."

About three weeks after Judge Greer announced his decision, I received my first death threat. I was in good company, however, because the woman who called Palm Garden of Largo Convalescent Center also put Judge Greer on her hit list. The timing of the call was a bit strange since Kevin Mort, the nursing home administrator, reported that a lady who apparently had called the facility on two prior occasions said, "There will be a big surprise at the trial. I am going to kill the judge and Michael, and if anything happens to Terri, I will kill you." The trial had been over for more than a month, so perhaps this wacko was living in a time warp. Nevertheless, it was reported to the Pinellas County Sheriff's Department, and per Mr. Mort's request, the threat was not publicized.

On March 2, 2000, just three weeks after Judge Greer released his decision, the Schindlers filed a petition with him to allow swallowing tests to be performed on Terri. They wanted to determine whether she could learn to eat on her own.

It turned out that the trial we'd just been through was not the beginning of the end, it was only the end of the beginning.

11 | It Is a Federal Case

This is not so much a book about the legal process of my wife Terri's case, but a book about how I felt about that process. As I mentioned previously, if you want the definitive legal history of The Schiavo Case, read *Using Terri* by Jon Eisenberg. What follows are more appeals than even I can keep track of. But they all have one thing in common: The Schindlers repeatedly lose.

With George Felos's sound advice and counsel, I had gone on the offensive to seek permission for the removal of Terri's feeding tube in the honest belief that this was what she would have wanted had she been able to make the decision for herself. We prevailed in Judge Greer's courtroom. We proved by the appropriate standard of clear and convincing evidence that removal of life support—which, in this case, meant the removal of her feeding tube—was what Terri would have wanted.

But rather than accept that decision, the Schindlers were gulled into appeal after futile appeal in both state and federal courts, even to the United States Supreme Court, as Jon Eisenberg outlines in his book, by a cabal of extreme right-wing religious and political fanatics, who offered to pay their bills in exchange for making Terri a right-to-life poster child in the latest battle of the culture war.

For them to believe that Terri would ever recover, or show even the tiniest degree of improvement from the brain damage she suffered as a result of her cardiac arrest in 1990, required a suspension of disbelief greater than the one you would need to accept the fact that Superman can fly.

If you take the Schindlers at face value and believe they only had the best interests of Terri at heart, you then have to decide whether or not you believe in science. It's the battle between creationists and evolutionists. One is fine for a pew inside a church: It belongs there; it's comfortable there; it's appropriate there. The other is what you expect to find in hospitals and rehabilitation clinics and medical laboratories. When you step out of the church and into the hospital, it's perfectly fine to bring your religious beliefs with you, to pray for a miracle at your loved one's bedside and to be comforted by a belief that God is watching over you, but you can't disregard science. And that's what the Schindlers publicly did for reasons I don't understand.

I'm convinced that Bob Schindler's earlier efforts to seize Terri's guardianship had more to do with his interest in controlling the funds in her trust account than in his desire to see her get a higher standard of care—which would not have been possible. If you're looking for me to cut a bereaved father some slack, you're going to be on a long and futile search. Had Bob Schindler just once shown up to participate in a patient-staff conference at Mediplex, I might back off. Had he and Mary offered to do Terri's laundry, I'd be less cynical. Had he even been a semiregular visitor at her bedside, I'd give him a break. But he hadn't been and he wouldn't be—until the television cameras he invited to accompany him were on hand.

The flood of petitions from the Schindlers began with their March 2, 2000, request to allow yet another swallowing test to be performed on Terri. Their belief was that if she could swallow, she could consume food orally and, therefore, would not have to rely on the PEG tube for life-sustaining nutrition and hydration.

It took Judge Greer less than a week to deny the petition. I was liking him more and more. It's not just that he saw that the facts were on our side and ruled that way, it's that his reasoning was clear; and when he

I was twenty-one and Theresa Marie Schindler was twenty when we were married on November 10, 1984, at Our Lady of Good Counsel Church in Southampton, Pennsylvania.

In 1981, Terri graduated from Archbishop Wood Catholic High School in Warminster Township, Pennsylvania. She was probably at her heaviest, about 250 pounds, when this picture was taken.

When I first met Terri, she was actually quite shy. Sometimes it seemed as though she was hiding behind those glasses. By the time we got married, the glasses were history, and she'd come out of her shell.

The Brothers Schiavo and their wives on our wedding day. From left to right: Steve, Bill, me, Scott, and Brian; and Pam, Joan, Terri, and Karen. Brian was still a bachelor. My dad called the girls his "Awesome Foursome."

Mary Schindler and Robert Schindler, Sr., Terri's mom and dad, on our wedding day.

Bill and Claire Schiavo, my dad and mom, at our wedding.

After Terri and I were married, we regularly came down to the St. Petersburg area for vacations.

Terri at a family party in early 1985.

Terri continued to lose weight after our wedding. It never dawned on me that Terri really didn't watch what she ate, but she still managed to keep getting thinner. The photo of her in the tank top (below) was taken shortly before her collapse. She was down to between 110 and 115 pounds from a lifetime high of 250.

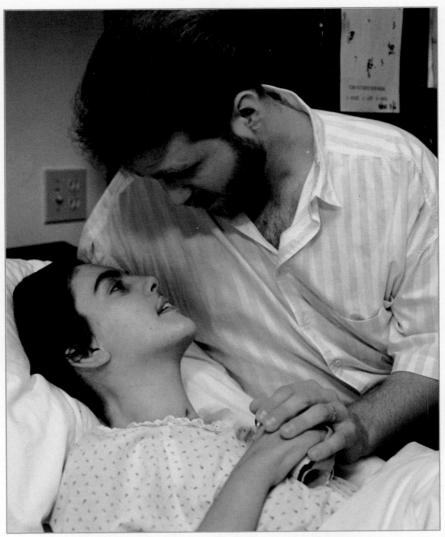

In November, 1990, I wanted Terri to receive rehabilitation therapy; Terri's insurance company determined she would not benefit from such therapy, and declined to pay for it. I took the battle to the media. This photo was taken at College Harbor Nursing Home in St. Pete by *St. Petersburg Times* photographer Joe Walles. After Terri died, the pro-Schindler forces circulated this photo and charged that I had already removed my wedding band only eight months after Terri's collapse. As you can see in this image obtained directly from the *St. Petersburg Times* photo department, I'm wearing my wedding ring. Apparently, the pro-Schindler people had digitally removed it before circulating the photo as part of an attack on my character. Even though it appears in this picture that Terri is responding to my face, voice, and touch, doctors were certain that she was in a persistent vegetative state and had no cognitive abilities. Years later I would have to face the truth that the insurance company was right: Terri would never and could never benefit from therapy.

For the first few years after Terri's collapse, I insisted that she be dressed and out of bed every day, wearing the same makeup she'd used before her collapse. I thought that it might help her snap back to a normal mental state.

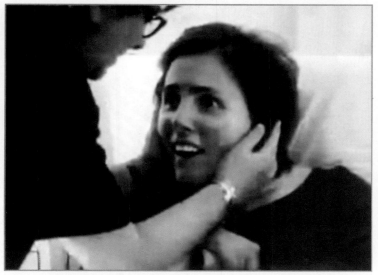

Frames from a videotape shot at the Woodside Hospice were widely used by the Schindlers to promote their claim that Terri could recognize and communicate with her mother. The claim was judged to be false at the time by neurologists who had determined that Terri was in a persistent vegetative state. The autopsy also proved that Terri was, as Dr. Ronald Cranford had declared in 2002, cortically blind. There was no way she could see her parents or anyone else, even though it appears in this, and other photos, that she is looking at them with cognition.

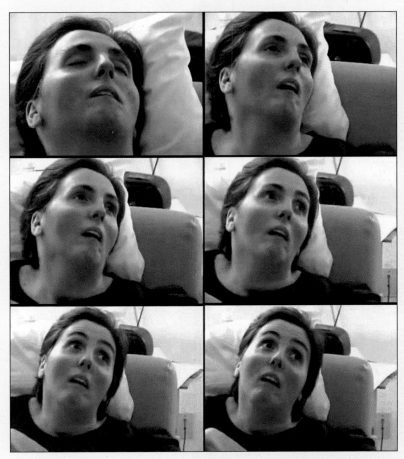

Patients in a persistent vegetative state go through sleep-wake cycles and display facial expressions or make sounds that often cause friends and family to believe that they are conscious and aware. These photos of Terri were taken from the video-tape shown in court at the 2003 evidentiary hearing. In the upper left, she is asleep. The other frames show her awake but unaware. Though her eyes are open, she is staring into space and has no visual fixation. She also has no sustained visual pur-suit, which means she never follows any thing or person with her eyes. During Dr. Ronald Cranford's neurological examination of Terri, it appeared that she tracked a balloon for fifteen seconds, but he says that was a random response or a primitive visual or auditory orienting reflex, which is sub-cortical. It does not mean that she was seeing the balloon and recognizing what it was.

Terri will die a HORRIBLE death!

According to medical pathology, she will go from thirst to extreme thirst. She is likely to cry and moan until she is so dehydrated, she won't have tears and her mouth will be too dry and cracked to make sounds. She may have nose bleeds as the mucous dries out. She will probably experience nausea, vomiting, and cramps as her intestines and stomach lining dehydrate. She will have dizziness, as well as cramping in the arms and legs as her electrolytes get out of balance. Eventually, it will all be too much for her body to handle, **and she will die.**

██████ David
████████ Dr
Clearwater, FL ██████

We wouldn't treat our pets like this - why are we allowing Terri to be executed in such an inhumane way?

Your neighbor
Michael Schiavo
██████████████
Clearwater, FL █████
is trying to <u>murder</u> his wife.

Many Americans don't realize that Terri is NOT being kept alive against her will.

She is NOT being kept alive by "extraordinary means."

And she is NOT in a "persistent vegetative state."

She's simply <u>disabled</u>, and needs *proper care* just like any other severely disabled person.

When her parents visit her, Terri laughs... she cries... she moves... and she makes child-like attempts at speech with her mother and father. Sometimes she will say "Mom" or "Dad" or "yeah" when they ask her a question. And when they kiss her hello or goodbye, she looks at them and "puckers up" her lips.

She's able to sit in a chair... she loves to listen to her favorite music... and she recognizes her brother and sister when they come to visit.

The arsenal of the religious right includes demonstrations, death threats, and disturbing postcards like this, mailed to hundreds of our neighbors. The back of the fanatic's postcard calls to mind this quotation from philosopher Eric Hoffer: "All mass movements . . . irrespective of the doctrine they preach and the program they project, breed fanaticism, enthusiasm, fervent hope, hatred and intolerance . . ."

Attorney George Felos with me in Judge Greer's courtroom during a 2003 hearing. (*Tampa Tribune* photo by Candace Mundy)

Since 1993, attorney Debbie Bushnell has handled all of the legal matters related directly to Terri's guardianship. It was Debbie who referred me to George Felos when it became clear that I would need a trial attorney familiar with "right to die" issues. Debbie says that The Schiavo Case "is a tar baby; it won't let go of you." (Courtesy of Deborah Bushnell)

Judge George Greer of the Probate Division of the Pinellas County Circuit Court was randomly assigned to The Schiavo Case in May 1998, and was involved with it until Terri's death on March 31, 2005. (*Tampa Tribune* photo by Bruce Hosking)

Demonstrations outside the hospice were organized by various groups from the extreme religious right, including Randall Terry's Operation Rescue. Terry's group provided buses to move demonstrators from Pinellas Park to Tallahassee to pressure the legislature. (*Tampa Tribune* photo by Bruce Hosking)

Reverend Jesse Jackson with Florida Governor Jeb Bush at the State Capitol in Tallahassee. Jackson was lobbying for passage of a second Terri's Law, and found himself on the same side of the issue as the radical anti-abortion leader Randall Terry. (*Tampa Tribune* photo by Colin Hackley)

The hostile demonstrators outside the hospice in the final two weeks of Terri's life were from the religious right. Many moderate religious people came to pray quietly for Terri as well.

(*Tampa Tribune* photo by Bruce Hosking)

In the final two weeks of Terri's life, demonstrators regularly picketed in front of our home in Clearwater. Unknown callers sent repeated death threats to Jodi, the children, and me, requiring round-the-clock police protection.

(*Tampa Tribune* photo by Bruce Hosking)

In Terri's last days, Bobby Schindler would visit her for ten minutes or so, and then come outside the hospice to tell demonstrators (and the media) that Terri was suffering and in agony. It was just another distortion of the truth. Suzanne Schindler Vitadamo, Terri's sister, is seen on the left.

(*Tampa Tribune* photo by Bruce Hosking)

Reverend Jesse Jackson showed up at the Woodside Hospice during Terri's final days, reportedly at the invitation of Bobby and Mary Schindler. Jackson sought to pressure Florida lawmakers to pass legislation aimed at keeping Terri alive, even though he had already gone on record with "serious misgivings about the appropriateness of Congress intervening with the legal court process on a specific, individual matter." (*Tampa Tribune* photo by Jay Nolan)

Pinellas Park Police made fifty-seven arrests during noisy demonstrations like this one outside the hospice while Terri was dying. Police said nearly all of those arrested were peaceful. One man who trespassed on hospice property because he was intent on bringing water to Terri had to be stopped with a Taser gun. (*Tampa Tribune* photo by Bruce Hosking)

Terri's grave in Sylvan Abbey Memorial Park. For a dozen years I fought to keep my promise to Terri. The inscription on the bronze marker is my expression of love to Terri, the first love of my life. (Photos by Michael Hirsh)

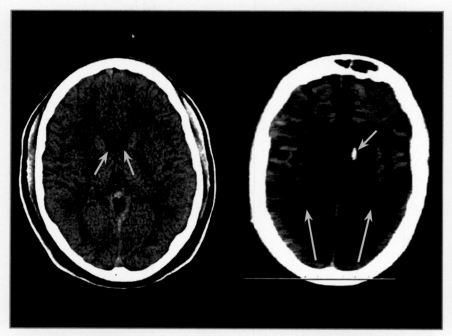

On the right is a computerized tomography scan—commonly called a CT scan—of Terri's brain. On the left is a CT scan of the brain of a normal twenty-six-year-old patient. Ventricles are the fluid-filled spaces in the brain. On the left (at the arrows), they're relatively small, which is normal. In the CT scan of Terri's brain, they have undergone massive enlargement to compensate for the loss of cerebral cortex, the convoluted tissue that gives the brain its nickname—gray matter. The empty spaces are completely filled with spinal fluid.

This extremely severe atrophy indicates irreversible damage to the cognitive centers of the brain where perception, reasoning, and knowledge reside. There was no chance of recovery and no possibility of any response to medical treatment. Complete loss of cerebral cortical functions was diagnosed from an EEG in 1993, and confirmed on another EEG in 2002, as well as with this CT scan done prior to the 2002 evidentiary hearing, three years before her death. The atrophy was confirmed by the post-mortem autopsy exam. Those who say that it was the removal of artificial nutrition and hydration two weeks before Terri died that caused this severe atrophy have chosen to ignore the irrefutable evidence, such as this 2002 CT scan, that proves the condition was longstanding.

The white, oval-shaped object that the upper right arrow is pointing toward is an experimental thalmic stimulator that was implanted in Terri's brain in 1990 by neurosurgeons at the University of California at San Francisco Hospital. It was the presence of the thalmic stimulator that precluded having Terri undergo a magnetic resonance imaging (MRI) procedure.

I gave Jodi Centonze an engagement ring in 1994. We were married in a Catholic ceremony on January 21, 2006. (Photo by Michael Hirsh)

felt that the Schindlers' expert witnesses were being less than straight with him, he didn't hesitate to say so. Consider the two doctors who signed affidavits in support of Terri having a new swallowing test.

Judge Greer wrote, "All of the evidence in support of this motion is from doctors Carpenter and Young who have observed her for 45 minutes and 25 minutes respectively. These observations occurred after the [January 2000] trial and neither doctor consulted any medical evidence with regard to her condition before executing affidavits and then testifying at this hearing."

The judge then summarized the history of Terri's swallowing tests, saying that "the uncontroverted evidence from Dr. Barnhill [our witness at the trial] was that the ward had been administered swallowing tests in 1990, 1991, and 1992 with the earliest test having been done at Bayfront Medical Center. This test resulted in a finding that she was not a future candidate. The last of these tests was done at Largo Medical Center and resulted in a finding that there was no swallowing reflex initiated and that the liquid went nowhere. Thereafter, and annually from 1993 through 1996 or 1997, the ward had a speech pathologist examine her and the finding was that she could not be rehabilitated in this regard and that there was a high risk of aspiration."

Judge Greer found that the doctors testifying on behalf of the Schindlers were about as thorough as the video-diagnosticians who would come later. The judge wrote, "The physicians for the Respondents [the Schindlers] testified that it appeared to them that Terri Schiavo was able to handle the normal secretions such as saliva and sinus drainage orally with no drooling. Dr. Carpenter had observed her in a sitting position while Dr. Young did not mention whether she was sitting or in bed. One of the physicians would not say when she would have stabilized after the February 1990 cardiac arrest and would not concede that her treating physician would be in a better position than he to make that diagnosis. The credibility of this witness was therefore compromised."

And then Judge Greer wrote about our expert witness, neurologist James Barnhill, M.D. "Dr. Barnhill who had testified at trial had physically examined Terri Schiavo on several occasions. He has also reviewed her records, especially on her ability to swallow. He testified that he agreed with the prognosis of the treating physician, Dr. Gambone, that there was no point in doing another swallowing study since she had not changed since the last study. Dr. Barnhill testified that Terri Schiavo has uninhibited reflex activity which includes a bite reflex resulting in a clenched jaw. This would create a real problem in oral feeding, assuming this was a possibility.

"Dr. Barnhill testified that in his opinion attempting oral nutrition would result in aspiration with insufficient nutrition passing to the stomach to maintain her, thereby prolonging her death, if the feeding tube were withdrawn. He testified that such aspiration would lead to infection, fever, cough and ultimately pneumonia. This would require suctioning which likely would be fatal.

"Dr. Barnhill further testified that it is common for patients to be able to swallow saliva but still need feeding tubes. On redirect examination, he testified that it was impossible for Terri Schiavo to be able to take in sufficient sustenance orally to stay alive."

Then, Judge Greer concluded, "It is clear that the credible testimony was that given by Dr. Barnhill for various reasons, not the least of which is that he has examined Terri Schiavo and reviewed her medical records." There it is again—what an amazing clinical concept! Examine the patient and study her records before reaching a conclusion. And with that, Judge Greer denied the Schindlers' petition for Terri to have another swallowing test.

Two weeks later, it was our side that went back to Judge Greer asking for his help in solving a problem the Schindlers were creating at the nursing home. The Schindlers were practically running tours through Terri's room, and it was interfering with the nursing staff. They were also planning on taking what they called "family photos" with Terri, and I was very sensitive to the fact that my wife would have been mortified to be seen by the public looking the way she now did. We requested that the judge prohibit them from taking pictures or videotaping Terri without prior approval from the court.

On March 24, 2000, the judge granted our request. While he authorized relatives related by blood or marriage to visit Terri at any time, and okayed visitation by anyone on the stipulated visitors list, which I approved, so long as no more than six persons visited her at any one time, no one else could get in to see her.

He also dealt with the issue of photography:

"The Respondents [Mr. and Mrs. Schindler], Robert Schindler, Jr., and Suzanne Carr, are prohibited from photographing, taking videos, or taking any other like pictorial representations of the Ward, or causing same to be taken by other persons, without prior approval of this Court."

So if the court never gave them approval—which it didn't—how did the Schindlers eventually come up with the videotape that was selectively edited and shown on television year after year? I don't know. Is it possible that under the guidance of their religious-right handlers, they could have snuck a camera into Terri's hospice room and shot it? The fact that the judge never nailed them with a contempt citation always bugged me. One of my attorneys suggested that perhaps Judge Greer felt he had bigger battles to fight with this case, especially when it became clear that he was being attacked personally and professionally. That may be, but it doesn't make me happy that their supporters were able to manipulate these images and turn them into a public relations coup.

The judge's March 24 order also prohibited the Schindlers from causing Terri to be examined by any physician without the court's prior approval.

Finally, Judge Greer stayed his order of February 11, which allowed us to remove the feeding tube, "until thirty days beyond the exhaustion of all appellate remedies." He did give me the option to seek an order lifting the stay.

Right around the time that this was going on, we learned that my father had been diagnosed with colon cancer. What's that old saying? Just when you think things can't get any worse . . .

The rest of the year was the calm before the storm, but I had no way of knowing that when the storm arrived, it would be a category five, and it would last for five full years. What we didn't know at the time was that the Schindlers were beginning to get legal support from foundations tied to the religious right. They were planning an appeal of Judge Greer's ruling allowing us to remove the feeding tube, and Pam Campbell was already out as their attorney.

In January 2001, I attended the hearing by Florida's Second District Court of Appeals in their Tampa chambers. For both sides, it seemed like a dress rehearsal of things to come. There were protesters in the streets, local people from area churches, apparently organized by a woman named Pam Hennessey, who seemed to have become their PR person.

The Schindlers' motion was denied. About six weeks later, on April 10, after several intervening court skirmishes, the Second District Court of Appeals issued an order that Terri's feeding tube could be removed at 1 P.M. on April 20, noting that "any party seeking review of this order must file a motion for review in the [Florida] Supreme Court."

Two days later, the Schindlers' attorneys let loose with a flurry of motions. One asked that Judge Greer recuse himself. They had no reason other than the judge had consistently ruled against them, which they felt was proof of his bias against them. They also went to the Florida Supreme Court with an emergency motion to prevent the lifting of Judge Greer's order keeping us from removing Terri's feeding tube.

That motion gave us an inkling that the battle was going to become personal and ugly. They tried to make something out of the fact that I waited more than eight years after Terri's accident to petition for removal of the feeding tube—an argument Judge Greer had already deemed meaningless.

They also took a shot at my relationship with Jodi, saying, "A few years *before* he filed the petition he became engaged, and still is, to another woman he owns a home with."

Interestingly, much of their petition disparaged the way the

Schindlers' own attorney tried the case before Judge Greer. For example, it said, "Terri's parents believe their daughter has cognition, recognizes them and reacts to them. However, no experts were hired by them." That, of course, flew in the face of their acceptance at trial that Terri was in a permanent vegetative state, which, by definition, meant she had no cognition.

And then they brought up the swallowing test—again. "A swallowing test was never ordered even though two physicians, who saw Terri after trial, swore in affidavits that she could swallow on her own." There was no mention that Judge Greer said those two doctors had almost no credibility.

The Supreme Court responded quickly, giving us less than five days to file a response to the Schindlers' petition. While my attorneys were working on that response, word came that Judge Greer denied the Schindlers' motion to recuse himself.

In the midst of all this legal activity I'd made plans to move Terri from the Palm Garden nursing home in Largo to Woodside Hospice in Pinellas Park. I had never forgotten the conversations I'd had with hospice workers in Philadelphia while my mom was dying. Now I could see many reasons to move Terri to such a facility. For one, hospice personnel are trained to do grief counseling, and I hoped that if it were available, the Schindlers would use it. There was another, very practical reason for moving Terri out of Palm Garden. The staff and management there had become quite uncomfortable with the notoriety brought about by having my wife there, and there had been subtle suggestions about moving her elsewhere.

The Schindlers were definitely unhappy about Terri moving to the hospice. They told Anita Kumar of the *St. Petersburg Times* that they were worried that Terri would not get the necessary treatment at a facility that advertised its care was focused on "comfort rather than cure." They told Kumar they believed I would refuse to allow treatment of an illness or infection, which could cause Terri's death. When asked about that, my guardianship attorney, Debbie Bushnell, said that I had "not decided whether to withhold treatment, and would decide on [Terri's] care on a case-by-case basis." She also said, "Schiavo would tell the Schindlers—who do not have access to medical information—before he decided to withhold treatment."

A day after we filed our brief in response to the Schindlers' appeal, the Florida Supreme Court handed them another defeat: Their request to stay Judge Greer's order allowing the feeding tube to be removed was denied.

Very quickly, the Schindlers went to Federal District Court Judge Richard Lazzara, who granted them a stay until April 23 in order for them to exhaust all possible appeals. Going to the federal court system was not something we expected them to do; this case was a state matter. It was surprising that a federal judge agreed to hear it, much less grant them a stay.

At one point, my oldest brother, Bill, said to me, "Well, now our name is in the United States Supreme Court." It was a weird feeling. At that point, I had no idea how much more bizarre it was going to get.

George explained the appeals process to me, and said that initially, only one Supreme Court justice would rule on the Schindlers' petition, and that would be Anthony Kennedy, because he was the one who had oversight for cases coming up from Florida.

On Monday, April 23, 2001, I was sitting at home in our living room, not moving very far from the television, when CNN put up the "Breaking News" headline. The crawl across the bottom said that the Schindlers' request was denied by Justice Kennedy. Once again, emotions flowed over me in waves. Once again, I allowed myself to believe that this was really going to happen now. It was a sad moment. After all the fighting and arguing, it was finally happening. Terri was going to be allowed to die. I felt very empty, even though another small part of me was happy for her.

One day between the end of the trial and the Supreme Court decision, Jodi and I went to the hospice. "I was just experiencing a lot of emotion that I had no idea that I would feel," Jodi said, adding, "I felt happy for Mike and happy for Terri, but also sad. I felt like she had been a part of my life for so long, that I knew her. There wasn't all the hoopla then. It was strange walking in there. It's strange because her eyes were open and Mike walked in and kissed her, and it was as though she was looking at him, 'cause that's the way her head was positioned. But as he kissed her and said 'hello' and walked away, she was still looking at the same empty space.

"I don't really think I knew what to expect. She just lay there, and her eyes blinked, and it was very sad to see what she looked like then. I'd seen all the pictures of Terri over the years, and there was just no resemblance to the woman in the bed. Regardless of what one of the bogus affidavits said, that was the only time I ever visited Terri."

The order from the Supreme Court meant Terri's feeding tube could be removed the very next day, on April 24.

George, Debbie, and I had been preparing for that day for a long time. We'd talked about when the doctor would come in; we'd discussed whether the tube should be removed, or whether it should just be taped off in a way that would prevent anyone from doing anything untoward. That was a very real concern—that someone would attempt to give her food or water.

Early on the afternoon of Tuesday, April 24, Debbie Bushnell called from the hospice to tell me that Terri's feeding tube had been clamped off. I fell apart. It had been a long struggle, with the courts and the appeals and the motions and the hearings. And the hatefulness. And then it was finally here.

Two days later, I was sitting in the room they'd given me to use at the hospice, when I saw the news on TV: The Schindlers had filed an emergency motion with Judge Greer based upon the discovery of what they called "new evidence." The alleged evidence was based on a claim that Cindy Brashers, the young lady I'd dated before meeting Jodi, would testify that I'd lied about Terri's wishes. Judge Greer dismissed their motion as "untimely."

But that didn't end it. The Schindlers' newest attorney, a right-to-life-funded activist named Pat Anderson, whose behavior in and out of courtrooms astonished and often appalled a veteran journalist who covered the trial, went to Circuit Court Judge Frank Quesada and filed a new civil suit, claiming that I'd committed perjury. It was based on an affidavit signed by Robert Schindler, Sr., who was relaying statements he claimed were made by Cindy Brashers—now married and known as Cindy Shook.

Perhaps I need to go over that again, because it's more than a bit bizarre. They didn't file an affidavit from Cindy Shook claiming that I'd lied. They filed an affidavit from Terri's father, claiming that Cindy Shook claimed that I'd lied. I'm no lawyer, but I didn't think any reasonably intelligent judge would take action based on that sort of BS. At the very least, I would expect the judge to say, "Can you produce Ms. Shook so I can hear it from her directly?"

But that's not what Judge Quesada did. What he did was order Terri's feeding tube reinserted. His order was issued based on heavy-handed distortion of what I said to Cindy.

Over the course of my legal battle to do what I believed was right, and what Terri would have wanted, I was asked why I wouldn't publicly confront the Schindlers. Why not debate them on television? It may even sound like a reasonable thing to do. The reason I wouldn't even consider it is: You can't debate people who have no qualms about distorting the facts. It's not a fair fight, and the truth will surely be lost.

Now, you may be thinking that the Schindlers were only trying to save their daughter, and that for me to say they were distorting the truth is too harsh an accusation. Maybe you believe they were caught up in the desperation and emotion of the moment and said some things—or their supporters said some things—that may just have been exaggerated. That happened, and I call those "wishful lies." I did it, too. Early on, I told people that Terri recognized my voice as I approached her room in the nursing facility, and that she cried when she saw I was getting ready to leave. Mrs. Schindler insisted that Terri responded to her voice, that her eyes followed her around the room. But Terri was cortically blind, so that couldn't have happened, no matter how much her mom wanted to believe it was happening. As I wrote in the Preface, I do have sympathy for them. Terri was their daughter. Losing her would be extraordinarily painful.

But when the personal attacks on me, and later, on Jodi, and my children grew, and I was accused of murder, abuse, negligence, and a host of other horrible things, it got to be too much. I could not just let those kinds of attacks roll off my back.

In 1992, about two years after Terri's collapse, I became friends with a twenty-two-year-old woman named Cynthia Brashers. I mentioned her earlier in this book. We had one actual date. After that, it was a close friendship; she said we were confidantes. I was clear to her that I was married, in love with my wife, and devoted to taking care of her. Frankly, that's why the relationship with Cindy didn't go anywhere. She wanted a future, and it was evident to her that my devotion to Terri made that impossible. We hugged. We kissed. That's it. Don't take my word for it. It's in her deposition that was taken on the evening of May 8, 2001, at the offices of the McDermott Law Firm in St. Petersburg Beach, Florida. The now-married Cindy Shook, and her husband, Donald, had retained the firm to represent them once she got caught up in the Schindler-Schiavo battle because of a phone call she made to a local radio station DJ who was discussing the case. It was April 24, 2001, and Terri's feeding tube had just been removed.

As a result of making that call, attorneys for the Schindlers had a private investigator named Kimberly Takacs track her down. Takacs initially got Cindy to talk by claiming to be a close friend of the family. Because Cindy's baby was crying, the two women stepped outside, where Takacs took notes on their conversation, but did not tape-record it.

Shortly after that conversation, on April 26, the Schindlers filed an emergency motion with Judge Greer. They claimed that there was new evidence. What was it? That Cindy Shook will testify that I lied about Terri's wishes. Judge Greer dismissed this motion as untimely. The Schindlers then filed a new civil suit claiming that I had perjured myself when I testified that Terri had stated that she wouldn't ever want to remain on life support. This suit was not filed in the probate court, where Judge Greer would handle it. Instead, the Schindlers' lawyers went judge shopping, and ended up in the courtroom of another Circuit Court judge, Frank Quesada, who ordered that Terri's feeding tube be reinserted.

The only sworn statement presented by their attorneys was from Terri's father, in which he says that Cindy Shook claimed that I told her that I "did not know what Terri Schiavo would have wanted him to do." The way the Schindlers' attorney and Mr. Schindler characterized the statement, it made it sound as though I'd been lying all along when I'd said that Terri and I had discussed what are commonly called end-of-life decisions. After all, how could I say we had discussed it when I told Cindy Shook that I didn't know what Terri would have wanted me to do?

But it was all a deliberate, intentional lie by the Schindlers. According to Cindy's sworn testimony, both Robert Schindler and the "purported private investigator" knew the correct context of my statement to the effect that Terri and I "never spoke about this."

Here's a portion of Shook's testimony from her deposition:

Q. Did you maintain to Mr. Schindler that Michael Schiavo told you, "How the hell do I know what to do with her? We never talked about this when we were married. We were young and this was never talked about."

A. Yes.

Q. Did you tell Mr. Schindler in what context that statement of Mr. Schiavo was made?

A. Yes.

Q. Okay. What did you tell Mr. Schindler?

A. That Michael and I had a conversation about how he was going to get on with his life. And I specifically talked to Mr. Schindler about the couple options that I've already mentioned about building an addition to the parents' home, hiring staff at the nursing home. He verbalized back to me he was aware of what I was talking about, and I told him Michael made those statements in that context.

Q. Okay. Did Mr. Schindler ask you whether you ever had a conversation with Michael about what Terri's wishes were regarding end-of-life care or removal of life support?

A. No.

Q. Did you ever tell Mr. Schindler that you had a conversation with Mr. Schiavo about that subject.

A. No. (Shook deposition at 92-93)

So that's what the context of my statement was. But as my attorney wrote in one of the briefs filed in the case, "Despite both Mr. Schindler and the investigator knowing the correct context of the subject statements, they recite in their Affidavits Shook's statement—that Michael Schiavo allegedly told her, 'We never spoke about this . . . My God, I was only twenty-five years old . . . it never crossed our mind'— but both exclude from their Affidavits the context of those statements."

As Cindy said in her deposition, my statement to the effect that, "he did not know what Terri Schiavo would have wanted him to do" was "not . . . about whether his wife would have wanted to be on life support," which was what the Schindlers were claiming it referred to, but whether I should keep Terri in a nursing facility or try to have her live at home.

Mr. Schindler obviously knew the representations being made to the court on his behalf were inaccurate. Whether the attorneys knew this too isn't known; what my attorney, George Felos, made clear, however, was that "it is undisputed that, subsequent to the Shook deposition, they have failed to correct the misrepresentations as they are required to do."

That's the short version of the Cindy Shook affidavit, but the niceties of legal discourse don't display how really ugly and mean-spirited the effort was to smear me in order to get the court to do what they wanted done. One personal attack that the Schindlers have launched is that when Terri collapsed, I didn't immediately call 911. Jeb Bush appeared willing to believe this lie, since after Terri's autopsy report was made public, he asked the Pinellas County prosecutor to investigate in order to see if I could be criminally charged.

Cindy was being questioned by one of the Schindlers' attorneys, James D. Eckert, about her conversation with Kimberly Takacs, the private investigator hired by the Schindlers. She was asked if they spoke about what happened on the day that Terri collapsed, and she said they did. But she makes it clear that what Takacs reported she said was inaccurate.

Reading from Takacs's report, Cindy explained, "It says on here that . . . I asked him why it took him so long to call 911. I have no knowledge of how long it took him. She [Takacs] told me that it took him seven minutes to call 911. Ms. Takacs informed me of that, and it was the first time I had ever heard that statement made."

Eckert then asked Cindy to tell him what else was wrong with Takacs's statement. She said, "He did tell me he thought he felt a heartbeat. He did not tell me 'and thought she was okay.' "

Shook continued reading from the investigator's work of fiction. " 'On another occasion he said the reason he didn't call 911—' He and I never had a discussion that he did *not* call 911. We had a discussion that he *did* call 911."

Trying to build a case that I deliberately didn't seek immediate medical attention for Terri wasn't enough for the Schindlers and their investigator. Try this. The attorney said to Cindy, "Now, then, you see clearly on page nine it says [you said] 'It was always about the money.' "

Cindy responded, "That's an incorrect statement." She went on to say that "I don't know what his financial situation was when I was with him, but the only issue about money was the lawsuit, and I was not involved in any details about that."

The lawyer inquired further, digging a deeper hole for his own client to fall into. "And then it says: 'I could tell you a lot of other things that would blow your mind about him, but I am just not willing to jeopardize my family.' "

Cindy's response: "I didn't make that statement at all."

After a couple hours' examination by the Schindlers' attorney, it was my lawyer's chance to question Cindy Shook. George Felos began by making sure that everyone was clear on the fact that I had never talked with her about Terri's end-of-life wishes. Cindy said, "I specifically talked to Mr. Schindler about the couple options that I've already mentioned about building an addition to the parents' home, hiring staff at the nursing home. He verbalized back to me he was aware of what I was talking about, and I told him Michael made those statements in that context." She went on to say that Mr. Schindler never asked her whether she'd had a conversation with me about what Terri's wishes were regarding end-of-life care or removal of life support.

A bit later, Felos asked Cindy whether she'd had any conversations with Ms. Takacs after her meeting outside her home that evening.

She replied, "No, sir. But there are some additional comments that she didn't put in her affidavit."

"What are those?" asked my lawyer.

"At the end of our conversation when I told her I couldn't help her, she said, 'This could be your daughter, and wouldn't you hope somebody would do the right thing?' and 'If someone is watching you be raped, wouldn't you hope they would do the right thing?' and 'We need to get this feeding tube hooked back up so I have time to get more dirt on Michael,' and 'If you can't bring it—yourself to do the right thing, please consult with your husband. Maybe he can convince you to do the right thing.'"

It is ambiguous, I admit, but my own interpretation of what Takacs meant by "the right thing" was for Cindy to say what Takacs wanted to hear.

Felos then asked Cindy, "Now, Takacs again states that you reiterated 'that her parents could assume the responsibility and that he did not want it.' Did you say that to her?"

"No, sir. I did not."

Then the topic moved back to the fiction that I'd delayed calling 911 the morning that Terri collapsed. "Did you tell Ms. Takacs that you heard two different stories at different times about the 911 call?"

"Yes," she replied. "The first story was that he heard a heartbeat, and the second story was that he didn't do CPR because he didn't know how. I guess they weren't two different stories. They were two different conversations."

"Did you ever tell Ms. Takacs that Mr. Schiavo told you that he didn't call 911 because he panicked?" asked attorney Felos.

"No," Cindy responded.

A moment later, Felos asked, "Did you ever tell Ms. Takacs that Mr. Schiavo said that he was obsessed with getting the settlement [from the malpractice lawsuit]?"

Again, she responded, "No."

"Did you tell Ms. Takacs that when the two of you began dating, at first he seemed like he was doing the things he should [to take care of Terri]?"

"No. I told her that I thought Michael took excellent care of Terri when I met him. She said, 'Oh, come on.' That was the conversation around that." And Cindy went on to say that for the duration of the time that we were friends, she believed I took good care of Terri, and that contrary to what Takacs reported, I never said that Terri was a nuisance.

The deposition continued, with Cindy steadfastly denying just about everything that the Schindlers' investigator claimed she'd told her. Late in the evening, Felos turned to the subject of a call that Cindy made to reporter Michael Brassfield at the *St. Petersburg Times* on the day that Terri's feeding tube was reinserted. "I explained to him the relationship that Michael and I had and the context of the statements that were made to Kimberly [Takacs], and that I felt like the Schindlers—they had even told me that they were very desperate and they would do anything to keep her alive and that they just needed that one statement from me—not the context or anything, just that one statement—either on tape or if I would speak to Mr. Magri on the phone, and that would save Terri's life; that I was what would save her life." (Joseph Magri was one of the Schindlers' attorneys who had filed the most recent court motion seeking to have Terri's feeding tube reinserted.)

"Go ahead and tell me when you had that conversation with Mr. and Mrs. Schindler," Felos said.

"[With] Mr. Schindler, when I spoke to him, the only one time that I spoke to him on the phone . . . he said, 'That's what I need. You've got the information that will save Terri's life. I need that one statement, if you'd be willing to speak to our attorney and give him that one statement to'—Mr. Magri is who he wanted me to speak with.

"And then when I was talking to Kimberly, she got Terri's brother on her cell phone, and he got on the phone with me and said that he would do anything to save his sister and if there was anything he could do to make me give that statement. And then Kimberly asked me if she could just tape that one statement, that she didn't need anything else; if I would just be willing to give that one statement on tape."

"What did you tell him?" Felos asked.

"I told him that I didn't want to speak to the attorney, that I didn't have any information; all I had was information in the context that I had it."

Just to make sure that no one could miss the point, Felos asked, "I want to understand this to make sure I have this clear. Are you saying that Ms. Takacs was asking you to give only that portion of the statement and not put the statement in context?"

Cindy replied, "She said, 'If you will just give me that one statement on tape, that's what we need.' " And in response to further questioning, she agreed that she had previously told the investigator what the context of the statement was.

On April 27, 2001, in a *St. Petersburg Times* article written by William R. Levesque and reported by Michael Brassfield, readers learned that at 8:30 P.M., Pinellas-Pasco Circuit Court Judge Frank Quesada "did what the U.S. Supreme Court and four other courts before him refused" to do: "ordered doctors to resume feeding Terri Schiavo while her parents pursue a lawsuit against the woman's husband."

The lawsuit filed just hours before Quesada's ruling "accuses Terri Schiavo's husband, Michael Schiavo, of committing perjury by saying his wife did not want to be kept on life support."

Mr. Schindler, told the *Times,* "God heard our prayers. We really thought it was probably the end of the road. I'm not a Bible thumper. But this has got to be the work of God. He's here and he's alive and well."

If it was the work of God, it could only have been because Schindler believed God repealed the ninth commandment. That's the one that says, "Thou shalt not bear false witness."

The *Times's* story goes on to say, "In an affidavit, Bob Schindler said Shook quoted Michael Schiavo as saying: 'How the hell do I know what to do with her. We never talked about this when we were married. We were young and this was never talked about.' "

In what has to be classic irony, the lawsuit that Mr. and Mrs. Schindler filed against me sought unspecified damages for inflicting against them "extraordinary mental anguish, suffering and virtually total disruption of their lives."

The *Times's* reporters contacted Shook, who told them that her words had been taken completely out of context. And the paper also stated that "The Schindlers' attorneys say their private investigator has thorough notes of her conversation with Shook. They plan to depose Shook today."

Ultimately, Schindler attorney James Eckert was compelled to provide us with copies of the investigator's "thorough notes." They're handwritten with many crossed-out words and phrases, and are clearly *not* notes taken during the purported conversation with Cindy Shook, but were written after the fact.

One of the Schindler attorneys, Pat Anderson, told the reporters, "I'm not surprised she's [Shook] backpedaling, because she's frightened of Michael Schiavo." Anderson dared to make that statement even though Cindy made it clear that she did not tell Anderson's investigator that she feared for her family's safety if she spoke with me. But that sort of distortion shouldn't have surprised anyone who knew Pat Anderson and the fact that she had a history of bending the truth if it would help her case. Fortunately, the Florida Bar was concerned about attorneys who make misrepresentations to the court and then fail to correct them. The bar had filed a complaint in the Supreme Court of Florida against Anderson and a fellow attorney. On February 23, 1989, Anderson had been publicly sanctioned (and her cohort was temporarily suspended from the practice of law) for "uncorrected misrepresentations to the court. Basically, respondents submitted a brief to the appellate court misrepresenting the facts of a case before the court and making extended argument based on the inaccurate facts. Despite the exposure of this inaccuracy by the opposing party, respondents did not acknowledge the patent misrepresentations, maintaining instead in a written response to a motion for sanctions that the opposing party was attempting to obfuscate and deceive the court."

I saw no point in debating the merits of my position publicly with the Schindlers, their attorneys, or their supporters. If they'd distort the facts in a sworn affidavit, and file a lawsuit based solely on those distortions under oath, why would I believe that they'd come down with a sudden case of accuracy on television?

12 | Now for Something Completely Different

The Schiavo-Schindler battle was a lot like the way soldiers describe combat: periods of total boredom punctuated by episodes of pure chaos. The winter of 2001 was the former, at least as far as the legal battles went. In late October the Second District Court of Appeals had ruled that five doctors were to examine Terri to determine if she might improve with new medical treatment, and I'd begun to adjust to the fact that nothing was going to happen quickly. My attorney was planning appeals to the State Supreme Court to try to stop the five-doctor exam, but that was an exercise in filing paperwork that didn't require my participation. As things turned out, it was going to be almost a year before we were back in court hearing from the doctors.

My relationship with Jodi was as solid as ever. What had begun in 1993 as two lost souls looking for friendship had grown into a marriage in everything but the eyes of the law. Early on, in accepting my situation with Terri, Jodi told me that she understood that it was possible for a man to love two women at the same time. And I was the luckiest man alive to have discovered that she really meant it.

Jodi knew I had a wife, and whether or not that changed did not matter to her. Let me be perfectly clear—that's not to say she was thrilled with the chaos. But she'd told me many times that the circumstances with Terri were what they were, and now that she loved me, she didn't have any right to change the rules. And that was it.

Jodi said, "Mike had a wife and her name was Terri. She came before me, and I knew that. That was just that. Not that there weren't issues here or there. Not like there wasn't anger. Sometimes I was mad at her, because I felt she did this to herself, and look at what she left Mike to deal with."

One of the things we were dealing with was the rumors that were spread about us. There was always a new one cropping up. One nurse in particular at Sabal Palms was one of the best at inventing stories. Years earlier in my relationship with Jodi, I'd heard her claim Jodi and I had a child with one more on the way. Others elaborated on the story, and claimed that I was paying child support for a secret daughter named Gina whom I'd had with another woman twelve years earlier. One of the nurses supporting the Schindlers even told a story that I'd brought this imaginary daughter to work in order to show her off.

By late 2001, we'd gone from the national trauma of the attacks on our country to the personal devastation of dealing with my dad's cancer to the discovery that Jodi's mom, Ellie, also had the disease. Perhaps it's too dramatic to say that these events compelled us to think about what we wanted from life, but we decided that we both wanted children, we weren't getting any younger, and we didn't want to wait any longer. Our friends encouraged us, our families encouraged us. Even George Felos and Debbie Bushnell, my attorneys, were happy for us.

The first time we did the home test, it came back negative. But one night we were coming home from my dad's house, and Jodi said, "Oh, God, I just can't stay awake." It was the first time she'd ever fallen asleep in the car on the way home. I thought maybe she was just tired.

A day or so later, Jodi came home from the deli we owned and went into the bathroom to take a shower. I knew she'd bought another test kit and was waiting for her to come out and tell me the results. But she didn't. I could hear the water running so I figured if she's in the shower, it means we're not pregnant. I was bummed out. Nevertheless, I walked into the bathroom and asked, "What'd it say?"

She stuck her head out the sliding shower door and said, "It's over there," pointing to the sink. I looked at the strip sitting on the sink. Two pink lines. I looked at her and she just smiled.

I went berserk. I went out of my mind. I came running out of the bathroom into the living room where her mother was sitting in the rocker and screamed, "I'm gonna be a daddy, and you're gonna be a grandmom," and I began waving the test stick in front of her face.

Just then the phone rang. It was George. "I can't talk to you right now. I just found out I'm going to be a father!" George was excited for me and didn't mind at all when I said that I'd have to call him back.

While Jodi didn't have reservations about getting pregnant because of the nutcases who'd been working overtime coming up with disgusting names to call her, she was concerned about how the Church would feel about us having children.

"A year earlier I had talked to one of the Catholic priests that I'd been seeing for quite some time just because we were in such a stressful situation. In addition to all the craziness, I'd just left a job with a firm I'd been with for eighteen years, and Mike's dad had been diagnosed with cancer. I didn't go there just to ask if it was okay to have kids. It was just part of many conversations about life. They were okay with it. They felt like children were a gift from God, and in Mike's situation, he was doing the right thing.

"It was a complicated situation. I guess my concern was getting older and not having kids, or not being comfortable with having kids and not being married. He basically told me that everything was fine, which I guess surprised me a little bit. But in my own heart I felt it was okay, because I know that God didn't mean for Mike to be alone forever just because he was carrying out Terri's wishes."

I was fortunate that while we were adjusting to Jodi's pregnancy and the hormonal changes that went along with it, the legal battle with the Schindlers was not in crisis mode. Actually, just the opposite.

In late 2001, both sides petitioned the Florida Supreme Court to stay their most recent ruling in order to try mediation.

The idea had come from Larry Crow, an attorney working for the Schindlers. He suggested a mediation session and even though I wasn't all that excited by the idea, I agreed to go along. On January 10, 2002, the Supreme Court gave us sixty days to see if it would work.

It was set up for 8 A.M. on Wednesday, February 13, at the Pinellas County Courthouse with a retired judge serving as mediator. That just happened to be Ash Wednesday, and the day before Valentine's Day, which would be the ninth anniversary of the ugly confrontation with Bob Schindler in Terri's nursing home room that marked the beginning of our battle.

The session was supposed to be confidential, but the media learned that something was going on, and they were swarming in the corridor outside the courtroom, trying to shoot through the glass pane in the door and attempting to eavesdrop as well.

I hated the notion of having to sit down at a table with Bob and Mary Schindler. By this time in our battle I had nothing but contempt for them. I blamed them for the indignities that had been heaped upon Terri, and wasn't inclined to be the least bit respectful. As you might suspect, that didn't bode well for mediation.

The long tables usually reserved for prosecution and defense—or plaintiff and respondent in civil cases—had been pushed together in front of the judge's bench, and we all sat around them. George Felos and Debbie Bushnell sat on my side; Pat Anderson, Larry Crow, and Terri's parents faced us, with the judge sitting at one end.

The judge began by laying out the rules: The session was confidential—not to be talked about outside the courtroom. The judge was very cordial, and definitely an optimist. He said that we all had to try to do our best to get this situation resolved and move on. He explained that the Schindlers would go into one of the jury rooms, and we would stay in the courtroom. He was going to meet with them for a couple of hours, and then come back and meet with us. Then we'd break for lunch.

And then they went into the jury room and we sat around waiting. I don't do well sitting around waiting for things to happen. Only a few minutes had passed when Bobby Schindler came into the courtroom and headed into the room where his parents were. George immediately went over there, asked the judge to come out, and told him that Bobby had no part in this mediation. Bobby was ordered to leave.

At long last, the judge came out of the Schindlers' room, sat down with us, and asked that we tell him our side of the story. We spoke for about ninety minutes. All the while I was thinking *Where are we going with this? What is this going to fix? They hate me and I hate them.*

Late in the morning, the judge brought the Schindlers and their attorneys back into the courtroom, and we all sat down together. I started to say something and Bob Schindler interrupted. That did it. Things got loud, tempers were flying. No one was actually shouting, but it was mean—primarily between Mr. Schindler and me.

Realizing that things weren't going as he'd planned, the judge split us up again, and escorted the Schindlers back into the jury room. A few moments later he came out and said, "Mrs. Schindler wants to know if she can talk to Michael by himself."

I'd known Mary Schindler for a long time, and I knew that deep in her heart, she knew that what I was attempting to do was the best thing for Terri. I felt sad for her that she had been controlled by people who had put her up to being part of this fight, but I just did not like her anymore. She'd said hateful things about me, and that was sad, because I knew she was a good woman at heart. Nevertheless, she'd become this person whom I'm sure she didn't want to be.

Reluctantly, I agreed to sit down with her. The judge had everyone but the two of us leave the courtroom. There we sat, Mary and me, staring at each other. She was at one end of the table; I was in the middle on our side. Since she was the one who asked to speak to me, I just sat there, waiting to hear what she had to say.

She began telling me what they'd tried to explain to the mediator, but I wasn't in the mood to listen to her nonsense. "What are you trying to accomplish with me?" I said, adding, "The stuff you're bringing up has already been discussed in court. Is there anything else you want to discuss with me?"

She brought up rehab, and the fuse burned lower and hotter. "How could you say that Terri has never had any rehab when you were there the whole time at Mediplex? You went with me." She had no answer.

Then she said, "I don't want you to do this." I knew she was talking about removing the feeding tube.

"I'm just carrying out what Terri wants, and you know that's what Terri wants." Then I asked, "Do you want to be like this?" She knew what I was talking about. She was being used like a puppet—and it was only going to get worse. There was no response. All I could think of was that I was sitting across from a woman who had no moral qualms about removing life support from her mother. Where was the "when there's life there's hope" doctrine back then?

"You know something, Mom"—I called her Mom, which is what I used to call her. I don't know why I did it then, it just came out—"This is stupid. This is over."

I could tell she was angry; she was tapping on the table with her index finger to make her point. But it was all a huge waste of time. I called my attorneys back in and said, "I'm done. I'm going. You guys can sit here as long as you want and talk, but I'm done." It was three in the afternoon. I'd had enough.

Maybe I had the wrong attitude, but I just knew from the get-go that there was no talking between us. These people—people I used to call Mom and Dad—came into a courtroom and said things that were absolutely hateful about Jodi and me, and now they wanted me to sit down and talk with them like we were family again? That wasn't going to happen. I had never once said anything hateful about them in public. Why play that game? Why lower myself to their standards?

Besides, I knew it wasn't about me and it wasn't about how they felt about me. They wanted to keep Terri alive in a condition she would never want to be in. They were being selfish, just as I had been selfish in the beginning. The only thing that mattered to me was what Terri wanted. She did not want to be kept alive like this. And that wasn't going to change.

Late that afternoon, George filed the required Notice of Impasse with the Florida Supreme Court. It was a single sentence in length: "Petitioner hereby files notice that the parties' mediation effort is at an impasse."

When I got home I was still doing a slow burn, but I tried hard to keep it from Jodi. She didn't need any additional stress. There was enough going on with the pregnancy, with my father dying of cancer, and with Jodi's mom also dealing with cancer.

We actually lived at my father's house for a couple of weeks to help care for him during his final days, and that was right around the same time that Jodi had her amniocentesis done. It was just precautionary—but she was thirty-seven and her doctor suggested doing it. Jodi and I had the same conversation that I'd had with Terri when she and I were trying to get pregnant years earlier. We both agreed that if the amnio came back and said there were extreme problems, we would consider all our options.

Just before my dad died, Jodi had told him that we were going to give him a grandson. She was so certain the baby was a boy, we had named him Nicholas. But just after Dad died, on April 15, we learned that the baby Jodi was carrying was a girl. So much for feminine intuition.

It was interesting how Jodi's mom dealt with us having kids. She'd been a very devout Catholic in her youth. But during her marriage she'd drifted away from the Church. After Jodi's dad died, her mother saw that Jodi had gotten involved with the Church again, and she decided she'd do the same. You might think that getting more involved with the Church would make her a more observant Catholic, but Jodi says it didn't work that way. "As she got older and went through more life experiences, she became much less rigid and more accepting of things, including the relationship I had with Mike and especially the notion that we were going to have children together. Even her church friends kept asking when we were going to have kids."

The last weeks of Jodi's pregnancy were difficult. I was scared to death, because I knew all the things that could go wrong. I tried not to be the RN; I tried to be the husband; the father. But it wasn't working.

After a few false alarms, Jodi and her doctor decided that they would induce labor. She picked September 14, and we were supposed to be at Morton Plant Hospital in Clearwater by seven in the morning. During the night, however, Jodi began going into strong labor. By the time we got to the hospital, the contractions were hitting her hard, but they were still five minutes apart.

Giving birth is a miracle, but going through the pain is terrible, and I felt very bad for her. As soon as we got into the hospital, she said the magic word: epidural. They put it in and began the Pitocin to speed things up. I was sitting there watching the monitor—that's the nurse part of me—and I could actually see the contractions coming. We were both doing all right, although she was getting anxious and I couldn't control my excitement. I probably looked a little dorky wearing my COACH T-shirt—but I didn't care.

The room we were in had a private sitting area for the family right outside the door, equipped with a big TV, a microwave, and a refrigerator. Jodi's mom was there, along with her brother, sister-in-law, and her niece, and to Jodi it seemed as though we were having a little party out there and she hadn't been invited.

We'd expected the delivery to be easy, but it wasn't to be. Jodi pushed for three hours and was getting quite upset. It seemed as though the epidural was wearing off and she was feeling everything. Her obstetrician, Dr. Jensen, had a terrific bedside manner, and was explaining everything that was happening to us, but it wasn't making things go any faster.

Part of the problem was that the baby was a lot bigger than we thought she'd be, nine pounds, thirteen ounces, and 22½ inches long, and there was a time when we thought that doing a C-section might be the way to go. But the baby's heart rate was good and Dr. Jensen kept trying. He used suction, then forceps, and kept urging Jodi to push. I looked at Jodi and said, "Push!" Then I got behind her and said it again. "Push!" She pushed, and at last, Olivia Claire Schiavo, the most beautiful little girl in the world, finally made her appearance.

They kept Livy in the room with us while we were waiting to move to the mother/baby side of the ward. Olivia slept, Jodi and I held her. There were times I never thought that I'd be a father, but I'd just watched my daughter being born. It was a beautiful thing.

13 | Five Doctors, More Waiting

If I had any hope that 2002 wasn't just going to be more of the same, it was dashed in late January when that legal train wreck known as Patricia Fields Anderson filed a petition for an order appointing Terri's sister, Suzanne, and brother, Bobby, as "proxy for the ward." The document, including attachments, was thirty-eight pages long.

How would I describe it and the other legal nonsense Anderson created? Suffice it to say that if motions were manure, the courthouse gardeners wouldn't need fertilizer for a decade.

This latest motion said that I was appointed guardian "to provide for the welfare and safety of the ward," and went on to say about me, "His conduct in discharging that responsibility has made a mockery of the law."

Never mind that the doctors who testified in previous trials, and Judge Greer, himself, attested to the fact that I'd given Terri exemplary care; that she'd never had so much as a single bedsore.

They also raised the matter of money, and quoted Judge Greer in 2000 as saying, "this Court observed that money overshadows this entire case." But Pat Anderson's brief neglects to mention that Judge Greer was talking about money creating a conflict of interest for both me *and* the Schindlers. The judge's entire decision is in Appendix 1, page 333.

One more example from their compilation of legal desperation, this one involving both money and sex, was in this petition: They said that according to testimony in 1993, I acknowledged "an eight-month intimate relationship with a woman named Cindy, but he gave no beginning and ending dates of the relationship." Their petition continued, "According to Cynthia Shook, she had a relationship with Schiavo that began in January 1992 and ended on the day of the malpractice jury verdict. Thus, Schiavo was conducting an adulterous relationship at the very time he testified to the jury in such a moving fashion about the importance of his wedding vows and his love for Terri and his desire to spend the rest of his life with Terri."

Sounds really terrible, doesn't it? But this was what it said in the footnotes at the bottom of that very page from which I just quoted. "Deposition of Cynthia Shook, May 8, 2001 at pp. 19–22. Mrs. Shook testified that the relationship was not romantic . . . If Mrs. Shook is correct in her recollection, this relationship began less than two years after Terri's collapse." There it is. I had a *not romantic* relationship with a woman that began less than two years after Terri's collapse. Where I come from, that's called a close friendship, not adultery.

As with so many of the legal maneuvers the Schindlers attempted, that one also went nowhere.

The next legal landmark in the case would come in the fall of 2002, when Judge Greer would be required to hold a hearing into potential new medical treatments that might improve Terri's condition. Before that hearing, according to the order from the Second District Court of Appeals, five doctors would have to be appointed to examine Terri— two by each side, and one by the judge.

Let's begin with our side.

First, there was Melvin Greer, M.D. (no relationship to Judge Greer), a board-certified neurologist who from 1961 to 2000 was chairman of the department of neurology at the University of Florida College of Medicine. Dr. Greer had served on many national American Academy of Neurology committees, and from 1985 to 1987 he was president of the academy. He's the co-author of the

Handbook for Differential Diagnosis of Neurologic Signs and Symptoms, and many professional and peer-reviewed research publications.

The second doctor we chose was Ronald E. Cranford, M.D. He is a diplomat of the American Board of Psychiatry and Neurology. He spent more than thirty-five years as a professor of neurology at the University of Minnesota; he's been director of the Neurologic Intensive Care Unit and the Neurology Clinic at the Hennepin County (MN) Medical Center; he served as chairman of the Subcommittee on Death and Dying of the Minnesota Medical Association, and chairman of the Ethics and Humanities Subcommittee of the American Academy of Neurology; he's also served for thirteen years on the board of directors of the Minnesota Inter-Religious Committee for Biomedical Ethics and he's been president of the American Society of Law, Medicine and Ethics. His CV includes ten pages of professional and peer-reviewed articles. And because of his belief in Terri's right to have her wishes carried out, he volunteered to participate without fee.

The doctor appointed by Judge Greer was Peter Bambakidis, M.D. He was also a board-certified neurologist at The Cleveland Clinic Foundation in Cleveland, Ohio. *Time* magazine writer Tim Padgett wrote, "Legal experts say one of the pluses in the doctor's favor was that he had never testified in a case like this before. So he brought a clean slate, and the judge felt he could count on the doctor to give an unbiased opinion."

Now let's look at the two physicians chosen by the Schindlers and their attorneys.

First, there was William Hammesfahr, M.D., who is board certified in neurology, although not a member (unlike Greer, Cranford, and Bambakidis) of the American Academy of Neurology. His letterhead claims that he is a Nobel Prize nominee in medicine.

Hammesfahr's claim that he's a Nobel Prize nominee is based on a letter written for him by Florida Republican Representative Mike Bilirakis, the doctor's congressman. Unfortunately, the so-called nomination is meaningless, because according to rules posted on the Nobel

Prize Web site, nominations are only accepted from people invited to do so, and that list includes members of the Nobel Assembly, previous prize winners, and a selection of professors at universities around the world. Considering this fact, it's more than a bit scary that Bilirakis is chairman of the House Veterans' Affairs Subcommittee on Oversight and Investigations.

And if that's not enough to cause doubt in your mind that Dr. Hammesfahr's claim is bogus, consider this rule, from www.nobel-prize.org/nomination: "Information about the nominations, investigations, and opinions concerning the award is kept secret for fifty years."

Dr. Hammesfahr's online résumé claims he was "chief resident" during his neurological and neurosurgical training at the Virginia Commonwealth University School of Medicine. The records provided by the school do not show that he was chief resident. His résumé shows under professional honors that he is a consultant to the State of Florida and listed in *Who's Who in American Medicine*, which is only slightly more prestigious than being listed in the Yellow Pages. The Web site for his own Hammesfahr Neurological Institute, which specializes in "treatment and recovery for the victims of stroke, brain injury, cerebral palsy, and learning disabilities," lists ten articles published by what he describes as *"Medforum*, the oldest peer-reviewed internet based medical journal."* You can learn more about Hammesfahr at Quackwatch.com.

Second, the Schindlers selected William Maxfield, M.D., a board-certified radiologist practicing in Tampa, with an impressive CV that lists more than fifty peer-reviewed publications and abstracts throughout a long and distinguished career. Unfortunately, not one of them has anything to do with treating or evaluating patients with Terri's brain damage or in a persistent vegetative state. It appears that Dr. Maxfield was selected by the Schindlers or their handlers because of his work with hyperbaric oxygen chambers to treat various conditions. It's interesting that the Web site for the Hyperbaric Oxygen

Therapy Center that prominently features Dr. Maxfield's biography indicates that HBOT is used in "comprehensive rehabilitation programs for stroke, Parkinson's, cerebral palsy, multiple sclerosis, reflex sympathetic dystrophy, ALS, and traumatic brain injury." Terri had none of those conditions.

Each of the five doctors examined Terri individually. All but Dr. Greer allowed their examinations to be videotaped, and the unedited videotapes were provided to the court.

I was there for each of the exams, and even though I understood medically what they were doing, I was watching it more like a husband than an RN, and it hurt me to see this happening to her.

Hammesfahr's exam really bothered me. First of all, he took ten hours, saying he needed the time to build a rapport with the patient. But it was what he did that made me cringe for Terri. He held Terri's leg up underneath her knee. Her lower leg was pretty much locked in place by contractures, so it wouldn't just fall. He pushed her lower leg down, let go of it, and it bounced up and went straight. And he got very excited. "Look at her move! Good job!" he shouted. And I looked at him, thinking, *You're crazy*. One of the other examining neurologists derisively called what Hammesfahr did with Terri's leg "nothing more than a parlor trick." A few weeks later, CNN medical correspondent Dr. Sanjay Gupta, himself a neurosurgeon, showed his viewers the video of the Hammesfahr exam, which was released by the Schindlers. He described the same event this way:

> Her leg is actually very spastic, meaning very stiff. And when he pushes her leg down like that, it's going to naturally come back into an up position. So when he pushes it down and then says lift your leg, it was kind of going to do that anyway.

I got even more angry when Hammesfahr decided that he wanted to come back the next day and poke Terri some more. I said no, and got on the phone to George, saying, "Get this man out of here."

George had to come down to the hospice and relieve me. This man was making a total idiot out of himself, and as I saw it, he was abusing my wife.

Maxfield wasn't much better. He was a radiologist attempting to do a neurological exam. It seemed as though it took him six hours. I'd never seen a radiologist come in and conduct exams, especially neuro-logically.

Bambakidis spent some time looking at Terri's most recent EEG, which was flat. I was there when it was done at Morton Plant Hospital. The technicians yelled at her, shouted her name, pinched her, tickled her eye or eyebrow, and stimulated her lips. They got no response. Bambakidis wanted to talk with me about Terri's medical history; he also talked with employees of the facility and told us he'd review everything—which meant her complete medical records—and get back to us.

Neurologist and bioethicist Dr. Ronald Cranford recently retired after a distinguished thirty-four-year career. He'd been involved in both the Paul Brophy and Nancy Cruzan cases—important right-to-die cases in this country. In 1986, Brophy became the first American to die after a court-authorized discontinuation of artificial nutrition and hydration, or ANH, to a comatose patient. Cruzan died in 1990 after a lengthy court battle to remove ANH. She'd been in a persistent vegetative state since an auto accident almost eight years earlier.

Dr. Cranford was a bit of a character, with a macabre sense of humor. He walked into Terri's room, took one look at the EEG and said, "What the hell is this? I can read EEGs, but I want it to be read by another person who can read them, because I'm looking at it and it's flat." Cranford later said that when he saw the flat EEG, which is rare, and the CT scans of Terri's brain, he could have precisely described at that moment how her brain would look upon autopsy.

Cranford did his exam, and became the first doctor to say, "She's cortically blind." That meant that while her eyes might work, her brain was not receiving or interpreting any signal from them. It was an observation that would be confirmed in the autopsy report. He also said, "There's no question, she's in a vegetative state."

Remember that what the appellate court ordered was that the five doctors examine Terri, and determine if there were any new treatments that might improve her condition.

Here's the conclusion of Dr. Bambakidis's five-page letter to Judge Greer. He was the physician who was selected by the judge, not by either side in this dispute:

> The preponderance of the data and my clinical examination reveal no evidence of awareness of self, environment, or ability to interact with others. More precisely, there is no evidence of sustained, reproducible, purposeful voluntary behavioral responses to visual, auditory, tactile or noxious stimuli. Mrs. Schiavo exhibits no evidence of language comprehension or expression. Given the fact that her current neurologic status has remained essentially unchanged for at least ten years, I would state that her chances of meaningful neurologic recovery to be virtually nonexistent. Thus, it is my opinion that she is in a Permanent Vegetative State. I know of no form of treatment which may be used, either singly or in combination with other treatments that has been demonstrated to result in meaningful neurologic recovery in a situation such as this.

What follows is Dr. Hammesfahr's conclusion after his examination of Terri. Remember that he's the physician whose claim to a Nobel Prize nomination is slightly less valid than my claim to be the World's Greatest Dad, based on a T-shirt my daughter gave me on my last birthday. Hammesfahr wrote in boldface type:

> **The patient is not in coma. She is alert and responsive to her environment. She responds to specific people best. She tries to please others by doing activities for which she gets verbal praise. She attempts to verbalize. She has voluntary control over multiple extremities. She can swallow. She is partially blind. She can feel pain. She can communicate.**

Hammesfahr never mentioned the flat EEG or the CT scans, which, as previously stated, were conclusive evidence of the deterioration of Terri's brain and her permanent vegetative state. That's a monstrous lie by omission. The only statement worth responding to, because it can cause real confusion, is his claim that "she can feel pain."

A 1994 statement published in the prestigious *New England Journal of Medicine,* which was approved by the American Academy of Neurology, the American Neurological Association, the American Association of Neurological Surgeons, Child Neurology Society, and the Multisociety Task Force on the Persistent Vegetative State, made it quite clear that patients in a vegetative state may manifest signs such as moaning, groaning, crying, laughing, and wincing, but these are "subcortical mechanisms." That means that, for example, a cry or moan that may be triggered by what doctors refer to as a "noxious stimulus," such as severe menstrual cramps, is a subcortical response in the deeper portions of the cerebral hemispheres of the brain, as opposed to the outer layer of the hemispheres, the cerebral cortex, where conscious pain and suffering reside. Bottom line: Terri could not *feel* pain as we normally understand that concept.

It may not surprise you that Doctors Cranford and Greer aligned themselves with Dr. Bambakidis, and that Dr. Maxfield came down on the side of Dr. Hammesfahr.

Before reviewing Judge Greer's evaluation of the reports, the videotape, and the testimony by all five doctors in court, it makes sense to deal with something that, in Terri's final years, the right-to-life folks attempted to turn into a really big deal.

When Dr. Cranford examined Terri, he can be heard to say on the videotape, "See, Terri can see." Considering that he was convinced that she was in a permanent vegetative state and cortically blind, how does he explain that comment?

He says, "The only thing that was atypical in any way was when I had the balloon above her, it looked as though she really does look up, and looks at it, and follows it for five or ten seconds back and forth. And I said, 'See, Terri can see.' Now, I always talk to patients as if they're conscious, so I see something like that, I don't care what I say. I'm acting to see if she's aware of what I'm doing.

"The only time she ever showed anything remotely indicative of sustained visual pursuit was during that time frame. But she didn't have consistent visual pursuit. She had a random movement at that time, or what we call a 'primitive visual orienting reflex,' where she could actually follow for a short period of time, but, first of all, that's not the same as visual pursuit, and second, the primitive visual orienting reflex is a brain stem mediated reflex. If that were in any way indicative of consciousness, then she would've done it much more repetitively and it would have been much more constant and reproducible."

That's quite technical, but I wanted to spell it out the way Dr. Cranford explained it, because the Schindler partisans went balloon crazy. In simpler language, as I tried to explain earlier, you could say that Terri's *eyes* were capable of seeing, even tracking an object briefly and inconsistently, but her brain was unable to understand what her eyes were seeing.

It was very similar with her hearing. Cranford said "it means nothing" if her mother came into the room and said her name and Terri turned her head toward the source of the sound. "She's not opening her eyes to the command; she's opening her eyes to a sound. Like an infant would do. Or like anybody waking up. If you woke somebody up in the morning, you wouldn't have to say their name. You could say anything you wanted. You could say, 'Terri, close your eyes,' and she would open her eyes if she's responding. So she's *hearing* at the brain stem level. That's an arousal response. That's typical.

"Some patients in a vegetative state will, when you walk in the room and say, 'Terri, look at me,' open their eyes and look in that direction for a second or two, and then their eyes drift away. That's what's called a 'primitive auditory orienting reflex.' It may look as though they're interacting, but they're not. The normal response, if you wake a person up who's normal, when they look at you, they'll track you and follow you."

From October 12 to October 22, Judge George Greer held a hearing to determine whether any of the five doctors felt Terri's condition could improve with any type of new treatment—meaning one that hadn't been tried before. Each doctor was given a full day in court to explain his conclusions and to be examined by the attorneys for both sides, and by the judge.

I had sat in court looking passive, but inside, I was in pain, thinking of Terri. And every night after the trial, I sat at home with Jodi and Olivia and cried. Nothing could make that pain go away, but when the court-appointed doctor, Peter Bambakidis testified, he did bring a smile to my face. As expected, he said that Terri was PVS and would not benefit from any treatment. During his examination by Pat Anderson, she finally went way over the line, causing the doctor to say in a very firm monotone, "Ma'am, you don't know what you're talking about."

The judge took a full month to evaluate all the doctors' testimonies and, as he did in the previous trial, he carefully reviewed the videotapes that accompanied all but Dr. Greer's presentation.

But a week before Judge Greer could issue his opinion and order, Schindler attorney Pat Anderson threw another petition at the courthouse wall, hoping that this one would stick. Her Petition to Remove Guardian and to Appoint Successor Guardian accused me of abusing Terri. The alleged "abuse" had nothing to do with what would normally be considered spousal abuse. This piece of legal toilet tissue applied the term "abuse" to everything up to and including a charge that I was late filing guardianship paperwork.

This one said that I "affirmed on national television (Connie Chung, CNN, 11/4/02) that he is an adulterer and has had a child with his mistress." It also said that I have "systematically isolated Terri and deprived her of sensory input," claiming that I had prevented visitors of whom I didn't approve from seeing Terri. Do I need to point out that it was Judge Greer who approved an order that gave any of Terri's blood relatives unlimited visitation rights? Considering that Bobby and Suzanne had rarely visited her during the past ten years, I thought the order was overkill. Nevertheless, the list of approved visitors who could accompany the Schindlers to see Terri had almost fifty names on it.

Another item from the fifty preposterous charges by Anderson and the Schindler family for this "abuse" petition was: "Schiavo has moved in with his mistress and fathered her baby . . . There is now more than an inheritance at stake: a baby will continue to be denied a legally-recognized father every day that Terri lives." Her concern for the emotional health of my daughter, Olivia Claire Schiavo, was touching.

By 2002, I'd pretty much stopped letting that kind of crap get to me. In the beginning, it drove me crazy. It was hurtful and I'd get very angry that people who didn't even know me were judging me. They were speaking for one side—like Anderson was—or they were just listening to one side, forgetting that they were hearing from people who had already testified under oath that they would lie to keep their daughter alive. In time, I think I learned how to deal with it, how to handle it, although I'm not sure that Jodi would agree. But my family was always there to hold me up when I was down, and my friends all knew the truth. Those are the people who really counted.

What really bothered me was the fact that *Mrs.* Schindler signed this piece of legal trash. Mary Schindler knew exactly what was wrong with Terri. She was there; she was the only one who was there with me day in and day out in the early years. But she couldn't survive without someone telling her what to do, what to say, and what to sign. As for the rest of them—they fed off the pro-life fanatics who had moved in and taken over. The others were pathetic—but Mrs. Schindler was a real disappointment. There was a time I would have forgiven her—but no more.

On November 22, 2002, Judge Greer issued his order based on the examinations by the quintet of doctors. He said the mandate from the appellate court required him to determine whether or not "new treatment offers sufficient promise of increased cognitive function in Mrs. Schiavo's cerebral cortex—significantly improving the quality of Mrs. Schiavo's life—so that she herself would elect to undergo that treatment and would reverse the prior decision to withdraw life-prolonging procedures."

Judge Greer observed that three of the five doctors testified that Terri was in a persistent vegetative state, while two felt she was not. "These two sets of opinion had little in common. Those who felt she was not in a persistent vegetative state placed great emphasis upon her interaction with her mother during Dr. Maxfield's examination and the tracking of a balloon. Those who felt that she was in a persistent vegetative state felt that her actions were neither consistent nor reproducible, but rather were random reflexes to stimuli. However, the court has not and will not make its decision on a simple head count but will instead consider all factors."

Then the judge described his personal reaction to the four videos that had been presented in court. "At first blush," he said, "the video of Terri Schiavo appearing to smile and look lovingly at her mother seemed to represent cognition. This was also true for how she followed the Mickey Mouse balloon held by her father. The court has carefully viewed the videotapes as requested by counsel and does find that these actions were neither consistent nor reproducible. For instance, Terri Schiavo appeared to have the same look on her face when Dr. Cranford rubbed her neck. Dr. Greer testified she had a smile during his (non-videoed) examination. Also, Mr. Schindler tried several more times to have her eyes follow the Mickey Mouse balloon but without success. Also, she clearly does not consistently respond to her mother. The court finds that based on the credible evidence, cognitive function would manifest itself in a constant response to stimuli."

Then Judge Greer turned his attention to Dr. Hammesfahr, labeling him a "self-promoter" who "should have had for the court's review a copy of the letter from the Nobel committee in Stockholm, Sweden." That would have been a good trick, since it doesn't exist and never has.

The judge wrote, "Dr. Hammesfahr testified that he felt that he was able to get Terri Schiavo to reproduce repeatedly to his commands. However, by the court's count, he gave 105 commands to

Terri Schiavo and, at his direction, Mrs. Schindler gave an additional 6 commands. Again, by the court's count, he asked her 61 questions and Mrs. Schindler, at his direction, asked her an additional 11 questions. The court saw few actions that could be considered responsive to either those commands or those questions. The videographer focused on her hands when Dr. Hammesfahr was asking her to squeeze. While Dr. Hammesfahr testified that she squeezed his finger on command, the video would not appear to support that and his reaction on the video likewise would not appear to support that testimony."

Turning to the testimony of the radiologist who examined Terri on behalf of the Schindlers, Judge Greer wrote, "Dr. Maxfield also felt that [the] '02 CT scan showed improvement in the quality of the remaining brain matter and that one reason Terri Schiavo was not in a persistent vegetative state was that she could swallow her own saliva and breathe on her own. These views were not supported by any of the other doctors, who made it clear that destroyed brain tissue does not regenerate, and any interpretation of the CT scan that claimed otherwise is a misreading of a scan that was taken at a different angle than the base scan taken after Terri's collapse. Dr. Cranford further testified that saliva handling is from the brain stem, a reflex."

And then, Judge Greer once again reached the same decision he'd reached at the end of the 2000 trial. "Viewing all of the evidence as a whole, and acknowledging that medicine is not a precise science, the court finds that the credible evidence overwhelmingly supports the view that Terri Schiavo remains in a persistent vegetative state."

Judge Greer pointed out that the treatment options presented were "vasodilatation therapy offered by Dr. Hammesfahr and the hyperbaric therapy proposed by Dr. Maxfield." He added that, "While none of the doctors are really involved in stem cell therapy, it was discussed at length by each of them. Perhaps one of the few agreements between these experts is that stem cell research is currently at the experimental stage and is years away from being accepted either medically or politically."

The judge noted that, "Dr. Hammesfahr feels his vasodilatation therapy will have a positive affect on Terri Schiavo . . . It is clear that this therapy is not recognized in the medical community." But then Judge Greer added, "What undermines [Hammesfahr's] credibility is that he did not present to this court any evidence other than his generalized statements as to the efficacy of his therapy on brain damaged individuals like Terri Schiavo. He testified that he has treated about fifty patients in the same or worse condition than Terri Schiavo since 1994, but he offered no names, no case studies, no videos and no test results to support his claim that he had success in all but one of them. If his therapy is as effective as he would lead this court to believe, it is inconceivable that he would not produce clinical results of these patients he has treated. And surely the medical literature would be replete with this new, now patented, procedure. Yet, he has only published one article and that was in 1995 involving some sixty-three patients, sixty percent of whom were suffering from whiplash." The judge added that none of those patients was in a persistent vegetative state—but I think most of us already figured that out.

One final comment by Judge Greer on the self-proclaimed Nobel nominee: "Neither Dr. Hammesfahr nor Dr. Maxfield was able to credibly testify that the treatment options they offered would significantly improve Terri Schiavo's quality of life. While Dr. Hammesfahr blithely stated he should be able to get her to talk, he admitted he was not sure in what way he can improve her condition although he feels certain he can."

The judge concluded, "the Mandate [from the appellate court] requires something more than a belief, hope or 'some' improvement. It requires this court to find, by a preponderance of the evidence, that the treatment offers such sufficient promise of increased cognitive function in Mrs. Schiavo's cerebral cortex so as to significantly improve her quality of life. There is no such testimony, much less a preponderance of the evidence to that effect . . . That being the case, the court concludes that the Respondents have not met the burden of proof cast upon them by the Mandate and their motion."

Judge Greer then denied the Schindlers' motion, and noted that he must follow the dictates of the Second District Court of Appeal and "enter an order scheduling the withdrawal of life-support."

Judge Greer did so, saying "it is further ordered and adjudged that Michael Schiavo, as Guardian of the Person of Theresa Marie Schiavo, shall withdraw or cause to be withdrawn the artificial life-support (hydration and nutrition tube) from Theresa Marie Schiavo at 3:00 P.M. on January 3, 2003."

It didn't say that I *could*—it said that I *shall*.

14 | Delay, Not Yet DeLay

While my attorneys were swatting foolish motions and petitions as though they were a swarm of flies, I was working in the emergency room at Morton Plant-Mease Countryside Hospital, which had the second busiest ER in Pinellas County. I loved it. I loved the purposeful action of the ER. When you help save a person's life, that means something. I'd come in and work on patients who were near death and, quite often, weeks later as they walked out of the hospital, they'd stop by to thank the ER personnel. That's fulfilling.

Maybe you can't understand it unless you've been there. One case I'll never forget was a man in his early forties who came in with chest pains. I was doing triage in the ER, and he had a heart attack right in front of me. He hit the floor. I was hitting the emergency button while trying to hold him up, punching him in the chest to try and stop the defibrillation. The ER team came out and began working on him. We got him stabilized, and sent him to Morton Plant Hospital in Clearwater.

The first big holiday following that event, this same guy came walking through the door with food for everyone—and he showed up on every holiday after that for all the people who had to work, just to thank us for saving his life. That's fulfilling. We transferred patients to the ICU who would have died without our help, and before they left, they'd stop in the ER to shake all our hands, saying, "Thank you, thank you." That's what's fulfilling about my job.

But there's also the other part of it, where we can't save a life, and we're there when they die. We do what we can, but we don't always win the battle. And we still get thanks from their family—gifts, or cards that say, "Thank you for being there with me when my mother died," or "Thanks for holding my hand."

I always try to keep those thoughts in mind when the crazies are out there calling me the Angel of Death. I'm just Mike Schiavo. I'm a good nurse. I'm a caring person. Those people out there who slander me? The ones who send hate mail but don't have the character to put their return address on it? They don't know me the way my family, my friends, and my coworkers know me. A lot of these people who are screaming *murderer* think that they're good Catholics. But they wouldn't listen to Bishop Lynch, who made a point of saying that this was a more complicated case than it appeared, and that calling it a killing and calling me a murderer was wrong.

But let me return to the matter of chaos. The chaos created by the religious-right cabal fighting to keep Terri existing in a persistent vegetative state was pointlessly enervating. If you're keeping score, you'll realize that until this point in the battle, they'd never won their case in court—not with Judge Greer, not with the appellate court, and not with the Florida Supreme Court. They'd managed to cause delays—and maybe that's what they were playing for. And that losing track record would never change, all the way up to the Supreme Court of the United States of America.

If the people who had found their way to the street outside Terri's hospice in order to shout "Let Terri live" (while rudely annoying the dying patients and their families inside) invested half the money, time, and effort they've spent on this cause into promoting proper and affordable health care for all Americans, especially the children, they would really be pro-life—and I would join them. But theirs is a fraudulent pro-life effort pushed by ideologues who saw Terri as a means to raise money to pay for battles in the culture war that they've begun.

There will never be a complete accounting of the money spent by the religious right on attorneys, motions, petitions, and lawsuits fighting to keep my wife from having her end-of-life wishes granted. My battle to achieve what we promised each other long ago, however, was rapidly draining her guardianship fund, to the point where her attorneys, George Felos and Debbie Bushnell, promised that if we ran out of money, they would continue working pro bono.

That didn't make coping with the endless stays of orders and delays any easier or less frustrating for me, or for the attorneys. We'd won the case in 2000, only to have it appealed all the way to the U.S. Supreme Court. Florida's Second District Court of Appeals bent so far over backward to give the Schindlers and their handlers another chance, that I'm surprised the judges didn't rupture a disk. They ordered Judge Greer to do it all over again and have five different doctors determine if there was a treatment out there that might improve Terri's condition. There wasn't. As a result, Judge Greer did what he'd done in 2000: He set a date for the removal of Terri's feeding tube.

And then he stayed his ruling so that the forces of antiscience and ignorance could once again trip their way up the appellate ladder, causing still more delays.

What do you imagine a justice thinks when he sees a motion from Pat Anderson headed as follows?

ARGUMENT
I. THE VIDEO EVIDENCE OF TERRI SCHIAVO'S
RESPONSIVENESS IS SO OBVIOUS NO EXPERT TESTIMONY
IS NEEDED.

Did Anderson think the justices just fell off the turnip truck and stumbled onto the bench? She told the appellate court, "This case has been driven from its inception by the vivid testimony of Dr. James Barnhill, a consulting neurologist who testified at the initial trial in January 2000 that Terri has no brain and her skull is filled with spinal fluid—testimony that was inaccurate, and unfortunately, unrebutted and thus relied upon by this court . . . That false predicate is utterly destroyed by the images of Terri that show her true condition. This case should be over."

I can't read that drivel without shaking my head in amazement. *That's an appellate argument by a licensed attorney?* I don't suppose it's necessary to point out that what Dr. Barnhill said in 2000 was absolutely confirmed by the autopsy report five years later.

Anderson's brief says "There is no dispute that she can swallow, so the logical conclusion is that she should be spoon-fed, not starved to death . . . and as Dr. Gambone himself admits she would survive on spoon-feeding." *What?* There was no dispute that Terri could swallow her own saliva; swallowing saliva is a reflex; swallowing food and water requires cognition, and food would put her at risk for aspirating it into her lungs. And Dr. Gambone, who was Terri's treating physician, never said she could survive on spoon-feeding. I constantly asked my lawyers how Anderson could get away with stuff like that. They were never able to give me a satisfactory answer.

More than six months later, on June 6, 2003, the Second District Court of Appeals affirmed Judge Greer's latest ruling—and concluded that I could have Terri's feeding tube removed on October 15. Score one more victory for Judge Greer. A month later, the Schindlers' lawyers tried to get the appellate court to reconsider.

By mid 2003, I probably shouldn't have been surprised at the tactics that Pat Anderson and the other attorneys being funded by the religious right would deploy. The Gibbs Law Firm in Tampa was helping crank out motions the way a greasy spoon makes burgers.

One of the things the Gibbs firm did was to solicit affidavits from medical professionals around the country who would take an oath that they had "personal knowledge" of the "facts" in Terri's case that supported the theory that she was not in a persistent vegetative state, and could be rehabilitated. Here's what they sent out to an unknown number of people via the Web:

Dear Dr.:
I'm contacting you because I noticed your posting on CodeBlueBlog.

I am working for the Gibbs Law Firm in Florida—they are the attorneys for the parents of Terri Schiavo and they are in a legal battle to prove to the court that Ms. Schiavo is not in a PVS state and that she could benefit from advanced medical testing and medical treatment. To this point, all Ms. Schiavo has received is a CT Scan, and this was done before 2000.

The court is open to receiving guidance from medical professionals and so far we have had many doctors provide us with declarations that we have submitted to the court. We desperately need more declarations as soon as possible. If you would like to view examples of other declarations from medical professional, go to *http://www.terrisfight.net/*, and look under "Court Documents."

I've attached a declaration template that you could use. If you have any questions, please call me, Tracy Jackson, at (661) 312-9371 or (800) 901-5119, ext. 2

Tracy J. Jackson
Batza & Associates
23929 West Valencia Blvd., Suite 309
Valencia, CA 91355
Tel: (661) 799-7777 Fax:(661) 799-3377
www.batza-associates.com

Get the picture? It gets worse. Here's the declaration that was attached to their solicitation:

I, [name], have personal knowledge of the facts stated in this declaration and, if called as a witness, I could and would testify competently thereto under oath. I declare as follows:
1. []
2. []
3. []
I declare under the penalty of perjury under the laws of the State of California that the foregoing is true and correct.
Executed this day of 2005, in California.

"Personal knowledge of the facts?" That explained how so many medical professionals, ranging from doctors who specialize in neurology to licensed speech pathologists, were coming out of the woodwork to swear that the medical folks who wouldn't provide a medical opinion without actually examining the patient and her records were dead wrong about Terri.

In mid-August, Pat Anderson filed an Emergency Motion for Stay Pending Discretionary Review with the Florida Supreme Court. She'd lost in Pinellas County and in the appellate court, so using an affidavit from, in this case, a speech pathologist in Chicago, she tossed another wad at the courthouse.

This one said, "Petitioners recently have filed an affidavit in the trial court from a speech pathologist at the Rehabilitation Institute of Chicago (copy attached) indicating Terri is a candidate for therapy and can improve in meaningful and significant ways."

What caught my attention about this particular affidavit was that the speech pathologist, Sara Green Mele, was on the staff of the Rehabilitation Institute of Chicago, a quality medical facility. Ms. Mele's affidavit, which she signed on July 25, 2003, said, "While I have not physically examined Terri Schiavo, I have looked at her medical records at MediPlex [sic] covering the period from January to July of 1991 . . . Also, I have studied the video clips presented at the October 2002 Medical Evidentiary Hearing, along with audio recordings of Terri Schiavo interacting with her father in November of 2002."

She went on to say, "Based on my experience and my observations, Mrs. Schiavo is clearly aware of her environment and interacts with it, albeit inconsistently. She is able to comprehend spoken language, and can, at least inconsistently, follow simple one-step commands. This is documented both in the MediPlex [sic] records and in following behaviors noted in the video segments." There followed a list of video clips that the Schindlers provided her in absolute violation of Judge Greer's order not to disseminate all or any portion of the four hours of tape shown in his courtroom.

Ms. Mele was duped or just got it wrong. In an earlier chapter, I extensively quoted from the Mediplex records; the staff there discharged Terri because they saw no possibility of rehabilitation. That is clearly spelled out in the Mediplex records. I just cannot understand how she could read through those records and come to the conclusion that Terri was aware enough to understand language.

She wrote in her affidavit, "It is not my opinion that Mrs. Schiavo is in a coma or in a persistent vegetative state. In my opinion, she exhibits purposeful though inconsistent reactions to her environment, particularly her family. Her eye movements, easily observed on the videotape, are particularly suggestive that she recognized family members and responded. She also appeared to have sufficient sustained attention to track a balloon. It is not my opinion that these behaviors are merely reflexive. The entire range of behaviors listed above, and each and every one of them, are inconsistent with a diagnosis of persistent vegetative state." She also wrote, "It has been my experience that patients similar to Terri have been able to accomplish food intake."

I'm a reasonable person, but there was nothing in Mele's affidavit that comports with the facts of the case. Nothing! If you didn't believe it while Terri was alive, you have no choice but to acknowledge it after the autopsy report was released. It says that Terri couldn't see, couldn't swallow food without risk of aspiration into her lungs, and had absolutely no cognition. That's science, not faith.

To determine whether Ms. Mele might have been chastened after seeing the autopsy results, perhaps even willing to admit she'd made a mistake, we contacted her at the Rehabilitation Institute of Chicago. After phone and e-mail exchanges, she finally wrote, "I completely stand by my affidavit in its entirety."

Fortunately, the nine justices of the Florida Supreme Court were not terribly impressed with Pat Anderson's motion based on Sara Mele's affidavit. On August 22, the high court declined to review the decision of the lower court that Terri's feeding tube could be disconnected.

By the time this happened, we'd become aware that e-mails were flying back and forth between various elements of the religious right,

Jeb Bush, and the Schindlers' attorneys. But before we could figure out where they were going next, Terri had a crisis. On Saturday, August 30, I got a call from the hospice saying that my wife was having trouble with her lungs and airways. I told them to immediately transfer her to Morton Plant Hospital for treatment, which they did. She was admitted, X-rayed, and treated for blockages in her air passages and a serious infection. Only two weeks earlier Terri had been taken to Morton Plant because she appeared to have aspiration pneumonia.

On the same day as Terri was taken to the hospital, Schindler attorney Pat Anderson filed a federal lawsuit challenging the removal of Terri's PEG tube. According to a bylined article by Graham Brink in the *St. Petersburg Times*, Anderson "said they felt compelled to file the hastily written request when Mrs. Schiavo was sent to the hospital on Saturday and 'nearly died.' "

I'm going to do something unusual right now. For the first time in a long time, I'm going to take the Schindlers at their word.

Brink's article said, "The parents say Mrs. Schiavo has been able to eat Jell-O on her own, and they want to be able to feed her by hand. Her husband says she cannot feed herself, and would not be able to swallow the food properly, which could lead to serious complications or death." The *St. Petersburg Times* reporter said he heard the Schindlers make that statement on the steps of the Federal Courthouse in Tampa.

Terri couldn't swallow food. Credible neurologists determined that while she was alive, and the medical examiner confirmed it after her death. There were signs posted in Terri's hospice room saying NOTHING BY MOUTH. The nursing staff, and the Schindlers, knew why those orders had been written and posted: because she could aspirate it into her lungs, and either choke to death, or develop an infection and die.

I hadn't put it together until now, but I think it is fair to ask whether there could have been a connection between Terri being hospitalized *twice* in two weeks for breathing problems, and her "eating Jell-O" as her parents claimed.

The signs posted in Terri's hospice room were clear: NOTHING BY

MOUTH. If, indeed, Terri "ate Jell-O," someone would have violated that order. This attempted feeding very well could have put Terri in the hospital, made her seriously ill, or killed her.

On Tuesday, September 2, with Terri still in the hospital fighting breathing problems and infection, George, Debbie, and I were once again in the courtroom of Federal Judge Richard Lazzara. Three years earlier the Schindlers had tried to get him to take their case. Now they were trying it again. Once court was in session, the judge asked all the attorneys present to introduce themselves and state who they were representing. It seemed as though everyone in the first six rows on our side of the courtroom was here on our behalf. I remember that the ACLU was there in force, as were lawyers representing Morton Plant Hospital and Hospice.

At the attorneys' table across the aisle was a skinny guy in a black suit named Christopher A. Ferrara, the president of the American Catholic Lawyers Association, as well as Pat Anderson. For whatever reason, they'd determined that Ferrara was going to argue the Schindlers' case at this session—or at least that's what they thought until Judge Lazzara began talking.

The first thing out of the judge's mouth was something like, "Didn't you try to bring this matter to me three years ago and I told you then that I didn't have any jurisdiction? Why are you here?"

Ferrara's response was barely intelligible, and Judge Lazzara wasn't buying any of it. He accused the Schindlers' attorneys of bringing this forward under false pretenses as an emergency motion, when it really wasn't. To say that they had managed to severely annoy a Federal District Court judge, and he had no qualms about letting them know it, really understates the case. When it was clear that Ferrara was about to go down for the count, Pat Anderson stood up and began talking.

The judge brought her to a screeching halt with, "And who are you?" She told him, but it really didn't help their cause. Then, in what to my layman's eyes was an unnecessary exercise of judicial pity, the judge gave them a few minutes to rewrite their motion.

Unfortunately for them, all they did was remove their character assassination of Judge Greer. Judge Lazzara read it, and went after the Schindlers' attorneys again. "I still don't understand why you're here. You haven't changed anything." The judge described it as a "shotgun motion," which I took to mean they were just blasting away, hoping to hit something. Then the judge did something that I thought was quite strange. He said, "I'll be right back." The judge stood up, as did everyone else in the courtroom, and went back to his chambers.

No more than ten minutes later, he returned and proceeded to read his decision. George was amazed. He told me that the judge had obviously written his decision before the hearing because he knew that no matter what Anderson and Ferrara presented, he didn't have jurisdiction over it. It was a state matter, not a federal case.

15 | The First Bush League Move

In the summer of 2003, Jodi and I found out we were pregnant again. The baby was due around the end of February, which meant that the emotional roller coaster we had been riding was just going to get steeper and go faster.

Because of the rather strange circumstances of our life together, Jodi actually had more time to stand back and observe the goings-on than I did. She couldn't be out there with me; all she could do—and it was plenty—was be there to comfort me when I came home from the battles. That gave her a unique vantage point. She had plenty of time to think about what was going on, and about the personalities involved. Jodi explained:

"I think initially when people first heard of this case, many of them felt sympathy for Terri's parents. In fact, for a long time I actually had sympathy for the Schindlers—Terri's mom and dad, not Bobby and Suzanne. I'm a mom now; I have a little girl. I can't even imagine how terrible it must be to lose your daughter. But my sympathy stopped with the Cindy Brashers Shook deposition. When Mr. Schindler asked Cindy to sign an affidavit and lie to the court because they needed to 'get more dirt on Mike,' that was the end for me. That's when I knew they'd become pond scum.

"I was also getting concerned that Mike was never going to win this battle for Terri. I actually told George that if he wasn't going to be a street fighter like Anderson, we weren't going to win. They were dirty and disgusting. That's what made those times miserable for me, especially once we had Olivia, and were having Nicholas. It was no longer just me, Mike, and Terri; it was about me, Mike, Terri, Olivia, and Nicholas. It hurt when someone said that Mike 'announced so proudly on TV that he was an adulterer and that he had a kid.' That's not what happened. Mike was asked, and he answered. What was he going to do, lie?

"They would lose in court, and launch new ad hominem attacks on me and Mike. I was the mistress, Mike was the adulterer, and while it never made it into a court document, they even managed to call the babies vile names. What can you say about the people who claim to have superior family values who would describe Olivia and Nicholas as 'little bastards'?

"Later, when it suited their purposes, they would disparage me as 'the fiancée.' What troubled me is that it made me feel as though I was more of a hindrance than a help to Mike.

"People who know me ask why it got so ugly and I tell them that I always thought that for Mr. Schindler this was always all about money and control. So you shouldn't be shocked when I say that I believe his hope was that Mike would meet someone, divorce Terri, walk away, and he and Mrs. Schindler would have it all.

"When NBC's Matt Lauer came to visit us, he asked me, 'How'd you live with everything always being about Terri?' I told him I knew the score and I didn't expect Mike to change the rules for me; I truly didn't. I told Mike, 'Terri was here first. You do what you need to do for her. I'm a big girl. I can take care of myself, and I want to be here for you as you go through this awful time.' I love Michael; he is the most giving, loving person I've ever known. He's a good person who deserves whatever measure of happiness I can bring him.

"So now let me go to the next question that always gets asked: Why didn't Mike just divorce Terri and marry me?

"I find the question itself offensive. Why should he? She was his wife. Just because things didn't work out the way they planned, or because he met someone else, is he just supposed to dump her and get on with the next stage of his life? When women ask me that, I'd say, 'Is that what you'd want your husband to do for you? If something like this happened to you, would you expect him to just say, "You know what? I'm over this crap. I've met someone else. Here, take her. I'm done. I'm getting on with the rest of my life." '

"What was he supposed to do with her, divorce her and let her parents deal with her? Let me be very clear about them. She was too much trouble for Mr. Schindler, Bobby, and Suzanne to deal with in 1992. Even Mrs. Schindler stopped seeing Terri on a regular basis after Mike had the fight with her husband because he refused to discuss giving him any part of his malpractice settlement. She can't deny it; she admitted it under oath.

"He had an obligation to Terri. Clearly, their marriage was no longer a normal marriage; it hadn't been since Mike was twenty-six years old. He's now forty-two. Do you expect him to have lived all those years alone? Not even the priest who counseled me when times got tough expected that.

"I believe God sent me to Mike. I don't mean to sound like I've done something heroic by being with him. I'm just an average person. But had we not found each other, I'm not sure what would have happened to him. Maybe there would have been someone else to be his rock. But I know he could not have lasted all these years alone, because when we first met he was a very sad, depressed, and lonely person. He deserved some happiness while he dealt with a situation that most men would have walked away from.

"But beyond the impact on our families, there's a much larger issue that needs to be addressed. We were in this situation because medical science has butted in on God's territory. In my opinion, it clearly was God's plan to take Terri that February morning in 1990. But medical science was able to intervene and give her back a heartbeat. Unfortunately, that was the best it could do for her. We have to ask whether it was her time, and we—society—did the wrong thing. We interrupted

God's plan. He called her, and we kept her here. We didn't bring her back to being Terri. We didn't bring her back to have any quality type of conscious life. We just brought back a heartbeat and left her to lie there.

"Remember Father Murphy's testimony at the 2000 trial? He was asked whether Terri should be kept alive artificially in case God wanted to work a miracle and bring her back. He said, 'If God is going to work a miracle, he does not need machinery or technology. I think he will just do it. So I have never been persuaded by the argument that we have to keep all the machinery going so God can work his miracle. I don't believe God needs that.'

"Maybe the ethicists out there who are studying The Schiavo Case need to ask the larger question. Where do you draw the line between saving a life and subverting God's will? What does 'alive' really mean? Mike and I have lived with those questions for years, and we still don't know the answer. I am not certain that we ever will."

———

On September 17, 2003, having again jumped through all the hoops required by the appellate court, Judge George Greer once again ordered the removal of Terri's feeding tube. The language was still jarring: "ORDERED AND ADJUDGED that the Guardian, Michael Schiavo, shall cause the removal of the nutrition and hydration tube from the Ward, Theresa Marie Schiavo, at 2:00 P.M. on the 15th day of October, 2003."

In his two-page order, the judge quoted from the Second District Court of Appeals order in *Schindler v. Schiavo*, saying he fully concurred in the observations made by the justices:

The judges on this panel are called upon to make a collective, objective decision concerning a question of law. Each of us, however, has our own family, our own loved ones, our own children. From our review of the videotapes of Mrs. Schiavo, despite the irrefutable evidence that her cerebral cortex has sustained the most severe of irreparable injuries, we understand why a parent who had raised and nurtured a child from conception would hold out hope that some level of cognitive function remained. If Mrs. Schiavo were our own daughter, we could not but hold to such a faith.

But in the end, this case is not about the aspirations that loving parents have for their children. It is about Theresa Schiavo's right to make her own decision, independent of her parents and independent of her husband. In circumstances such as these, when families cannot agree, the law has opened the doors of the circuit courts to permit trial judges to serve as surrogates or proxies in order to make decisions about life-prolonging procedures. . . . It is the trial judge's duty not to make the decision that the judge would make for himself or herself or for a loved one. Instead, the trial judge must make a decision that the clear and convincing evidence shows the ward would have made for herself. It is a thankless task, and one to be undertaken with care, objectivity, and a cautious legal standard designed to promote the value of life. But it is also a necessary function if all people are to be entitled to a personalized decision about life-prolonging procedures independent of the subjective and conflicting assessments of their friends and relatives.

It's a shame the justices didn't also mention Terri's entitlement to have her wishes carried out independent of craven politicians. The leader of that pack in Florida is none other than George W. Bush's younger brother, Governor Jeb Bush.

For months he and his staff had maintained close contact with attorneys funded or provided by the extreme right. They'd been brainstorming ways to overcome absolutely legitimate rulings by judges who were determined to obey the laws and dispassionately apply them in the matter of Terri Schiavo. But in Bush's worldview, these were "activist judges," the bogeymen of the millennium.

On October 7, Jeb Bush dipped his big toe into the Schiavo legal morass by filing a friend of the court brief in support of the Schindlers' attempts to keep Judge Greer's order from being carried out. I suppose some people could take him at his word that he "has a strong interest in ensuring that Terri Schiavo's fundamental right to life is not deprived without due process of law, and that it is properly balanced with her right to privacy and liberty," but if they did, they were delusional.

Here's a man who demanded privacy for his family when it was revealed in the press that his daughter, Noelle, a onetime cocaine addict, had illegally obtained prescription drugs, and that his youngest son, Jebby, got busted for public intoxication and resisting arrest. He's going to give me lessons in properly caring for Terri while messing with my own family's private business?

Bush's brief was signed by his general counsel, Raquel A. Rodriguez, which meant every Florida taxpayer helped pay for it. His concern about the due process of law would be touching if it weren't so disingenuous and laughable. This matter had been up and down the Florida judicial system more times than a kid playing on a department store escalator. It had even made its way to the United States Supreme Court. And each and every time, it was sent back to the Pinellas County courtroom of Judge George Greer with his original order affirmed.

The governor's brief was instructive, however, for what he acknowledged. On page three he said of Terri, "She is in a persistent vegetative state ('PVS')." I'm guessing that he hadn't received the Republican talking points yet, because the fact that Terri was PVS just never fit into the pro-life game plan, and you know what that means in Bushworld: If the facts don't fit, it's time to fix the facts. Actually, to give Jeb credit where it's due, he began fudging his PVS admission on page ten of the brief, saying, "Terri's parents have cast doubt on the quality of her PVS diagnosis and on the level of Terri's cognitive impairment." Sure they did, with testimony from a phony Nobel Prize nominee and a radiologist giving neurological opinions.

But the main thrust of Bush's brief was that we didn't know whether or not Terri could be fed orally, which is not artificial life support, and therefore wouldn't violate her end-of-life wishes that had been proven by clear and convincing evidence.

The governor's notion that perhaps Terri could be fed by mouth was naïve, desperate, ignorant, or political. Shortly after the brief was filed, George Felos sent Bush and his counsel a three-page letter outlining the facts. Frankly, I wondered why he would bother, but that's George. To deal with the issue of whether or not Terri could be fed orally, he quoted from the trial court order that had been affirmed on appeal:

1. Terri has had three swallowing tests and for many years thereafter, annual evaluations by speech pathologists that found that she could not be rehabilitated in this regard.
2. It is common for patients to be able to swallow saliva, but still need feeding tubes.
3. It is impossible for Terri Schiavo to be able to take in sufficient sustenance orally to stay alive.
4. If sustenance were administered orally, it would result in aspiration, which would lead to infection, fever, cough and ultimately pneumonia, which likely would be fatal.

I found it especially ironic that George would be telling the governor this shortly after two serious episodes of breathing problems, including one involving aspiration pneumonia. Remember the Schindlers' "she can eat Jell-O" speech?

George went on to point out that the two speech pathologists the Schindlers' attorneys had been quoting acknowledged that they'd never been able to wean a PVS patient off a feeding tube. One of those was the previously mentioned Sara Mele of the Chicago Rehabilitation Institute, who even after reading the autopsy report continued to insist that Terri had not been PVS and could have been rehabilitated.

Myra Stinson of Clearwater, Florida, was the other, and she seemed like a perfectly nice, well-intentioned person. We spoke with her about how she happened to sign an affidavit that said Terri could be fed by mouth and otherwise rehabilitated. She said that she was moved to call the Schindlers' lawyer, Pat Anderson, after seeing edited clips of the videotape of Terri on television. She was never shown the full four hours of video that was shown in court. All she saw were the clips shown on TV—and watched them just that one time.

What happened next? According to Stinson, "I was at home on a Sunday, and they called and asked me to write it—they needed it that day. So, I wrote something out, and they picked it up." And then they retyped it in affidavit form and had her sign it.

Since this conversation took place after the release of the autopsy report that clearly stated the extent of Terri's brain damage and that she did not have the capacity to swallow food without aspirating it into her lungs, we asked Ms. Stinson if she may have misinterpreted what she saw on television. After all, she signed an affidavit that said, "It's my professional opinion, within a reasonable degree of clinical certainty, that Terri Schiavo has a good or excellent prognosis for being able to be taken off her feeding tube."

She told us, "Well, that was before we knew all the information. I've had patients who've been able to swallow after a long period of time, and they've recovered. But I didn't have any information as to the extent of the brain damage, and I don't know how she could've gotten that much brain damage just from passing out from her heart or something, you know."

We gave Stinson a brief explanation of how long Terri's brain had been deprived of oxygen after her collapse, to which the speech pathologist responded, "Well, you know, the coroner said that he wondered why it took so long for Michael to call [the paramedics]." When it was pointed out that the medical examiner had said no such thing, Ms. Stinson's response was, "Yeah, well, okay, well, I had heard that there had been a lapse in time. But, anyway, there again, just from being without oxygen, does that do that much damage to a brain?"

I could tell you more, but the point's been made. In George's letter to the governor, he wrote, "We had such affidavits reviewed by the board-certified neurologists previously testifying in this case, including the independent neurologist appointed by the court. We also had the parents' affidavits reviewed by an independent speech language pathologist. The universal response by these neurologists and the independent speech language pathologist is that Terri Schiavo cannot be sustained by oral feeding and cannot be taught to sustain herself. In particular, the speech language therapist states that 'therapies to wean a patient off a feeding tube would prove absolutely fruitless and meaningless if administered to a patient in a persistent vegetative state.' "

George concluded, "The fact is that—as determined many times by the court, and as found by numerous competent health care professionals—Theresa Marie Schiavo's life cannot be sustained by oral administration of sustenance, and further, to attempt the same would be against medical advice and would cause her to aspirate. Again, please be assured that no one in this case promotes, advocates or seeks to deprive naturally administered sustenance to any patient, let alone Theresa Marie Schiavo."

What was wrong with George's letter to Governor Bush? Too many facts. And you know what facts are to an ideologue like Jeb? They're pesky little things that need to be brushed aside because they just get in the way of telling people what they want to hear and believe, so that they'll give you their vote and maybe their cash. George W. Bush needed weapons of mass destruction; Jeb Bush needed Terri to be able to eat with a spoon. The trouble is, just saying it doesn't make it so—except for the true believers, who will never be convinced that they're not being given all the facts.

16 | Florida Politricks

On the afternoon of October 15, 2003, I moved into one of the villas on the grounds of the Woodside Hospice in Pinellas Park. The decision had been made that Terri's treating physician, Dr. Vincent Gambone, would actually remove the PEG tube this time, rather than just clamping it off. We felt there was a legitimate concern that someone might attempt to thwart the court order by feeding Terri, and removing the tube was a way of making sure that didn't happen—at least not via the tube. The Schindlers objected to the tube's removal, but Judge Greer left it up to Terri's doctor.

There were still concerns that other visitors, including her parents or siblings, might attempt to administer food or liquid by mouth, and we hoped that switching her bed around so that her head was visible through the window in the door would prevent that. Given the security concerns we had, there was also a local police officer posted outside Terri's room to make sure than anyone visiting was on the list, and to see to it that no one brought a camera—even a cell phone camera—into the room.

The day prior to the tube being removed, the Schindlers had held a news conference and released a video of Terri in spite of Judge Greer's order. According to WorldNetDaily, an online mouthpiece for the religious right, Mr. Schindler "revealed Terri tried to convey to him she did not want to die by bolting upright and trying to get out of her chair when told she might be killed." I read that stuff back then and was outraged; now I tend to say, "Whatever." What I find really pathetic are the ignorant faithful out there who just eat that crap up, read it like the gospel, and then send them money.

Debbie Bushnell, who had been living this saga with me since 1994, responded to the release of the illicit videotape by informing the Schindlers that they would no longer be allowed to visit Terri without me or my representative in the room with them. It wasn't an idle threat. Jodi and I recruited friends, including nurses I've worked with, to take shifts around-the-clock sitting with Terri from the time the tube was removed until the end came.

I wasn't present when Dr. Gambone removed the tube, a procedure that took less than five minutes. I hadn't been in the room the first time, either. For everyone who didn't know Terri, this was a great theatrical moment filled with political drama. For me, it meant my wife was going to die. It meant that Terri's long quest for peace was near its end.

Debbie was outside Terri's room when the procedure was done. She and George had decided that it would be best if only medical personnel were present for the short procedure, and then she came back across the parking lot, to the hospice villa they'd given me to use for the duration, and the two of us sat and talked quietly about Terri.

Out in front of the hospice, it sounded like a rowdy tailgate party for a Bucs game. There were all sorts of demonstrators, ranging from elderly women who prayed silently to a raucous group shouting, "Let Terri live!" Police were attempting to keep the street open for traffic, and had the difficult task of escorting little kids from the elementary school next door safely through the crowd.

Debbie and I would go from the villa to Terri's room and stay with her. If we were told that the Schindlers were coming, we'd leave. It was never for long. They'd spend five or ten minutes, then go outside and talk to the cameras, telling fanciful tales about how Terri was pleading for her life, or how they could see that she was beginning to suffer.

That night I left the hospice campus and went to George's office for a meeting about security with George, Debbie, and some other people. That's when Jeb Bush's name came up, and they told me he wanted to pass a law to force the reinsertion of the feeding tube, but the Legislature wasn't in session. Debbie said it could never happen. I remember her telling me that there was no way the Legislature would do something like that. She said, "Passage of legislation takes weeks, months, sometimes years."

What we didn't know about was the mounting pressure on both Jeb Bush and Florida lawmakers. They were getting overwhelmed with e-mails and phone calls, 85 percent of them, it turned out, from out of state, demanding that they do something to save Terri. On several occasions, the government switchboard in Tallahassee was jammed with their calls. On October 17, Randall Terry, who'd once been a big name in the antiabortion business with his Operation Rescue, publicly urged Jeb Bush to take action to save Terri.

Honestly, I don't think we had any idea how well organized the religious right was around the issue of my wife's death. And we certainly didn't have any mechanism to counter the pressure they were putting on Bush.

The same day the feeding tube was removed, Bush came to Tampa and had a half-hour meeting with Terri's parents. One of their "press consultants" said that the meeting gave them "a glimmer of hope that there is some way he could intervene" and have the tube reinserted. He also said that some of "the best Christian legal organizations" were looking for a "legal silver bullet."

In addition to the letter George had sent to the governor—a letter one of his aides later told us the governor "didn't have time to read," I'd issued a standing invitation for Bush to come and visit Terri. I wanted him to see for himself what I knew to be the truth: that Terri didn't respond to a familiar voice, that Terri didn't see—her eyes didn't follow you around the room—and that she didn't attempt conversation. All the actions the Schindlers tried to convey through selectively edited videotapes were fake, contrived, and bogus. Whatever you choose to call them, they weren't a reflection of Terri's capabilities, and I wanted Jeb Bush to see her himself. The man is intelligent; he probably knew that once he walked into Terri's room, he would no longer have plausible deniability; he'd no longer be able to say that she had cognition, that she could see and hear and attempt to speak. Rather than put himself in that position, he covered his eyes and ears, looked away, and kept talking to his base.

On October 20, five days after Terri's tube was removed, George faxed a letter to the president of the Florida Senate, Jim King. It was a futile gesture, but there wasn't much more that could be done. George told King he was writing "to dispel the campaign of misinformation being spread against my client and the subject court proceedings in this case."

I don't want to sound too cynical, but campaigns of misinformation were what the other side specialized in, from the bottom all the way up to the top. If they'd lie to get our country into a war, telling lies to interfere in the case of one woman from Clearwater was small potatoes.

The same day George sent the letter to Jim King, the Senate president began getting notes from Senator Johnnie Byrd, an extreme rightwinger who saw this as an opportunity to get a leg up in his battle for the Senate seat that would ultimately be won by Mel Martinez. King seemed reluctant to get involved. Following the death of his parents, he'd been a sponsor of Florida's "death with dignity" law that had been passed in 1990, and he appeared concerned that writing a law requiring the reinsertion of Terri's feeding tube crossed a line that shouldn't be crossed.

Nevertheless, he is a politician and the phones were ringing and e-mail servers were crashing. Something had to be done. According to a story by Steve Bousquet of the *St. Petersburg Times,* King came up with the theory that if a governor can grant a stay of execution in a death penalty case, perhaps he could be given similar authority in the

Schiavo case. He picked up the phone and called Jeb Bush to discuss it. Not long afterward, according to Bousquet, in a reception area outside King's office, two of his policy advisers and one of Bush's lawyers began writing the bill.

"They specified four conditions that apply only to Schiavo," Bousquet reported. "A patient (1) who had no written advance directive, (2) who was found by a court to be in a persistent vegetative state, (3) who has had nutrition and hydration withheld as of October 15 and (4) whose family member challenged the withholding of nutrition and hydration."

It didn't take a constitutional law expert from Harvard to figure out that the law was absolutely unconstitutional, but it didn't matter. By Monday evening, October 20, the bill was drafted, and at 7:44 P.M. Bush added it to the agenda of the special session that had been called to deal with economic issues. The governor had apparently been assured that the Florida House would go along with whatever language the Senate passed.

At 10:10 P.M., without any committee hearings and no consideration that the law wouldn't stand up to appeal on constitutional grounds, the House passed it 68–23 with twenty-eight members absent. The next day, the Senate voted 23–15, and the governor signed it into law. As Debbie put it, "At that point, the media and the political dynamic was almost all in the Schindlers' favor. They're the ones who had the huge media machine; they had their followers sending e-mails, making phone calls, and shutting down the switchboard at the Legislature. Politicians were willing to rally around them just because of that. It was a David and Goliath kind of fight."

It was during the time that the devout followers of Randall Terry and others like him were bombarding the Tallahassee politicians with their "save Terri from the evil monster" calls and e-mails that the death threats began to escalate. There's something terribly ironic about death threats coming from the pro-life movement.

As for Florida's governor, I think the only thing that kept the country from being surprised by the arrogance of Jeb Bush was that we'd already come to recognize it as a family trait. Jeb was in the pocket of the extreme right the same way George W. was. Around Tallahassee, the people in the know referred to the measure not as "Terri's Law," but as "Terry's Law," after pro-life fanatic Randall Terry. And Jeb, who had converted to Catholicism and seemed inclined to out-Catholic the Catholics on this one, was more than willing to do Terry's bidding.

What the Florida Legislature had done was give the governor the power to overrule every judge in the state. My lawyers knew that it had to be appealed to the State Supreme Court, but that would take time. They began working on a motion to be filed locally, and at the same time, sent a letter to the area hospital council warning that anyone performing medical procedures on Terri without my authorization would be held legally liable.

In the meantime, Bush ordered the Florida Department of Law Enforcement to take custody of Terri, and to take her to a hospital where the feeding and hydration tube could be reinserted. It had been out for seven days, and if she was to survive, the procedure had to be performed quickly. I was in the villa on the hospice grounds when the hospice supervisor called and asked me what I wanted to do and where she should be taken. I said, "Obviously, I'm not making decisions about that anymore. You'll have to ask the governor." George had briefed me, saying, "Don't answer anything about the feeding tube. That's Governor Bush's problem now." I knew where George was going with it. If Jeb Bush wanted the tube reinserted, Jeb Bush could make all the decisions, but that was tough for me. I'd been making decisions about Terri for almost fourteen years; now, someone else had control. Someone who didn't know Terri and, frankly, didn't care about Terri.

I'd made several trips back and forth between the villa and Terri's room, listening to the crowds out in the street screaming. I suppose it never occurred to Randall Terry and the Schindlers that there were other people and families inside the hospice—other people who were dying. And they were making it that much more difficult for those forty or so families to deal with their own personal tragedies. But it was all nothing more than street theater for the pro-life leaders. Whenever a camera was pointed at them, or when they knew the local newscasts were on the air live, they'd scream and chant and bang their drums. I couldn't have felt more contempt for them all if I tried.

On one trip, while I was walking back to the villa, my cell phone rang. It was Debbie saying, "Don't move; I'm on my way to pick you up. We have a hearing by phone in an hour." I ran back to the hospice supervisor and told her not to do anything. But the hospice had already been told that the Florida Department of Law Enforcement was on the way, and once again, she pressed me for instructions. All I could say was, "I can't answer any of those questions. You'll have to ask Jeb Bush."

Debbie ran the gauntlet of media and demonstrators, drove into the hospice, picked me up, and we raced back to George's office.

Once I got there, I was able to watch the helicopter shots on television as the FDLE entered the hospice with an ambulance, snatched Terri, and took her to Morton Plant Hospital. Outside, hundreds of right-to-life fanatics were shown on television screaming and cheering as the ambulance pulled in.

In the meantime, hospital officials appeared to have made a political choice, deciding that their liability was greater for not inserting a feeding tube than for doing it. We learned later that evening that to the credit of physicians in the area, it took quite some time for Morton Plant to locate a qualified doctor who would agree to perform the procedure.

Late in the day, George had filed for an emergency hearing on an order for a stay of Terri's Law. As a result, a telephonic hearing had been set up with the circuit court duty judge, Charles Cope. I don't wait well. I paced, I worried, I kept coming up with unanswerable questions. George Felos, on the other hand, was calm as he laid out his papers and prepared his argument.

At about six o'clock, we got a call saying that instead of a telephonic hearing with Cope, Chief Judge W. Douglas Baird was going to hear the case, in the courthouse, at 7:30 in the evening.

Now we had a different sort of problem. I wasn't dressed to go to court. Shorts and a T-shirt just don't send the right message. But there was no way I could go home and change. It was primarily a security concern. The media and the crazies knew where I lived and it was too easy to get trapped there. Jodi and Olivia had already moved out and were staying with her mother in order to avoid the demonstrators at the house. Debbie suggested that she could drop me at her home a few blocks away, and I could spend the evening with her husband, Reggie, who was planning on watching game three of the Yankees-Marlins World Series.

Debbie pulled her SUV right up to the door of George's office, and I let the media get their shot of me getting in, giving them a mumbled "no comment" to a cacophony of shouted questions. She dropped me off at her house, and I spent the evening going nuts. I couldn't get into the baseball game, although Reggie was going crazy because he was a Yankee fan and they won it, six to one. For me, it was another evening of pacing, interrupted by cell phone calls. An administrator from Morton Plant called early on, asking what I wanted to do about visitors for Terri. I told her, "That's the only question I'm going to answer. Other than her mother and father, no visitors whatsoever." It was a hospital, not a hospice or nursing home. I didn't want a parade of people through her room—and that included the obnoxious priest named Malanowski who would later call me "a murderer." So much for respecting the local Catholic bishop's specific request to avoid that sort of inflammatory language.

Jodi called, my brother Brian called, the hospital called several times. It was an awful evening—no reflection on Reggie's hospitality.

It was about 10:30 when George and Debbie got back to the house. I could see that George was just whupped. "We lost," I said.

George answered, "Uh, yeah."

Debbie said that Judge Baird was very deliberate, giving both sides a chance to present their case. The attorney general's office chose not to participate; whether that had anything to do with the fact that Florida's attorney general, Charlie Crist, was planning to run for governor (term limits were requiring Jeb to step down), I can't say. "I just knew that we had the judge both emotionally and intellectually," Debbie recalled. "It was impossible not to see what happened from a practical, political standpoint, and also to see that the statute was clearly unconstitutional."

Debbie related that the governor's attorney argued that declaring a statute unconstitutional was a very serious matter. Governor Bush's lawyer argued that the judge should not make a decision that evening on a temporary injunction; the arguments needed to be fully briefed. From their point of view, their argument had some validity: If the judge ruled that Terri's Law could not go into effect until its constitutionality was proven, Terri would die and the law would be moot. George covered the legal arguments, and in his summary, he talked about the right to privacy we all have and how Terri had been exploited by the entire process.

Debbie was convinced by the look on Judge Baird's face that he wanted to rule for us. But ultimately, he exercised judicial restraint, and did not. He said we needed to fully brief our arguments. The unusual session was very intense, with a lot of adrenaline flowing on both sides. And what the lawyers didn't know as they argued their case was whether the hospital had found a doctor willing to perform the procedure and reinsert Terri's feeding tube.

By this point in *Schiavo*, Terri's guardianship account had no money left with which to pay George and Debbie. I laughed at the people who insisted to the very end that I was doing this to Terri so I could take the money and run. Thanks to the Schindlers, there would be no money left to donate to charity, as I'd formally offered to do several times.

Neither Debbie nor George had ever been involved in a legal matter where the opposition would repeatedly cite personal bias to explain why a judge ruled against them. Debbie said, "If they were shut down on any legal issue, it was not because the legal issue didn't have merit, it was because the judge was prejudiced against them. Or because we somehow finagled the situation because we were in collusion with the judge.

"I didn't take it personally," Debbie said. "I understood what they were doing, and why. But I was shocked. I was shocked at what the other side was willing to do to reach their predetermined end.

In his book *Using Terri*, attorney Jon Eisenberg traced the money—big money—that was being paid to keep the Schindlers' legal team on the job. On my side, there were no foundations being milked for legal fees. There was just George and Debbie, the ACLU, and eventually the Washington office of the Chicago law firm Jenner & Block with lead attorney Tom Perrelli, and individuals like Jon, working for a cause in which they believed.

Debbie had a guardianship law practice that provided some income while she was working on *Schiavo*. George was doing nothing but working on Terri's case. For those of you inclined to laugh at lawyer jokes, take a deep breath and say a thank-you to lawyers who believe so strongly in the law that they'll work pro bono.

Long after the case was over, Debbie reflected on what she and George did, and why they continued doing it once the governor signed Terri's Law.

"*Schiavo* was an endurance test, certainly from the lawyer's perspective, and I'm sure from Michael's perspective, too, although he had many more emotions in there than we did.

"We were not going to quit. The other side was coming at us with all kinds of legal maneuvers, both within the right-to-die case and also with the legal guardianship.

"At this point, regardless of loyalty to Michael or to Terri, this was an important constitutional issue. This is the kind of thing that lawyers can't allow to stand. You can't allow a precedent [like Terri's Law] to stand. It screws up the law. It makes everything harder for the people that come after us. It's something that has to be rectified and you just have to put the time into doing it, whether you get paid or you don't.

"That's where we were at that point. George and I were absolutely exhausted, and it got worse from there. They were trying to wear us down; they were trying very clearly to make us give up," said Debbie.

Fortunately for me and for Terri, Debbie and George had no intention of giving up. They knew that they needed to get their appeal to the Florida Supreme Court as quickly as possible. They believed the state's high court would take the case, and that the United States Supreme Court would not.

The day after Bush issued his decree and had Terri snatched from the hospice, the chief judge of the Pinellas County circuit court, David Demeres, complied with the one other major requirement of Terri's Law. He ordered the Schindlers and me to agree within five days on an independent guardian *ad litem* who would make recommendations to the governor and the court. When we couldn't agree, the judge chose Professor Jay Wolfson, currently the Distinguished Service Professor of Public Health and Medicine at the University of South Florida. Wolfson not only holds a doctorate in public health, he's also an attorney and the professor of health law at Stetson University College of Law in Tampa.

Debbie wrote the brief responding to Judge Baird's order, indicating that our problem was not with Dr. Wolfson, but with the constitutionality of Terri's Law. We wanted it to be clear that cooperating with the guardian *ad litem* did not mean we were acknowledging that the law was legitimate.

The Schindlers' attorney, Pat Anderson, took the opportunity to demand that whoever got appointed guardian *ad litem* investigate whether or not Terri should divorce me, since I was an adulterer. There's one thing I can say about Pat—in print: She always manages to sink to the occasion. About the only thing we both agreed on was that the GAL should act quickly, and turn in his report within thirty days.

Before the judge could actually appoint Wolfson as GAL, we got our first indication that President Bush was following the case. In the same Rose Garden news conference where he denied that the MISSION

ACCOMPLISHED banner posted on the USS *Abraham Lincoln* was not arranged for by his White House staff—it was—he was asked whether his brother Jeb had made the correct decision by intervening in The Schiavo Case. His terse response was, "Yes, I believe my brother made the right decision." I had no idea that we'd be hearing more from the president at a later date.

What followed next was a lot of fancy footwork in the courts. With the help of the ACLU, we filed a state court lawsuit arguing that Terri's Law was unconstitutional, and during oral argument, Judge Baird said, "Mrs. Schiavo, along with every other citizen of this state, has the right to be left alone in his or her private life by this state's government." He went on to say that Terri's Law "unquestionably interfered with and intruded upon [Terri's] constitutional right of privacy."

At the hearing, the governor asked Judge Baird to dismiss our suit, which he denied. The governor then appealed his order to the Second District Court of Appeals, which a few steps down the line issued an indefinite stay, which meant Terri's feeding tube would now stay in place until this played out in court. Then the governor did what Debbie had said was characteristic of the way the other side played the game: He filed a petition to remove Judge Baird for bias. The governor didn't seem to understand that judges judge. They decide how to rule based on their interpretation of the facts of the case. I know it's a tough concept for a Phi Beta Kappa graduate of the University of Texas to grasp, but he needed to try a little harder.

By this time, Debbie had become convinced that even though the Second DCA ultimately sent The Schiavo Case back to Pinellas County with a vote of confidence for the way Judge Greer had been handling it, the appellate judges were acting as though they had one eye on the case law and another on the Florida voters who could vote to turn them out of office.

With respect to the appellate justices, Debbie said, "I think this case is a great example of how politics and media coverage can distort results, even in the court system. Judges are susceptible to politics and the kind of political finagling that went on in this case. They don't want to alienate a part of the population that can mobilize voters against them. State judges don't have jobs for life. Federal judges do. And if you notice, it was the federal judges who eventually shut down this case."

Even while our appeal of Terri's Law was working its way up, the forces of the religious right were hard at work on the Florida Legislature, looking for more ways to insinuate themselves into the private decisions of families. Just before Thanksgiving, Florida senators Stephen Wise and Jim Sebesta introduced a measure that would *require* persons in persistent vegetative states to be administered medically supplied nutrition and hydration if they didn't have a living will, *regardless of family beliefs about what those patients would have wanted*. Those are the same folks who say there should be less government in our lives, not more. Just think about that when Election Day rolls around and you're deciding whether or not to bother voting.

Dr. Wolfson spent thirty days attempting to determine what would be best for Terri. He interviewed me, the Schindlers, the governor, and others at length. And he spent hours and hours at Terri's bedside, trying to discern by observation whether it was possible that she was not in a persistent vegetative state. His final report was more than forty pages in length. If you are interested in an absolutely unbiased, no-vested-interest look at Terri Schiavo in November 2003, I urge you to read it. (Google "Miami.edu Schiavo Timeline" and you'll find his report as well as many other pertinent documents.)

Here are some highlights from the Wolfson report, beginning with his impressions from time spent with my wife:

Terri is a living, breathing human being. When awake, she sometimes groans, makes noises that emulate laughter or crying, and may appear to track movement. But the scientific medical literature and the reports this GAL obtained from highly respected

neuro-science researchers indicate that these activities are common and characteristic of persons in a persistent vegetative state.

In the month during which the GAL conducted research, interviews and compiled information, he sought to visit with Theresa as
often as possible, sometimes daily, and sometimes, more than once
each day. During that time, the GAL was not able to independently
determine that there were consistent, repetitive, intentional, reproducible interactive and aware activities. When Theresa's mother
and father were asked to join the GAL, there was no success in eliciting specific responses . . . There were instances during the GAL's
visits, when responses seemed possible, but they were not consistent in any way.

This having been said, Theresa has a distinct presence about her.
Being with Theresa, holding her hand, looking into her eyes and
watching how she is lovingly treated by Michael, her parents and
family and the clinical staff at hospice is an emotional experience. It
would be easy to detach from her if she were comatose, asleep with
her eyes closed and made no noises. This is the confusing thing for
the lay person about persistent vegetative states.

Now, to some of Dr. Wolfson's conclusions:

In recent months, individuals have come forward indicating that
there are therapies and treatments and interventions that can literally re-grow Theresa's functional, cerebral cortex brain tissue,
restoring part or all of her functions. There is no scientifically
valid, medically recognized evidence that this has been done or is
possible, even in rats, according to the president of the American
Society for Neuro-Transplantation. It is imaginable that some day
such things may be possible; but holding out such promises to
families of severely brain injured persons today may be a profound disservice.

In the observed circumstances, the behavior that Theresa man-
ifests is attributable to brain stem and forebrain functions that are

reflexive, rather than cognitive. And the substantive difference according to neurologists and neurosurgeons is that reflexive activities of this nature are neither conscious nor aware activities. And without cognition, there is no awareness.

In the days leading to the delivery of his report, Dr. Wolfson attempted to negotiate what he called a "platform of understanding" between the governor, the Schindlers, and me. The agreement would have allowed Wolfson as guardian *ad litem* to select specialists to make a "formal determination about the feasibility and value of swallowing tests and therapy for Theresa." It would also have allowed him to "select competent, neutral, clinical specialists to conduct appropriate examinations and tests to make a formal determination of capacity and prognosis."

The most significant part of the agreement, in my opinion, was the statement that, "The parties agree in principle to establish in advance, parameters for their respective actions based upon the outcomes of the examinations and tests."

Until the night before Dr. Wolfson's report was due to be submitted, it looked as though all three parties might actually agree to the platform of understanding. But literally at the last minute—11:50 P.M. on November 30—my attorney George Felos threw an appropriate monkey wrench into it. Wolfson said that George called him and said, "Jay, I can't do it. I'll tell you why. Because you were appointed under the provisions of a law that we believe is fundamentally unconstitutional, and as much as I think it's a laudable idea and that it would ultimately bring all these things to closure, if I were to support any recommendation you made, I would be diluting my constitutional argument."

Wolfson's response? "George Felos was right. He was right legally. He was protecting the interests of his client's case. So, that ended the deal on additional studies. But even without the proposal for additional studies that didn't get agreed to, my recommendations were that they could and should be done only if both sides agreed as to how they were going to be used. Otherwise, it would be a moot exercise, and there was no room for that."

Wolfson went on, "I think you can see from the text of my report that I found that the evidence supporting the clinical diagnoses and prognoses was very, very sound, very firm. And that there really wasn't any basis in science or medicine to dispute those things and that some of the folks who did intervene on behalf of the Schindlers did not come to the table with adequate science or medicine."

Shortly after reading Wolfson's report, Governor Bush released a statement urging that I permit swallowing tests and therapy, but made no commitment as to what his recommendation would be if the outcome proved negative. He expressed concern that there was no clear and convincing evidence as to what Terri's end-of-life wishes were, ignoring the fact that Judge Greer had determined her wishes to the required "clear and convincing" standard, and he'd been affirmed on appeal. Bush disingenuously said, "The *current* court proceedings have not addressed this issue . . ." He attacked Dr. Wolfson indirectly, saying, "I am also concerned we do not know the expertise of the individuals who provided the 'answers' to the questions that are addressed in the report." That comes from a governor who at one point relied on the bogus Nobel Prize nominee Dr. William Hammesfahr for his medical advice in this case. And Bush's conclusion proved that it didn't matter what Wolfson's guardian *ad litem* report said, he was going to pander to his political base:

> As I have said from the beginning, the state must protect every Floridian's right to life, and in so doing, err on the side of life. As governor, I will continue to do just that. Nothing in Dr. Wolfson's report leads me to believe the stay should be lifted at this time, or that Mrs. Schiavo should be deprived of her right to live.

Translation: My mind is made up; no one, not even a neutral guardian *ad litem* that I insisted upon, is going to confuse me with the facts. One of those facts that Bush refused to face was that Jay Wolfson could find no evidence that I had ever abused Terri or that I was financially motivated to see her die. He wrote:

> Of Michael Schiavo, there is the incorrect perception that he has refused to relinquish his guardianship because of financial interests, and more recently, because of allegations that he actually abused Theresa and seeks to hide this. There is no evidence in the record to substantiate any of these perceptions or allegations.

In an interview for this book, Dr. Wolfson was asked for his thoughts about the hard-line position I took with the Schindlers, and on fighting to do what I believed Terri would have wanted done:

> Why would any reasonable person subject themselves to the kind of character assassination and death threats and everything else? You'd have to say, "Let's walk away. They want her, they can have her." No, Jodi has said to me that Terri was, in many ways, the love of Michael's life. You may have heard me quoted as saying "you can love more than one person, and you can have deep, caring, intimate love for somebody, even if they're not with you." It's not something you abandon; it's not something you give up. And I came to believe that Michael really, really loved Terri, and was doing what he was doing because he believed it was in her best interests, even though it wasn't necessarily in his own. And that's tough stuff.
>
> When I first interviewed Michael at Mr. Felos' office—I was asking him questions about his wife, including queries into how they spent their time—what their plans and dreams were—what they did on weekends—and as Michael was reflecting upon and answering those questions (in my very sincere effort to get to "know" his wife) he started to cry. I was very much struck by that. It was not contrived and it was quite emotional. I saw Michael break down again in Minneapolis when he spoke publicly for the first time after Terri's death—he was obviously and deeply affected emotionally by this matter.

He knew her more intimately than any other human being. They certainly had their good and bad days—who doesn't? What normal couple doesn't have really rough waters during which one or both think or talk about or even threaten divorce. I discount all of that because it is part of marriage. Anybody who disagrees is lying or has never been married.

The natural human emotion part of it is that Michael loved his wife. He invested undisputed, intense time and energy caring for her along with his mother-in-law, Mary. He kept her in pristine shape for years—to the annoyance of many nursing home staff because of his demands that they tend to her.

My job in this was to serve as Mrs. Schiavo's special guardian *ad litem*, and to stand in her shoes as best I could. As I came to know her, I found that she was a very sweet, very self-conscious lady. The last thing I believe she would ever have wanted was her parents and her husband to be arguing over her. The last thing she would've wanted was to be displayed partially clad on national television.

[By the end] nobody knew Terri, but everybody kind of knew who she was. She became a symbol for something, and in all of that, I'm not going to blame the Schindlers for specific things, and I'm not going to blame Michael for specific things, or the attorneys for specific things. This whole matter became something far greater than what it was, more than Terri Schiavo's decision through her guardian to permit her to have a death with dignity.

I think a lot of people got carried away. There were a lot of exogenous forces; there were a lot of entities from the outside that played roles that encouraged and affected the behavior of people. And when all is said and done, the science and the medicine and the law prevailed. It took a long time, it took a tremendous toll, and it forced us to ask, I hope, some very important questions about how we, as a society, want to deal with things like this. I'm not sure they've been resolved.

17 | Terri Changes Her Mind

If you had asked me at the start of 2004 whether or not The Schiavo Case would come to an end before the year was out, I'd tell you to toss a coin. Of course, the way things had been going in my life since 1990, it would have probably landed on its edge. Predicting The Schiavo Case was a fool's errand. About the only sure thing I'd have told you to bet on is that we'd be spending a lot of time in court.

There was one piece of good news I was prepared to predict. It happened on February 24, when Jodi gave birth to our son, Nicholas. In contrast to the birth of Olivia, this delivery was easy. Of course Jodi was concerned that there would be pickets outside the hospital. The crazies had found out about this pregnancy early on, and Jodi had spent nine months living with a fear in her gut that every time she stepped outside, someone would confront her—or worse. The first thing her ob-gyn said to me when he walked into the delivery room that day was, "I saw your name in the paper today." The point is, neither Jodi nor I could ever get away from the battle, even for a few hours, even long enough to have our son.

Jodi's mom would alternate between living at her own home and living with us. We all knew that Ellie wouldn't win her battle against ovarian cancer, but it was knowing that she was going to have a grandson that kept Ellie alive until Nick was born. The smile on her face when we brought Nick home to a yard full of balloons and a goofy stork sign in front of the house was the best.

In addition to dealing with Terri's care, helping with her mom's care, the ongoing legal battles, and a full-time job, I was coping with the sleep deprivation that the parents of nearly every newborn are familiar with. I was hoping that George and Debbie would be able to keep things under control, and that there'd be no medical crises for a while. Unfortunately, wishing doesn't make it so.

On March 29, I got a call from the hospice saying that workers discovered what appeared to be four fresh puncture wounds on one of Terri's arms, and a fifth wound on her other arm. I was alarmed. At various times the Schindlers or their lawyers had falsely accused us of giving Terri morphine or other drugs to hasten her death. That's why my immediate reaction to the report was not that someone was injecting a substance into Terri, but that perhaps someone was rather clumsily attempting to draw a blood sample from her in order to have it analyzed.

I called Debbie Bushnell, and she called the Clearwater Police Department while the hospice was making arrangements to transport Terri to Mease Hospital in Dunedin as soon as her physician, Dr. Stanton Tripodis, completed his exam.

The hospital ran a toxicology test for the presence of unauthorized drugs. When it came back negative, Terri was returned to the hospice. Clearwater police detectives conducted an extensive investigation that included interviews with family members, physicians, hospice employees, and others. Both Terri's doctor and a physician at Mease examined the marks on Terri's upper arm but could not conclude that they were evidence of an injection. Hospice officials said the marks could have come from the use of a Hoyer Lift to move Terri. I don't buy that, but I'm also at a loss to explain the marks.

———

One of the most bizarre motions my attorneys had to knock down came after the late Pope John Paul II got involved indirectly in the Schiavo case. We knew that the Vatican was keeping a close eye on it, and on March 20 the pope delivered a speech that impacted directly on The Schiavo Case. The subject was "Life Sustaining Treatments and Vegetative State: Scientific Advances and Ethical Dilemmas." The venue was the World Federation of Catholic Medical Associations and Pontifical Academy for Life International Congress in Rome.

Neurologist Ronald Cranford says there was reliable evidence that the conference itself had a hidden agenda, which was to have participants from around the world sign a consensus statement that took a doctrinaire position on issues relevant to the Schiavo case. However, when many of the invitees balked at endorsing a document containing glaring misstatements of fact, the organizers, including Bishop Elio Sgreccia, vice president of the Pontifical Council for Life, converted the statement into the text of a speech that was attributed to the pope, even though he didn't deliver it in its entirety.

Here's the line from the pontiff's address that the Schindlers' attorneys jumped all over with both feet. The pope said, "I should like particularly to underline how the administration of water and food, even when provided by artificial means, always represents a *natural means* of preserving life, not a medical act."

The lawyers argued that since the pope might have changed his mind about ANH, if Terri could have heard his speech, she would have changed *her* mind, and wouldn't be asking to come off the feeding tube. This argument was based, of course, on their erroneous assertion that Terri was a devout, practicing Catholic. Of course, the pope's speech found its way into motions and responses to motions in The Schiavo Case, and was ultimately argued before the Florida Supreme Court later in the year.

Jodi had an opportunity to speak with a number of priests about the pope's remarks dealing with artificial nutrition and hydration. They all agreed that Catholics are not obligated to accept artificial nutrition and hydration to preserve life. They even made a point of saying that they, themselves, wouldn't want to be kept alive that way, and that removal of ANH feeding tubes was an accepted medical practice at Catholic hospitals in the United States.

———

On May 5, 2004, Pinellas County circuit court judge W. Douglas Baird ruled that Terri's Law and Governor Jeb Bush's actions pursuant to its terms were unconstitutional. It had taken six months for the court to officially state the obvious. Judge Baird's ruling gave several reasons for his decision: The law unjustifiably authorized the governor to summarily deprive Florida citizens of their constitutional right to privacy; it allowed the governor to exercise powers belonging to the judiciary, which violated the "separation of powers" doctrine by one branch of government encroaching on the powers of another, and by one branch delegating to another its constitutionally assigned power.

Judge Baird cut Jeb Bush and the supporters of Terri's Law some slack that I wouldn't have given them when he wrote, "This court must assume that this extraordinary legislation was enacted with the best intentions and prompted by sincere motives. However, as the highly respected constitutional lawyer and senator, Daniel Webster (1782–1852) is widely credited with observing, 'Good intentions will always be pleaded for every assumption of authority. It is hardly too strong to say that the Constitution was made to guard the people against the dangers of good intentions. There are men in all ages who mean to govern well, but they mean to govern. They promise to be good masters, but they mean to be masters.'"

Judge Baird continued, "To preserve the promise of individual liberty and freedom, the Florida Constitution guarantees to every citizen the right to be the master of his or her own personal private medical decisions . . . The statute [Terri's Law] is facially unconstitutional as a matter of law."

By this time, I'd developed an understanding of the legal process. It didn't take a Ph.D. to figure it out: We win, they appeal, we win again, they appeal again. This time, my attorneys asked the second DCA to send the case directly to the Florida Supreme Court, which it did, and the state's highest court agreed to hear oral arguments on August 31. Considering what had been going on, that was warp speed.

Fortunately, George and Debbie were getting some outside legal help. The ACLU was involved, as was California appellate attorney Jon Eisenberg, who prepared a friend-of-the-court brief on behalf of fifty-five bioethicists from around the country. The list included doctors, clergy, attorneys, professors from a variety of disciplines, the editor-in-chief of *The American Journal of Bioethics,* and the editor of the *Cambridge Quarterly of Healthcare Ethics.*

The brief pointed out that by declaring Terri's Law unconstitutional, the high court "will put the focus where it belongs—not on a political agenda, but on Terri's wishes, which have been fully and fairly determined in the forum best suited for doing so." It also notes that in Terri's Law, "the authority to make a substitute judgment decision for Terri is in the hands of a stranger who knows nothing of her preference and values." I wasn't certain how that argument would sit with the court, since it had long become clear that the extreme religious right really didn't give a damn what you wanted if you're incapacitated—their only concern was with what they wanted.

———

The summer of 2004 was interesting, to say the least. The west coast of Florida was hit with four hurricanes, we were now fighting the pope, Jodi's mom was dying, my attorneys were preparing for the August 31 Supreme Court oral argument, and Pat Anderson was bound and determined to take depositions from both Jodi and me. I'd been down that path before, but Jodi's response was—how shall I put it?—hostile. She said, "I will not give those assholes the satisfaction of telling them one thing. And I'm certainly not going to leave my mother's bedside to do it. I'll go to jail first." I guess that qualifies as hostile.

Dan Grieco handled the matter as Jodi's attorney, and was astounded at his first dealing with Anderson. He told me that any other attorney would have said, "Okay, she's her mom's sole caregiver, her mom is dying in her home, let's reschedule." But not Pat. She wouldn't do it without a note from the doctor verifying that Jodi's mom was terminal.

And just in case you thought that I was exaggerating when I claimed that the Schindlers' lawyers were just throwing manure disguised as motions at the courthouse and hoping that flowers would bloom, I'm going to quote from their Motion for Relief from Judgment and Motion to Re-Consider on July 20, 2004.

Terri has now changed her mind about dying.

I'll pause while you digest that.

It continues, "As a practicing Catholic at the time of her collapse who was raised in the Church and who received twelve years of religious school and instruction, Terri does not want to commit a sin of the gravest proportions by foregoing treatment to effect her own death in defiance of her religious faith's express and recent instruction to the contrary."

The interesting line for me is where they said that "Terri has now changed her mind about dying." Because it meant they acknowledged that what I'd said all along that what Terri wanted, based on conversations she had with me, with my brother Scott, and with my sister-in-law Joan, was true. Terri expressed a desire not to be kept alive by artificial means. So after fighting over that one issue for eleven years, they now admitted it.

And then the motion went from the outlandish to the ordinary, run-of-the-mill misstatement of facts that we'd gotten used to. "Even after she and her husband moved to Florida from Pennsylvania to be close to her parents, Terri attended church services on a regular basis." First of all, we moved here well before the Schindlers did. Second, Terri rarely attended church services.

The motion went on, "Typically, she went to a late Saturday afternoon service with her parents and then went to dinner with them afterward . . . Her practices included taking Holy Communion, and her parents have no doubt of her adherence to her church's teachings." More distortions. She couldn't have gone to Saturday services with her parents—because they never went. They didn't belong to a church. Ask Bishop Lynch; that's what Mr. Schindler told him. I can tell you that Terri didn't take Holy Communion. And as for her adherence to her church's teachings, I believe that it was Mrs. Schindler who swore under oath that Terri told her she was no longer in love with me and wanted a divorce.

The motion continued, "In fact, Terri last attended church the afternoon before her collapse in the early morning hours of Sunday, February 25, 1990, true to her habit described by her mother and independently corroborated by the woman at whose home Mr. and Mrs. Schindler and Terri dined that last Saturday evening." Yet another misstatement of the truth.

If the Schindlers went back through the statements they'd made about Terri, they'd find one where they claimed that the night before her collapse, Terri went to church with her sister, Suzanne. Only she didn't do that either. Terri would have never chosen to go to church with Suzanne because they weren't close and rarely did things together.

The motion to which all this legal detritus was attached goes on to cite several sections of the pope's speech in Rome as though it was authoritative on the subject of permanent vegetative state patients. As expected, this "Terri has changed her mind about dying" motion was dismissed by Judge Greer. And here's a shock: Once they lost on that motion, they went back to arguing that I had no idea what Terri's end-of-life wishes were; that we'd made it all up.

———

Even though the Vatican ultimately made it clear that the pope's speech, because of the form it took and the venue in which it was delivered, did not fall into the category of papal pronouncements that are deemed infallible, it still caught the attention of Catholics in this country. Because of this, and the fact that so many people are influenced to one degree or another by pronouncements from Rome— even Catholics who took my side in this battle, and there were many of them—it seems to make sense to evaluate the major points about PVS made by John Paul II. I asked Ronald Cranford, one of the five physicians to examine Terri for Judge Greer's evidentiary hearing, to analyze the pope's speech and comment on just some of the more problematic medical conclusions:

The pope: We must neither forget nor underestimate that there are well-documented cases of at least partial recovery even after many years; we can thus state that medical science, up until now, is still unable to predict with certainty who among patients in this condition will recover and who will not.

Dr. Cranford: Essentially a false statement. Medical science today can predict with an extremely high degree of certainty the chances for any meaningful recovery after one year of existence in this state based on clinical criteria alone. The so-called "miracle recoveries" reported periodically in the lay press were found not to be in a vegetative state in the first place.

The pope: I should like particularly to underline how the administration of water and food, even when provided by artificial means, always represents a natural means of preserving life, not a medical act. Its use, furthermore, should be considered, in principle, ordinary and proportionate, and as such morally obligatory, insofar as and until it is seen to have attained its proper finality, which in the present case consists in providing nourishment to the patient and alleviation of his suffering.

Dr. Cranford: The Vatican statement that "artificial means always represents a natural means" is just flat-out wrong. The Vatican confuses facts with values at a most fundamental level. This assertion is not wrong because it is based on some spiritual, philosophical, or ethical value system over which the Catholic Church has exclusive province. It is wrong because ANH as a medical treatment is a medical fact. There is nothing "natural" about a surgical incision in the abdominal wall, nor the tubing required to supply nutrients and fluids through the abdominal site, nor the medically prescribed nutrients and fluids supplied through these tubes through this surgically created incision. The view that ANH is a medical treatment has achieved an overwhelming consensus in the United States. Further, the use of the PEG tube is a recent medical advance of the last thirty years or so, like so many other advances of recent medicine. It requires consent from the patient or appropriate surrogate. The indications, contraindications, complications, recent advances, and ongoing management of artificial nutrition and hydration are reported in medical journals, not religious or theological journals.

The pope: The evaluation of probabilities, founded on waning hopes for recovery when the vegetative state is prolonged beyond a year, cannot ethically justify the cessation or interruption of minimal care for the patient, including nutrition and hydration. Death by starvation or dehydration is, in fact, the only possible outcome as a result of their withdrawal. In this sense it ends up becoming, if done knowingly and willingly, true and proper euthanasia by omission.

Dr. Cranford: The withdrawal of medical treatment, including artificial nutrition and hydration, after permanency has been established in the vegetative state, is consistent with the highest standards of medical-legal-ethical practice in the United States. The withdrawal of medical treatment is radically different, medically, ethically, and legally, from physician-assisted suicide and active euthanasia; it is not "euthanasia by omission." The Vatican continues to do great disservice to its Church members by persisting in using sloppy, imprecise language in differentiating important categories of letting patients die and killing. Once again the Vatican has drawn the lines in the wrong places.

The Vatican statement appears to diminish the critical importance of this medical determination and the related ethical issues by stating that the value of the life of a PVS patient is the same regardless of the irreversibility, or permanency, of the condition. In other words, the Vatican again takes the strong, hard-line stand that all human life is equal, under any and all circumstances—from procreation through birth to death, regardless of the medical condition of the patient, no matter how extreme. It is an ethical position out of the mainstream of the ethical-medical-legal dilemmas of contemporary society.

The pope: Moreover, it is not possible to rule out a priori that the withdrawal of nutrition and hydration, as reported by authoritative studies, is the source of considerable suffering for the sick person, even if we can see only the reactions at the level of the autonomic nervous system or of gestures. Modern clinical neurophysiology and neuro-imaging techniques, in fact, seem to point to the lasting quality in these patients of elementary forms of communication and analysis of stimuli.

Dr. Cranford: The withdrawal of artificial nutrition and hydration from PVS patients ultimately resulting in terminal dehydration (not starvation) and death does not result in suffering in an unconscious patient. Functional neuro-imaging studies in the past decade or so have shown cerebral cortical levels of metabolism at 40–50% of normal in PVS patients, at metabolic levels comparable to deep coma and unconsciousness.

––––––

On May 26, 2004, Debbie Bushnell was once again in Judge Greer's courtroom, engaged in another motion skirmish with Pat Anderson. What the motion was about is less important than what happened after the two attorneys argued it.

While still in the courtroom, Anderson confronted my attorney, and asked if it was true that she intended to recommend that I have a representative present at the Schindlers' May 29 visit with Terri. This confrontation took place shortly after the Clearwater police had concluded that they couldn't figure out what the marks on Terri's arm really were, and I was highly suspicious of the Schindlers.

Debbie told her, and I'm quoting here from a letter she wrote to Judge Greer detailing the confrontation, "I intended to make that recommendation, and that, in my opinion, although the Court's ruling did not require the Schindlers' visit to be supervised, it did not prevent other visitors from being present at their scheduled visitation time."

Debbie continued, "Ms. Anderson informed me she would write the Court a letter informing the Court of my statement. I responded that was her right, at which time Ms. Anderson stated to me, angrily,

'Lady, you will burn in hell for this.' I responded that that was her opinion."

Not willing to let bad enough alone, however, Anderson followed Debbie toward the courtroom exit where, as Debbie wrote to Judge Greer, "Ms. Anderson angrily stated to me that I should be careful in parking lots because the same thing that happened to Father Murphy could happen to me."

You'll recall that Father Gerard Murphy was the Catholic priest who had devoted his life to counseling the terminally ill and their families. His testimony at the 2000 guardianship trial about the practices of the Catholic Church with respect to artificial life support was profound, and he had said on the witness stand that he regretted that he wasn't the Schindlers' pastor. Just weeks before Debbie's altercation with Anderson, Father Murphy was struck by a car in the parking lot of a Tampa shopping center. He died a week later.

Debbie knew what had happened to Father Murphy, and wrote to Judge Greer with respect to Anderson's angry outburst, "I responded that that sounded like a threat. I also stated that I and my co-counsel heard the press reports of Father Murphy's death and wondered if there was a connection to the Schiavo case. Ms. Anderson glared at me and stated [again] that, if I wasn't careful, what happened to Father Murphy might just happen to me. Upon exiting Courtroom B, and while standing directly in front of the television cameras which were recording our exit, Ms. Anderson glared at me and loudly repeated her angry statement that I would burn in hell."

Debbie recalled that the exchange was even nastier than her letter described it. She says, "It left me incredulous that an attorney would do that. It just confirmed—rubbed in my face—things that I already kind of knew but didn't want to know, about the political system, the court system, people's nature, the extent to which they're willing to hurt and mislead in order to get what they believe to be true generally accepted and forced on people. I lived with it for every second of every day for ten years. To tell you the truth, I don't want to remember a lot of this."

The death of Father Murphy was investigated by homicide detectives from the Florida state police. It was ruled an accident.

Now, let me introduce you to Dr. Carole Lieberman, the self-proclaimed "Media Psychiatrist to the Stars." She received her medical degree from Catholic University of Louvain, in Belgium, and completed her residency in psychiatry at New York's Bellevue Hospital. Then she must have been bitten by the show-biz bug and moved to Hollywood.

I don't know what kind of standards they set for the practice of medicine in Belgium, but I'm reasonably certain that Lieberman's supervisors at Bellevue would not approve of the diagnostic procedures she used to proclaim that I fit the profile of a wife abuser. Her "testimony" of July 12, 2004, which has been widely quoted by Web sites supportive of the Schindlers, began: "Based upon my interviews of Terri's father, Robert Schindler, and my research into media accounts of her case, I can provide the following preliminary opinions at this time . . ."

She went on to say, "I have studied men who exhibit pathology in their relationships with women . . . Michael Schiavo fits the profile, described in [my] book as the Prince of Darkness. O.J. Simpson was cited as a classic example of this type, and there are indeed similarities between the two men. It is especially significant to note that O.J. flew into a homicidal rage when he realized that Nicole was totally abandoning him, as is characteristic of these impulsive men who most dread being abandoned by their women."

This show-biz shrink and celebrity wannabe parroted a lot of the crap that the Schindlers peddled about Terri and my relationship as though she knew it to be fact. Her standard of evidence wouldn't pass muster on the fictional programs CSI or Law & Order, much less in a real medical examiner's office. She wrote, "Medical records and/or experts have revealed that her neck injury was consistent with strangulation." You'll find excerpts from the report of the autopsy that was done on Terri in Appendix 2 (page 345) and the complete report is available through the Schiavo Timeline on the Web. It's the only medical record that matters, written by the only medical expert who matters. If the conclusion had been that I strangled Terri, I couldn't be writing this book, because death row inmates in Florida don't have computers in their cells.

Lieberman goes on to say that "Michael has been under psychiatric care . . . One of his treating therapists, Dr. Peter Kaplan, told Terri's father that he should have called the police after Michael argued with Terri's sister, Suzanne, and Michael tried to attack her. This occurred right after Terri's collapse, when they were all in a house together. Terri's father told Suzanne to lock her door and keep a hammer nearby."

Dr. Kaplan—a psychologist, not a psychiatrist—whose ethical standards require him to actually examine a patient before diagnosing him, said about me in a letter he wrote on May 20, 2005, in response to a request for confirmation of reports of a conversation that he allegedly had with Terri's father:

"One report of this alleged conversation is that I told Mr. Schindler that he should have called the police after Michael Schiavo purportedly had an argument with Terri Schiavo's sister, and that I did so in a manner that suggested that Michael Schiavo might be dangerous. Another version of this alleged conversation is that I told Mr. Schindler something that more directly suggested that Michael Schiavo was dangerous. I know Michael Schiavo because he took the positive step of initiating counseling with me to help with his grief about his wife's condition. I deny that I ever told Mr. Schindler that Michael Schiavo was dangerous or anything that would suggest that he was dangerous. I have never thought that Michael Schiavo posed a danger to anyone, and have not made any statement that would reasonably lead someone to this conclusion."

So that brings us back to Dr. Carole Lieberman, whose Web site declares her to be a psychiatric expert witness. She diagnosed and condemned me without having examined me and without seeking permission to talk with a legitimate psychologist who has treated me. Can it be that Lieberman isn't even smart enough to recognize when she's being used by people who have an axe to grind?

Carole Lieberman has chosen not to become a member of the American Psychiatric Association, a voluntary membership organization described as "the voice and conscience of modern psychiatry" to which roughly 70 percent of practicing U.S. psychiatrists belongs. If she had done so, she'd be required to uphold the ethical standards for psychiatric physicians that are set forth in the *Principles of Medical Ethics With Annotations Especially Applicable to Psychiatry*, which is based on the American Medical Association's Principles of Medical Ethics.

The ethical guidelines say about psychiatrists and the media: "On occasion psychiatrists are asked for an opinion about an individual who is in the light of public attention or who has disclosed information about himself/herself through public media. In such circumstances, a psychiatrist may share with the public his or her expertise about the psychiatric issues in general. However, it is unethical for a psychiatrist to offer a professional opinion unless he or she has conducted an examination and has been granted proper authorization for such a statement."

I am outraged that Dr. Lieberman had no qualms about diagnosing or condemning me without ever meeting or speaking to me. I have filed a formal complaint against her with the medical licensing agency in California.

On August 31, 2004, my brother Brian drove up to Tallahassee with me to hear the oral arguments before the Florida Supreme Court. From attending more lower court hearings than I can count, I'd become accustomed to attorneys being given the freedom to present their arguments in their own way. That's why what happened seconds after the Washington, D.C., attorney representing Governor Bush, Robert Destro, began speaking astonished me. He had been quite cordially invited by the chief justice to begin his twenty-minute presentation, and managed to get one sentence into his prepared speech when Chief Justice Barbara J. Pariente pounced on him.

It sounded like this:

"My name is Robert Destro, here to represent Governor Bush in this case and with me are Kenneth Connor, who will argue in rebuttal, and Camille Godwin . . ."

"Before you get into your argument, the court would appreciate it if you would address the separation of powers, first, with the privacy argument, and with whatever free time you have, you can argue the other issues."

Destro tried again. "Thank you your honor. May it please the court, Terri Schiavo did not have an independent benefit of . . ."

This time, Justice Charles T. Wells stopped him dead in his tracks. "Let's try to get into the argument on separation of powers. Let me ask you this. Would you agree that the governor did not have the power to order a stay on October 15, 2003?"

Destro dissembled. Justice Wells changed the subject, asking if the law wasn't written solely to deal with Terri Schiavo and no one else.

After further parrying, Destro went on, "Well, your honor, the statute, itself, is open-ended. Certainly Terri Schiavo fits within the description of the statute, but it would be a question of fact as to whether or not there are other people in the State of Florida, at any given— during the time this statute was in effect. The statute is very clear on its face, that you don't have an advanced directive, that the court has found that, when nutrition and hydration can be withdrawn, there could be any number of people and it would be a question of fact as to how many were in the State of Florida at that time."

Destro kept making a point of *time* because Terri's Law was written to be in effect for just a fifteen-day period before it expired. Justice Peggy Quince decided to pile on. "Would this have to fit into this fifteen day time period? This act came into effect on a particular day, and fifteen days later, it is no longer in effect, isn't that correct?"

Destro didn't even hang his head in shame when he responded, "Yes, your honor, that is true."

It was beautiful. I couldn't help smiling as the Supreme Court justices destroyed him. The same thing happened to Destro's co-counsel, Ken Connor, when he had a chance to address the court and tried to insist that Terri's Law wasn't written just for Terri Schiavo. "By the face of it, your honor," Connor pleaded, "it does apply to more than just Terri. Terri Schiavo's case was the triggering event for it."

Justice Wells smacked him with, "We would have to ignore reality to do that, would we not?"

Pat Anderson was seated on the front bench and I kept waiting for her to jump up and shout at the justices, "You'll all burn in hell!" or "Off with your head," but I guess she was on her best behavior that day.

Justice Wells left no doubt how he felt when he said, "What is going on here is that the Legislature set about to set aside the final judgment of the court."

Chief Justice Pariente had either read the *amicus* brief filed by the ethicists, or was of the same mind, when she said to Connor, "The act does not even require the governor to take into account the patient's wishes."

I was sitting in the impressive courtroom when it suddenly dawned on me: The only people who get to speak in our courts who *aren't* sworn to tell the whole truth and nothing but are the lawyers. If you've got forty-five minutes and you're interested, you can watch streaming video of the entire hearing on the Web at www.miami.edu/ethics/schiavo/timeline.htm.

When it was over, George, Brian, and I walked across the street to the steps of the state capitol where the media had gathered to ask questions. I hadn't expected to say anything, but one of the reporters asked me, "What were you thinking in there?"

I said, "I was thinking, *If this was so important to you, Jeb Bush, where are you? Why aren't you here? I don't see you at all.*" And then I said, "You know something, Jeb? I can remember you sitting in front of all these reporters with tears in your eyes when your daughter was having her [drug] problems, and you asked for your privacy. And you got it. So now, why aren't you giving Terri and me our privacy?"

The reaction to that was stunned silence. There must have been a hundred reporters there, plus TV crews from all over the country, and they had nothing to say. I topped it off by once again inviting Jeb to come visit Terri, which I knew was a complete waste of time, but after seeing him and his partners in this crime against decency go after me in the media, it felt good to strike back for a change.

There was a strange coincidence of timing that day. August 31 fell on a Tuesday, and in Pinellas and Pasco Counties, it was Election Day. Judge Greer had been opposed by a local attorney who attempted to take a back-door route in order to inject the Schiavo case into the contest by sending a mailer to everyone in the area who'd paid extra to have the "Choose Life" license plate on their vehicle. The ploy didn't work. Greer won by an overwhelming margin, and in a postelection statement, the former county commissioner, who'd already served twelve years on the bench, said, "I feel just great satisfaction. The amount of support I received and the way voters responded today is something very special for me and my family."

Before The Schiavo Case would end, Judge Greer, who is a religious, conservative Republican, would be asked to leave the church he'd belonged to for years, Calvary Baptist in Clearwater. Because of his rulings, Greer had been criticized in the *Florida Baptist Witness*, the weekly Baptist newspaper distributed at the church, and as a result had discontinued his donations but remained a member. The executive editor of the paper, James A. Smith, Sr., then wrote, "It appears that Judge Greer has chosen to remove himself from the loving care of a biblically sound church rather than to submit to the biblical obligation to exercise his public duties in a manner that is consistent with his Christian faith." To which I say, thank God for Judge Greer's integrity, ethics, and commitment to his oath to uphold and defend the Constitution.

However, the editorial in the Baptist newspaper wasn't the end of the story. The pastor of Calvary Baptist, William Rice, sent a letter to the judge suggesting "it might be easier for all of us" if Greer resigned. Rice added, "I am not asking you to do this, but since you have taken the initiative of withdrawal, and since your connection with Calvary continues to be a point of concern, it would seem the logical and, I would say, biblical course." Of course it would.

———

Summer in Florida can mean hurricanes and the summer of 2004 was a doozy. Hurricane Frances made landfall on Florida's east coast as a Category Two, and on September 5, it brushed Clearwater with seventy-mile-an-hour winds. While Frances was roaring past us, Jodi's mom, Ellie, passed away.

This is a good example of what I mean when I say that Jodi is my rock. She just takes everything in stride and deals with it. She dealt with her mom's death and arranged her funeral while at the same time continuing to plan Olivia's second birthday party a week later, and she kept me focused on the things I needed to do for all of us. By the way, Jodi never was deposed. After Pat Anderson went out of her way to aggravate Jodi while her mother was in the end stages of cancer by insisting that she sit for a deposition, she just forgot about it. During her tenure representing the Schindlers, Anderson succeeded in delaying things, but she never won on the merits, and in the long run, she was deservingly defeated.

Just three weeks after the Florida Supreme Court heard oral arguments, the justices issued a unanimous decision striking down Terri's Law as unconstitutional. The conclusion to their thirty-one-page decision spoke to the head and to the heart:

> We recognize that the tragic circumstances underlying this case make it difficult to put emotions aside and focus solely on the legal issue presented. We are not insensitive to the struggle that all members of Theresa's family have endured since she fell unconscious in 1990. However, we are a nation of laws and we must govern our decisions by rule of law and not by our own emotions. Our hearts can fully comprehend the grief so fully demonstrated by Theresa's family members on this record. But our hearts are not the law. What is in the Constitution always must prevail over emotion. Our oaths as judges require that this principle is our polestar, and it alone . . .

The trial court's decision regarding Theresa Schiavo was made in accordance with the procedures and protections set forth by the judicial branch and in accordance with the statutes passed by the Legislature in effect at that time. That decision is final and the Legislature's attempt to alter that final adjudication is unconstitutional as applied to Theresa Schiavo . . .

The governor's response to being slapped upside the head by the Florida Supreme Court was to tell his phalanx of Christian lawyers looking for the silver bullet to come up with something—anything—that might buy more time. In short order they asked for a rehearing and clarification of the high court's opinion. It was denied. While the lawyers were scurrying around to find another way to delay things, Judge Greer helped them out by granting a stay that prevented the removal of Terri's feeding tube until December 6. That date would later be extended.

At the same time, Judge Greer ruled on the absurd motion that as a result of the pope's speech, Terri had changed her mind and no longer wanted to die. He wrote, "In affirming this court's February 2000 ruling," the Second District Court of Appeals held that Terri Schiavo "had been raised in the Catholic faith, but did not regularly attend Mass *or have a religious advisor who could assist the court in weighing her religious attitude about life-support method.* [Italics added.] Nothing has changed. There is nothing new presented regarding Terri Schiavo's religious attitude and there still is no religious advisor to assist this or any other court in weighing her desire to comply with this or any other papal pronouncement." The Schindlers and their supporters could insist that Terri was a devout, practicing Catholic, but the judges were looking for proof—and there was none.

With the Florida Supreme Court turning a deaf ear to his arguments, Jeb Bush had nowhere to go but to the United States Supreme Court. On December 1, 2004, a petition for certiorari, seeking review of the state court's decision on Terri's Law, was filed with the high court in Washington. George Felos was so certain that the highest court in the land would not give the governor any satisfaction that he waived my right to respond to the governor's petition. The Schindlers, or more correctly, the extremists who had taken charge of their legal activities, had no similar sense of confidence. American Center for Law & Justice attorney Jay Alan Sekulow filed an amicus brief in support of Bush. Shortly after the new year, the legal papers were distributed to the Justices of the United States Supreme Court, who discussed it in conference on January 21. Three days later, the high court denied the petition, causing panic to break out in the Schindler camp.

We got a bonus the first week in February when Florida's Department of Agriculture and Consumer Services cited the Terri Schindler-Schiavo Foundation for failing to register with the state to solicit donations, a fact that was discovered and reported by our volunteer appellate attorney, Jon Eisenberg.

Within days, the Schindlers went back to the Second District Court of Appeals, then to Judge Greer. They were rebuffed in both venues. After more courtroom nonsense, Judge Greer stayed removal of the feeding tube until 5 P.M. on February 23.

The Schindlers were desperate. The only judges they could find were ones who obeyed the law and honored the Constitution. I could almost hear them muttering, "How come whenever you need an activist judge, you can never find one?"

Their only option was to get help from Operation Rescue's Randall Terry, who appeared at a news conference with Terri's parents and vowed that there would be huge protest vigils against the removal of the tube. Terry is more than just a rabid antiabortionist who filed for bankruptcy in order to avoid paying massive debts owed to women's groups and abortion clinics that have sued him. He has been arrested more than forty times and counted as one of his avid followers James C. Kopp, the man convicted of murdering a doctor in Buffalo who performed abortions.

Terry is the avowed enemy of everything it means to live in a free society as an American. As the Fort Wayne (Indiana) *News Sentinel* reported on August 16, 1993, at an antiabortion rally in Fort Wayne, Terry said, "Our goal is a Christian nation . . . We have a biblical duty; we are called by God to conquer this country. We don't want equal time. We don't want pluralism . . . Theocracy means God rules. I've got a hot flash. God rules."

18 | Wink, Wink, Nod, Nod

There's a story about Chicago's legendary Mayor Richard J. Daley, the "Boss." He supposedly was telling a crony about someone new to the Democratic Machine, and said, "The trouble with him is he thinks it's on the legit."

That described me perfectly for the first few years of The Schiavo Case. I thought it was on the legit—the affidavits, the depositions, the motions, the pleadings. I was impressed when I heard attorneys talk about the Rules of Civil Procedure. I believed when someone signed an affidavit, they would stick to the facts; when someone answered a question at a deposition, their testimony would not change at trial; and when someone swore to tell the whole truth, *so help me God*, they would.

What a fool I was.

By the start of 2005, I'd concluded that every time the other side did something outrageous, there'd be a wink, wink, nod, nod, and they'd get away with it. Watching their high-priced right-to-life attorneys Robert Destro and Ken Connor answering questions from the Supreme Court justices was a perfect example of what I'm talking about. "Oh, yes, your honor, Terri's Law was designed to help an entire class of people—not just Terri Schiavo. Don't pay attention to the fact that it expired in fifteen days." Wink, wink, nod, nod.

While all that was happening on the media stage, over at Governor Jeb Bush's offices, there was an entire operation going on behind the scenes whose mission was to have a constant supply of delaying tactics ready to deploy as court after court rejected their frivolous motions.

I know this because we've received copies of many of the e-mails that went to and from Bush's office related to our case. Perhaps the people communicating with Jeb didn't notice that at the bottom of e-mails from his office, it says, "Please note that Florida has a broad public records law, and that all correspondence to me via e-mail may be subject to disclosure." You can find all sorts of interesting stuff reading other people's e-mail.

For example, on December 30, 2004, a friend of the governor's named Nancy sent him a note that said,

> Dear Jeb: Perhaps there is some way to investigate these on going violations, here is a list I received from Bobby last night. Surely these violate Florida Statutes, please don't let them kill her. God Bless you and may he give you the fortitude to use all means within your authority to prevent this outrageous injustice. Here's the e-mail. FYI Gatorpmac.

And what followed was a letter from Bobby Schindler.

> Nancy,
> Don't know if you heard the news, but the 2nd DCA really put the screws to us, and Felos issued a reprehensible press release gloating at the fact that Terri is going to die. He is truly disgusting.
>   They issued a one line ruling. No hearing, no opinion, nothing. They are bent of [sic] killing my sister. It seems that ever since Gov. Bush got involved these judges became even more arrogant than ever before, like they are telling the Gov. don't get involved in our business. It is amazing how they are just thumbing their nose at us, and the law, and have absolutely no problem ending a life, and they can get away with it.

It took me 4 days but I've finally completed a short narrative for each of these on this list. This has to get out. Take a look and would appreciate your thoughts. All this is ongoing, and Schiavo is getting away with it because the courts are protecting this monster. How can we expose this?

What followed in the e-mail from Bobby was a list of twenty-six items that he was trying to peddle as though it proved I had abused Terri. It was nothing but a repackaging of the usual list, most of which had been dealt with at one court hearing or another. Some examples from Schindler's list:

- No therapy or rehabilitation since 1991, despite medical records indicating that Terri responsive [False]
- No swallowing test/therapy since 1993, despite medical testimony that Terri can be taught to eat [False]
- Refuses to release medical information to parents since 1993 despite court order (Ongoing) [False]
- Limited visitors list that must first be approved by Schiavo and will remove visitors at own discretion (Ongoing) [For cause.]
- Denied certain CDs to be played for Terri and refuses to allow Terri to listen to music with earphones (Ongoing) [He's kidding, right?]
- Ordered no pictures/video taken of Terri (Ongoing) [Judge's order.]
- Michael Schiavo is engaged and has cohabitated and fathered two children with another woman while still married to Terri (Ongoing since 1995) [True.]

You get the picture. Now, what would the governor of Florida do with a list as impressive as that? In his infinite, absolutist pro-life wisdom, he passed it along to his general counsel, Raquel Rodriguez, and said they should discuss it.

In the meantime, another e-mail sent to the governor let him know that while Randall Terry was appreciative of Jeb's efforts thus far, the professional protester wasn't finished. The e-mail was sent by Alan Keyes, the right-wing extremist who's managed to lose three bids for the U.S. Senate and two for president without getting the hint that it's time to unpack his carpetbag because mainstream America isn't buying what he's selling. It consisted of a carefully crafted letter purportedly from Terri's father, followed by Randall Terry's "battle plan to save [Terri] from starvation."

The following highlights of the plan demonstrate the organizational skills and the tactics that the religious right deployed in this kind of battle. They're very good with the small details, such as changing Terri's name to something that makes a statement.

First comes the motivation. Convince the true believers that the court decisions in *Schiavo* were just the latest in a laundry list of judicial affronts to the God-fearing citizens of America. "The advocates of evil have hijacked the judiciary to achieve their agenda," claimed Terry. And then he gave them a list that included the federal court decisions to remove the Ten Commandments from the public-school classrooms of Kentucky and from the Supreme Court of Alabama; the decision to strike "under God" from the Pledge of Allegiance; and what he described as "the court ordered mandate to create homosexual marriage or civil unions in the states of Vermont and Massachusetts."

Then comes the linking hyperbole. "The threat of starvation for Terri Schindler-Schiavo is another one of those epic battles. If she is in fact starved to death, it could open a floodgate of starvations and other forms of cruelty towards the severely disabled and severely handicapped in America."

Next is the call to action. "Please understand, Terri's family is happy for the sympathy of tens of millions of Americans. But sympathy alone will not save Terri from Starvation! We must fight, we must struggle, we must sacrifice for Terri's right to live, or she will perish. We are at war for the life of this woman and the soul of this nation, and war requires troops who will act in concert to push back the enemy."

And finally, just before the "list of action items that every single person reading this letter can do," came the exhortation. "If we will all act in concert with each other, we can create a tidal wave of momentum and public outrage that [will] result in saving her life. We can create an avalanche of support for Governor Bush and the Florida Legislature that stimulates and emboldens them to stand against the judicial tyranny that threatens Terri's life. I am convinced that most of the country is disgusted with arrogant Judges ramming their godless agenda down our throats; I have seen the anger of good and decent Americans who are fed up with Courts acting like dictators and tyrants."

Terry next said that the Schindler family had "many friends in the Florida Legislature. We must provide them with the support and the 'political cover' they will need to take up this issue again. I believe they will have the courage to intervene as long as they know millions of Americans and especially Floridians are supporting them . . . If we as citizens will denounce this oppression [by the courts], and Governor Bush and the Florida Legislature will again stand against these judicial tyrants, it could be a key moment in our history as a nation. We could look back and see that this was a key battle in restoring the rule of law and the right of self-government in America; that it was a team battle in breaking the stranglehold that the courts have on our lives, our laws, and our liberties. May God make it so."

Now for Randall Terry's instructions to the mindless masses. First, there was a PDF file that would print a history of Terri's story, two copies to a page, to be copied to "put in your church bulletin, or hand out at church, or give to your friends at work. If the clergy won't help, maybe you could put it on cars in the parking lot." Second, a link to send e-mail to Governor Bush, the speaker of the Florida House, and the president of the Florida Senate, to "politely urge them to intervene and save Terri's life." Another link was provided for Florida residents to directly contact their state senator and representative.

Then, the real marching orders began. "If you hear that Terri's feeding has been ordered to be stopped, if at all possible come to Florida immediately. We will need people in Pinellas Park (near Tampa) where Terri is, and we'll need people to go to Tallahassee to plead with the Governor and the Legislature to rescue her. We will have 24 hour vigils until we rescue her, or she departs this life." Links were provided to a list of hotels near the hospice and in Tallahassee.

And finally came the inevitable request for funds to be sent to the Terri Schindler-Schiavo Foundation, with the notation that gifts were not tax deductible. The address was coded so that funds sent as a result of Randall Terry's pleas could be identified.

To me, these were people who were pretending to be doing God's work. Not long after that fund-raising appeal went out, the Schindlers worked out a money-making deal with a right-wing direct-mail outfit to lease the mailing list of all the contributors to the Terri Schindler-Schiavo Foundation to other outfits trying to raise money. What is it that Donald Trump says? It's just business!

Randall Terry wasn't the only person sending e-mails outlining strategy for the extremists. Ordinary folks were writing to Jeb Bush and suggesting actions that would be laughable but for the fact that they were taken seriously by the zealots on the governor's staff. Consider an e-mail from a Karl Maurer of Chicago. He propounded a theory that set the Constitution on its head, but it was deemed important enough for Florida's deputy attorney general, George LeMieux, to call Maurer on the phone to discuss it. And then LeMieux passed it on to Rodriguez, the governor's lawyer. In a nutshell, Maurer noted that the Florida Constitution gave the governor power to grant clemency to criminals "or in cases where it would restore civil rights." He went on to say, "What's at issue is whether or not the Governor is willing to expand the definition of clemency from the narrow and legalistic to a more broad definition more in keeping with the traditional Common Law origins of the act of clemency. This will set a precedent in Florida, but isn't that precedent what is really needed?"

Maurer continued, saying either I give Terri to her parents, or "I can allow Governor Bush to establish a new precedent for clemency that allows him to intercede in 'right-to-die' cases and unilaterally spare people."

He continued, "I hate the thought of playing poker with Terri's life, [if] Michael believes Gov. Jeb Bush is seriously considering clemency, he and Felos might capitulate, and the entire crisis can be avoided. Personally, I would prefer Gov. Bush grant clemency and establish the new definition of clemency as one that serves to redress all overreaching by the courts where the end result is the loss of a human life that is unable to defend itself."

That's how those people think. When almost three dozen judges, all the way up to the United States Supreme Court, rule against them, it's the judges who are "overreaching." And the solution to that is to legitimize anarchy. Think about it: This is an idea that was passed along by the state's deputy attorney general to the governor's general counsel for serious consideration.

While Jeb didn't act on that one, he apparently was moved by Bobby Schindler's attempt to win the Pulitzer Prize for fiction. Remember that e-mail—the one complaining that not letting Terri have headphones to listen to CDs was proof of abuse?

It must have been sheer coincidence, but a few weeks after Bobby's e-mail reached Jeb's office, the Florida Department of Children & Families—an agency under Jeb Bush's thumb—filed a petition to intervene in the court proceedings in order to investigate charges that Terri had been abused. I was shocked that the governor would use a state agency for nefarious political purposes.

Actually, the DCF petition asked Judge Greer not only to stay his order for the removal of Terri's feeding tube for up to sixty days, but to appoint a legal counsel to represent Terri, and to seal all of the proceedings—so the whole thing could be done in secret. Jeb must have learned that one from his big brother.

The good news was that the local media wasn't going to let him get away with it. Attorneys for the *Tampa Tribune* and WFLA-TV News Channel 8 immediately filed a Motion to Intervene and Petition for Access to Judicial Record that called a spade a spade, saying, ". . . concealment of DCF's petition simply allows that agency to hide the rationale for further executive branch participation in this proceeding. Consequently, closure is by no means necessary to comply with established public policy or to serve some other compelling interest. DCF's petition, therefore, should be made public." It was almost enough to make me rethink how I felt about the media.

Judge Greer didn't take long to rule against DCF, reasoning that privacy concerns had "long since been lost" as a result of extensive publicity about the case. How's that for a judicial understatement?

Once the DCF complaint was opened to scrutiny, it became very clear why Jeb's people wanted to keep the public from reading it. Most of the allegations of abuse had long ago been thrown at me. Not one of them had stuck.

And who were the people who made the allegations of abuse? Well, it's difficult to be certain because the DCF is so concerned about protecting the finger-pointers, but one of them heard on a Yahoo! message board that Terri was being mistreated, another said he knew that I'd spent Terri's money on court cases instead of on her medical care, still another said I wouldn't let Monsignor Malanowski visit her, and one more said that "a full investigation should be done because Ms. Schiavo is not allowed to have the blinds in her room opened." That last one is interesting, because the Schindler forces were desperate to get a current photo of Terri in her hospice room; and since I'd made sure the police were enforcing the rule that prevented them from bringing into her room purses or bags in which they might conceal a camera, their side was reduced to staging sneak attacks on the hospice windows in hopes of taking a photo. That's why the blinds in Terri's room were usually closed.

When Jeb Bush says he'll help if he can, you can take him at his word. Imagine how many taxpayer dollars were spent having DCF attorney Kelly J. McKibben work with Michael Will, an Adult Protective Investigations supervisor in their Orlando office, to draw up the eleven-page motion that said there would need to be a two-month delay in removing Terri's feeding tube in order to allow DCF to investigate all the abuse charges. And then more Florida taxpayer money had to pay for Ms. McKibben to travel from Orlando to Clearwater in order to appear in Judge Greer's courtroom and present the motion at a hearing that had been called to discuss other matters, including the date at which the feeding tube could be removed.

Debbie Bushnell was amazed that DCF had shown up. "I've worked with DCF a lot," she said, "and I have never seen anything like this kind of intervention. I have trouble keeping DCF involved in guardianships; after the guardianship is set up, they say, 'Oh, well, it's the court's business now. The court can deal with it. We're outta here.' But in this situation there was just no doubt in any of our minds that Jeb was intent on interfering in any way possible. The place of last resort at that point was DCF, and he was pulling the strings."

At one point in the hearing, Judge Greer asked McKibben, "Do you feel that it's your job to second-guess this court's rulings?"

DCF's attorney said, "Yes."

Debbie recalled that "it was amazingly honest, and it showed the extreme position that they were taking in this situation. DCF's position was blatantly political, and blatantly absurd."

The action by the Department of Children & Families was annoying, but it was small potatoes compared to what was going to hit us in the next couple of weeks, especially since Judge Greer dropped the equivalent of a neutron bomb on the Schindlers at a hearing on Friday, February 25. The judge's order said:

> Five years have passed since the issuance of the February 2000 order authorizing the removal of Theresa Schiavo's nutrition and hydration and there appears to be no finality in sight to this process. The Court, therefore, is no longer comfortable in continuing to grant stays pending appeal of Orders denying Respondents' various motions and petitions. The process does not work when the trial court finds a motion to be without merit but then stays the effect of such denial for months pending appellate review. Also, the Court is no longer comfortable granting stays simply upon the filing of new motions and petitions since there will always be "new" issues that can be pled. The Respondents will need to demonstrate

before the appellate courts that their requests have merit and accordingly are worthy of a stay.

At last, Judge Greer had had enough. He was no longer willing to sit by and watch the lawyers for the religious right make a mockery of the court system and the appellate process. In three dozen words, he put an end to it:

> **ORDERED AND ADJUDGED** that absent a stay from the appellate courts, the guardian, MICHAEL SCHIAVO, shall cause the removal of nutrition and hydration from the ward, THERESA SCHIAVO, at 1:00 P.M. on Friday, March 18, 2005.

The hate mail and the threats escalated with that order. There were WANTED posters on the Web that put a price on my head, as well as on Judge Greer's. A woman in California who wrote on an AOL message board devoted to the Schiavo case, "IF SHE DIES, I WILL KILL MICHAEL SCHIAVO AND THE JUDGE THIS IS FOR REAL!" told FBI agents when they came to arrest her that she was only kidding. As they took her away, the agents told her that they weren't. She was found guilty of transmitting a threat in interstate commerce and sentencing is pending.

My sister-in-law Joan, my brother Bill's wife, was confronted behind their Philadelphia home by a lone man in a car whom she'd seen drive past the house several times. He pulled up to her as she was about to leave for work, and said, "If Terri dies, I'm coming back to shoot you and your family."

Threatening mail comparing us to those who operated the Nazi death camps was so common and so unoriginal, it meant nothing.

What was also unoriginal was the response of the Schindlers' attorneys to Judge Greer's order: They wanted more delays. George reached back to a motion he'd written in December 2002 to fight it:

> And what is the possibility that appellants can find a doctor to swear to a "new treatment" that offers no *real* promise to the ward? The

possibility is substantial, as this case has already shown. Further, as this case and other cases of this nature show, there is fierce cultural battle being waged by a small-but-vocal minority that believes, on religious or moral grounds, that it is grievously wrong to terminate any patient's artificial feeding.

This case has attracted such individuals and organizations, as well as other parties having their own agendas. Already, an organization that equates removal of feeding tubes with "murder" unsuccessfully attempted to intervene after the first trial, a state legislator unsuccessfully attempted to intervene in earlier proceedings before the Florida Supreme Court, and fanatic organizations are now funding this litigation. Doctors who observed the ward immediately after the trial or whose affidavits were later filed, are either members or directors of the organization that unsuccessfully tried to intervene at trial. For a doctor who believes that "extremism in the defense of virtue is no vice," the needed affidavit is a small price to pay to prevent the "murder" of Theresa Schiavo.

The difference for us this time was that it seemed that judges from the circuit court in Pinellas County, Florida, up to the Supreme Court of the United States had known all along what the law said. Now, they were prepared to embrace it—and that scared the Republicans.

In Washington, GOP legislators were staying in close touch with Jeb's staff as they tried to determine if there was a way to bully judges into deciding the case their way. Erin Berry, the legislative counsel for Representative John Hostettler, a conservative Republican from Indiana who has served as chairman of the Congressional Family Caucus, spent some time reading the Florida Constitution, and then sent an e-mail that found its way to Jeb's attorneys, Raquel Rodriguez and Christa Calamas, which said, "I'm still trying to research whether Florida's governor has ever defied a court order in the past." On Hostettler's Web site, his biography says he "called for a return to the Constitution as the nation's governing document." Before Congress finished with *Schiavo*, we'd see an epidemic of this kind of hypocrisy.

On March 8, the first draft of an attempt to create a federal Terri's Law was introduced in the House. Two days later, Judge Greer ruled that Florida's Department of Children & Families could not intervene in the Schiavo case. The judge said that if DCF's petition were granted, it would violate the separation of powers between the judicial and executive branches of government. There's no truth to the rumor that he sent a freshman high school government textbook over to the governor's office in Tallahassee with the suggestion that it be carefully studied. But he should have.

Governor Bush, who was quoted in the newspapers as saying he would do anything he could to save Terri Schiavo's life, said he was disappointed in the ruling. "I don't know how DCF can't be involved. There's a law that says if the hotline is called and there's a warranted need for an investigation that there ought to be an investigation." I didn't know whether I should laugh because he thought the public would believe that he was sincere, or cry because he thought the people who would read his statement the next day were so stupid they'd buy it.

While Jeb was busy trying to figure out how to beat the judges who were insisting on following the law, he took a moment to share by e-mail something purported to have been written by his eldest son, George P. Bush, a Dallas attorney whom political reporters claim Jeb is grooming to run for higher office. It was an op-ed piece in which George P. proves that he's learned a little something from either his father, his uncle, or the people who advise them about slinging sewage.

Consider these excerpts:

- "And the rest of us will have to come to terms with the fact that a court has allowed a faithless husband to kill his helpless, inconvenient wife . . ." [*A court? How about *every* court, up to the *United States Supreme Court?* And I won't dignify the other adjectives or the verb to "kill" with a response.*]
- ". . . even though experts like world-renowned neuroscientist Dr.

William Hammesfahr have stated that they treat patients with conditions worse than Terri's daily with success." ["World-renowned?" More like: completely discredited.]

- "The courts have not found with "clear and convincing evidence" that Terri would have wanted what the courts will allow this Friday." [That's *precisely* what the courts found. The only way to have misinterpreted this is to not have read the court order.]

- "This case lends more weight to the will of a man who is likely to gain financially from Terri's death . . ." [Shame on you, George P., that's no way to talk about Randall Terry.]

The danger in passing around misinformation disguised as plausible fact is that there are people on the receiving end whose ability to think critically doesn't speak well for the American educational system. And some of those people knew where we lived. One God-fearing believer in Wichita, Kansas, went to the trouble of finding the names and addresses of our neighbors—hundreds of them—and sending each a postcard telling them that "Your neighbor Michael Schiavo is trying to murder his wife."

Believe it or not, that didn't bother me as much as the rest of the message, which reflected the distortions and misstatements that Randall Terry, the Schindlers, and an assortment of elected officials were still spreading. "She is *not* in a persistent vegetative state. She's simply disabled, and needs *proper care* just like any other severely disabled person. When her parents visit her, Terri laughs . . . she cries . . . she moves . . . and she makes child-like attempts at speech with her mother and father. Sometimes she will say 'Mom' or 'Dad' or 'yeah' when they ask her a question. And when they kiss her hello or good-bye, she looks at them and 'puckers up' her lips. She's able to sit in a chair . . . she loves to listen to her favorite music . . . and she recognizes her brother and sister when they come to visit."

How can you debate with people who have no qualms about making up whatever they feel like saying? The flip side of that postcard was even worse. The headline was, "Terri will die a horrible death." It went on to describe the symptoms a patient can experience when hydration and nutrition is withdrawn, but it ignored the fact that Terri would feel or experience none of it. She was incapable of feeling pain because that part of her brain where feeling would occur in a normal person was gone. With appropriate palliative care, which the hospice was expert at providing, even patients not in a vegetative state who have artificial nutrition and hydration withdrawn do not usually experience pain and suffering as their body systems shut down.

But there's no point in trying to explain this to people whose minds are closed. Why is it that they're more likely to listen to a raving lunatic dragging a life-size Jesus on a cross back and forth in front of the hospice than to qualified doctors who deal with this manner of death almost daily in their practices? That's a rhetorical question; there is no intelligent answer.

In mid-February, the police told us they'd learned that a major demonstration was scheduled to take place at our home. We decided to take the kids and leave. We returned two days later because Jodi was bound and determined that she wasn't going to cancel Nicholas's first birthday party on February 24. When we were back home, we learned that elderly friends of Jodi's mom had gotten the date wrong and, when they mistakenly showed up at our house on Saturday for the party, found themselves in the middle of a demonstration.

The couple, Mary Lou and Larry, who are both devout Catholics, pulled into our driveway. As soon as they got out of the car, the Franciscan brothers leading the demonstration began screaming that they must be my parents. Since both my parents had died, it just shows how little these people knew about my family. It was an unsettling experience for two people with pacemakers implanted to help deal with heart problems. Larry tried to ignore the demonstrators, but Mary Lou thought it was absolutely horrible that people who would call themselves Catholics would set upon an elderly couple in that way.

As the March 18 date for removal of Terri's feeding tube drew near, things at home began getting scary. Even though the Clearwater Police Department was wonderful in keeping track of what was going on in the neighborhood, living under a continuous barrage of threats was taking its toll, especially on Jodi.

Every time she was ready to leave the house, she'd let the police know so they could make sure she wasn't being followed out of our neighborhood. It got to the point that the cops knew what days Olivia went to preschool, and what Jodi's college schedule was, and they automatically watched out for her. We'd had security cameras installed around the house, and while Livy and Nick would watch their Elmo videos in a bedroom, someone from our extended family was always watching the cameras on the large-screen TV in the living room.

Television crews and their satellite trucks had invaded the neighborhood, and while the police kept the vehicles out of our cul-de-sac, there were times that we could look out the window and see a couple dozen TV cameras lined up facing the house, as though they expected me to come out and make an announcement.

The people we felt sorry for were our neighbors—some of whom were trying to sell their house while this drama was being played out on our street. To their credit, they were all supportive. One family that we didn't know, because they lived a block away, received the ugly postcard about me, and their response was to bake cookies for us. But because they correctly assumed that we wouldn't accept food from people we didn't know, they delivered them to our friends next door, who knew both of us. The gesture was really appreciated, especially because there were times that we felt as though we were under siege in our home.

Imagine what it's like to have a florist delivery guy who shows up at the front door with a beautiful flower arrangement—and before he gives it to us he apologizes because the idiots who sent them had signed the attached card, "Love, Terri."

Jodi found these days to be the most difficult in our twelve years together. She said, "I was pretty much in survival mode, trying to take care of the kids and keep their lives as normal and on schedule as possible. Olivia went to school two days a week, and I still went to my classes regardless of what was going on. I tried not to catch any of the news on TV. The one thing I was grateful for is that my children were young enough not to realize what was going on and to realize how horrible people could be."

The mail that disturbed both Jodi and me were the letters actually addressed to "The Illegitimate Bastard Children of Michael Schiavo" that talked about how kids disappear from their homes every day—and then the same letter would talk about God and quote Scripture. The people who sent those worried Jodi the most. They're the ones who are total fanatics and obviously have a screw loose. You just never knew what they were going to do.

While all this was going on at the house and the hospice, the legal battles continued. We felt as though we were riding a roller coaster—they file, we respond, we win, and they file again. We'd gotten used to new things happening weekly, then daily. But in the days prior to the scheduled removal of the feeding tube, things happened on an hourly basis, and it was exhausting. Think about it. In a two-day period, *Schiavo* was being dealt with at the Second DCA, the Florida House of Representatives, the Florida Senate, the Florida Supreme Court, the Department of Children & Families, the United States House of Representatives, the United States Senate, and the United States Supreme Court.

America had troops dying in Iraq and Afghanistan, and had no plan to get them out of harm's way. Ten million American children had no health insurance, which meant they never saw a doctor until it was an emergency. Nothing meaningful was being done to reduce our dependence on foreign oil, and the price of gasoline was about to skyrocket. But The Schiavo Case, a tragic situation for one American family, seemed to have taken over the national agenda. It was nuts.

On March 16, the Second District Court of Appeals affirmed Judge Greer's order and refused to stop the scheduled March 18 removal of the PEG tube. On the same day, by a voice vote, the U.S. House of Representatives passed H.R. 1332, the Protection of Incapacitated Persons Act of 2005. The bill would amend federal law to allow jurisdiction of a state matter to be assumed by federal courts.

Sitting at home, we just dreaded hearing the phone ring. Jodi recalls that "We just couldn't take any more bad news or any more bogus filings or manipulations or stories they made up. And you just never really knew what to expect."

That night Jodi broke under the pressure. For the first time in our long relationship, she asked me to walk away from Terri. I was also overwhelmed by the news that Congress was getting involved.

Jodi said, "It was just taking its toll on Mike with the death threats and the horrible mail. We were forced to live like criminals in our own home because people who had no idea what was going on seemed to feel that they had a right to tell Mike what to do with his wife.

"I thought, *Enough is enough, let it be over.* Mike fought the good fight. He can't say he didn't try. He took care of Terri for all these years, beyond belief, and tried to do everything he could to carry out her wishes. I didn't want him to have to walk away feeling like he let her down. He did what he could, but it was the little guy up against an entire army. And for the first time, we really argued over this."

I'd gone through this sort of thing with George over the years, telling him that I couldn't keep fighting. But I'd always changed my mind. This time, Jodi was telling me that for the sake of all of us, it was time to quit. And after hours of arguing, she'd convinced me.

I called George to tell him it was time to give it up, and we had a long talk. He reminded me that we had to realize that it wasn't just about Terri anymore. It was about all the rest of the people who didn't want the government telling us how we could die and when we were allowed to decide that we didn't want further medical treatment. And it was about who has the right to make decisions between a husband and wife. And whether we were going to let a vocal minority change the rules for everybody.

That was a big thing. We weren't the ones trying to tell people what decisions they had to make for themselves or their own family members.

By the time I got off the phone I actually felt empowered that I needed to do more, that I needed to do this not just for Terri but for all of us. I still wasn't looking to change anyone else's mind. I just didn't want them to be able to force me—or you—to change yours.

To say that Jodi wasn't thrilled with my decision is an understatement. To my shock, she packed a bag, put the kids in the car, and left.

"I had to do some real soul-searching," Jodi explained. "After a sleepless night, I realized that to walk away from Mike then would be like Mike walking away from Terri. And he knew what she wanted; he knew what they believed in; he knew what they'd spoken about and what his promises to her were. And throughout all the years and all the fighting and all the horrible things people said and accused him of, he kept on going and held his head high. I admired Mike for what he did, and for me to walk away at that point in time would make me so much less of a person than he was, if that makes sense. I knew that a part of him cared for me and what I was telling him, but at the moment it was only about Terri and what they promised each other, and as long as he was good with Terri and good with God, nothing else seemed to matter.

"That was really hard for me to deal with when all hell was breaking loose around us. But Terri was there first, and when I had time alone to think about it, I realized that just because our relationship had changed, and even with having kids together, as much as I feared for them, I couldn't change the rules. So I was only gone for one night. One long, miserable night. I went back the next morning. We never sat down to discuss the situation—there just wasn't time with everything that was going on."

The night Jodi left—I sat up crying all night long. I knew she'd be back; that wasn't it. I think it was the first time I realized that I hadn't been as successful as I thought at splitting myself into two people—Terri's Mike and Jodi's Mike. And I can't tell you how awful that made me feel.

There's one point that needs to be emphasized here—just in case the zealots read this and think, *We almost had him. We almost beat him. We almost saved Terri.* Wrong. The order to remove Terri's feeding tube was not from Mike Schiavo. It was from the Pinellas County Circuit

Court. The Schindlers are the ones who forced us to turn the matter of Terri Schiavo over to the court and allow a judge to decide her fate. Yes, it was a tactical decision when we did that, because we knew that the evidence, the facts, and the truth were on our side. Judge Greer set the date and time to remove Terri's feeding tube after ruling that it had been proved by clear and convincing evidence that this was what Terri would have wanted. I couldn't have "given back" Terri to her parents if I'd wanted to. And there was no way Judge Greer would have named them her guardians had I asked to be removed from the position. But I doubt that the Schindlers' supporters ever understood that. It was only two days later that someone using the signature "The Coming Conflict" posted this note at blogsforterri.com:

> If we kill Michael Schiavo, the parents will be her closest relatives. FL gun owners, it's in your hands.

19 | Peace at Last

On Thursday, March 17, 2005, the Republican majority leader of the United States Senate demonstrated that as a heart-transplant surgeon, he makes a lousy neurologist. Dr. Bill Frist had previously shown that politics trumps medical science by refusing to say whether he thought HIV could be transmitted through sweat or tears as is claimed in a federal education program lauded by conservative groups. This time, he ruled out Terri's diagnosis of persistent vegetative state based on watching the infamous edited videotape. Frist said he questioned the diagnosis "based on a review of the video footage which I spent an hour or so looking at last night in my office here in the Capitol. And that footage, to me, depicts something very different than persistent vegetative state."

Frist said he had "called one of the neurologists who did evaluate her and evaluated her more extensively than what at least was alleged other neurologists had, and he told me very directly that she is not in a persistent vegetative state." That neurologist is the one who provided Frist with the video. He also gave him "something like thirty-four affidavits from other doctors who said that she could be improved with rehabilitation." None of those "other doctors" had gotten closer to Terri than their television sets.

What neurologist would you guess Bill Frist consulted with?

Would you believe—Hammesfahr? The majority leader of the U.S. Senate, a man with presidential aspirations, chose the only neurologist to examine Terri who was *not* a member of the American Academy of Neurology. He chose the only neurologist who had falsely claimed to be a Nobel Prize nominee. He chose the only neurologist whose diagnosis was at odds with that of *every* other neurologist (seven) who examined Terri, studied her medical history, and reviewed the laboratory studies that confirmed the destruction of her cerebral cortex. He chose the only neurologist whose testimony in court was so suspect that the judge essentially dismissed it and him.

Frist was so anxious for politics to trump medical science that he led the Senate in approving a bill that would violate the constitutional principle of Federalism, and order a United States district court judge to take jurisdiction of a case that had been fully heard by the courts in Florida, and appealed twice to the Supreme Court of the United States. I figured things couldn't possibly get any more bizarre. I was wrong.

The next day, March 18, 2005, was the day Judge Greer set for the removal of Terri's feeding tube. It was also the day that the U.S. House of Representatives Committee on Government Reform subpoenaed Terri to appear before its members, an act for which the term "surreal" was invented.

The subpoena was a wink, wink, nod, nod, but on a much higher level than we'd previously experienced. I could picture a cabal of religious-right lawyers sitting around saying, "What can we possibly do to keep them from removing the tube—'cause we can't count on the goddam courts?" And then one of them jumps up and says, "I've got it. Congress can subpoena Terri!"

But the committee improved on the subterfuge. In addition to Terri, they issued a subpoena for me, for her two physicians, and for the director of the Woodside Hospice, to appear at a "field hearing," which would take place on March 25 at the hospice. They required that when Terri appeared—here's where their brilliance shines—she bring with her "all medical and other equipment that provides nutrition and hydration in its current and continuing state of operations." Wink, wink, nod, nod. Terri was expected to show up with her feeding tube in place and working. I thought it was a nice touch when the chairman of the committee, Rep. Tom Davis, sent Terri a "Dear Mrs. Schiavo" letter that concluded, "Thank you in advance for your participation in this important hearing. If you have any questions regarding this hearing, please contact the committee at (202) 225-5074."

Since Judge Greer's order required removal of the tube at 1 P.M. on March 18, the subpoena created a definite conflict. The committee attempted to deal with that problem by requesting formally that the judge delay the tube removal until March 29. Their motion said, "If the subpoena recipients comply with the Court's Order, they impede Congress's constitutional authority to obtain information and thus face criminal charges for obstruction of justice and contempt of Congress. If they comply with the congressional subpoena, they face contempt of court for violating this Court's February 25, 2005 Order."

When Debbie Bushnell heard about the subpoenas, she felt that we'd gone down the Alice in Wonderland rabbit hole again. She said, "It's very difficult to predict a situation like this, because everything that's happening is so outside the realm of possibility that it becomes a case where anything can happen. And once you go outside those boundaries of normal dealings and rationality, then people feel freer to do anything."

That said, both Judge Greer and the Florida Supreme Court acted rationally, and denied everything that the congressional committee asked for. Meantime, Debbie had been at the hospice, staying in touch with George by phone, waiting for the court to brush aside the congressional requests as well as an announced last-minute attempt by the Department of Children & Families to stop things.

One o'clock came and went, and the tube had not been removed. I was watching this at home on TV, and they were reporting that the chief judge had put in a stay until Judge Greer could be located to deal with the DCF. Once he'd been found, the hearing was held by telephone and Greer lifted the stay, saying, "The tube should be re-moved forthwith." And Debbie said that she'd repeated to Greer, "Judge, you said 'forthwith'?" And he responded in a demanding tone, "Forthwith!"

As soon as Debbie got off the phone she went down the hall and told the doctor, "Do it. Do it now before something happens."

I believe that the emotional toll on Debbie and George was proba-bly just as great as it had been on Jodi and me. Asked about it, Debbie said, "I think all of us would have to say that we were emotionally drained and in shock from the whole process. There was a feeling that things had ratcheted up just about as much as they possibly could. But we knew that every day she was alive, there were going to be legal proceedings and that it was going to get faster and harder. We did have some points at which we said, 'Well, surely this is all they can do.' In-evitably, when one of us said, 'Well, this just looks like the end,' every-one would say, 'Are you kidding? Of course they're going to come up with something else; we just don't know what it is.'"

The radicals who had taken control of the Schindlers were very good at exploiting TV news, and the news stations let them do it, maybe even encouraged them to do it. At 5, 6, and 11 P.M., the demon-strators would gather close together, they'd pick up their signs, and they'd begin chanting. And the cameras ate it up.

"To look at it from inside the hospice," Debbie said, "it was just disgusting. It was so blatantly political and so blatantly not about this young girl who was lying in the hospice bed." At the height of the demonstrations, the Pinellas Park police estimated there were more than six hundred protestors in front of the hospice, and more than a hundred news media representatives. The demonstrators ranged from clergy who came to offer prayers quietly and respectfully for Terri; to professional rabble-rousers who we have good reason to suspect were paid to show up and chant and shout on cue; to the entertaining Jug-gler for Christ; to a vanload of college students on spring break from Ohio State who drove all night long to show up, get arrested, and leave town on probation—not your typical spring break in Florida. Also among the fifty-five people arrested outside the hospice was the former Green Beret Bo Gritz, whose support of the Schindlers was puzzling given that at the top of his home page he cites John 8:32 ("And the TRUTH shall make you FREE").

Occasionally, there would be a handful of demonstrators who were supportive of me personally, but never more than that. Debbie believes we had a lot of people who sympathized with us, but, she says, "These are rational people who believe that everyone else is rational. They had a hard time fathoming what was happening and the craziness that we were actually dealing with. And when they got a taste of it, they didn't want any part of it. It's just too crazy. It's a tar baby. It will take over your life, it will make you miserable. And once you get into it, if you're a responsible person, you could never walk away."

I was still at home on the afternoon of the 18th when I got the call from Debbie at the hospice saying she'd just given the order to remove the tube. It may not make sense, but I felt like I'd just been sucker-punched in the gut. I put the phone down and just sat on the couch in our living room, staring. It's just not normal to get a phone call saying, in essence, "We've just started the process that will cause your wife to die in two weeks." I always knew that someday I was going to get that call, but knowing in advance and being prepared aren't the same. I think I also resented the fact that I wouldn't be allowed to deal with this process like the thousands of other families who, every year in America, go through the exact same decision-making procedure, and come to the exact same conclusion. I wouldn't be allowed to contemplate Terri's end privately. All the world may be a stage, but I wasn't interested in being one of the performers. It didn't appear, however, that the choice would be mine.

———

Because there was so much media around the house, I couldn't just jump in the car and leave for the hospice. There were at least a dozen cameras lined up on the sidewalk. Microwave antennas stuck up over the houses down the block. I didn't know what they were waiting for;

it was like they expected me to come out and give a speech. They stood there for hours, just waiting.

When I finally made the decision to go, I called the Clearwater police and they offered to have a van pick me up in front of the house. The problem was that I didn't want people to know that I'd left. Jodi made the suggestion that I could climb over the fence behind our house and cut through the neighbor's yard to the next street over.

There were a few problems with the plan: The fence is eight feet tall, I'm afraid of heights, and I had to do it at a spot where people in front of the house wouldn't be able to see me. So Jodi's brother, John, helped me get our big ladder out and lean it against the fence. We were trying to be very quiet, tiptoeing around, and all of us were laughing. It was a gallows humor moment. I'm thinking, *Jesus Christ, I can't even leave my house out the front door to go be with my wife.* Then I climbed to the top of the ladder, which is two feet higher than the fence. I'm six-foot-six, so my eyes seem about a mile and a half above the ground on the other side. I got up there and hesitated. "Holy shit, John. It's a long way down."

And he whispered, "Go! Go! Go! You gotta go!" I tried to see if I could climb down, but that wasn't going to work, so I had to jump. I landed on soft ground and I felt my right knee pop. I said, "John, I think I just broke my leg," and I could hear him laughing on the other side of the fence. Looking toward the street I could see the truck waiting for me, and I began hobbling toward it as fast as I could. As soon as I got in, he pulled out, and there were all these unmarked police cars lined up to escort us out of the area.

They'd radioed ahead to the hospice, and when we got there, I could see that security had been considerably beefed up. It wouldn't be till much later that I learned that the Pinellas Park police had snipers on the roof of the hospice and SWAT guys in camouflage hidden on the grounds of the place to stop the protesters who were intent on getting in to bring Terri food or water. (About a week later, my brother Brian took a walk through the wooded area on the grounds where memorial services are often held, and he swears that one of the bushes moved. Months later, when this was mentioned to Pinellas Park police captain Michael Haworth, the man in charge of security around the hospice, he laughed and said, "I'll have to talk to that guy.")

As soon as I got inside, the nurses wanted to take a look at the knee, but I said that I didn't care about that, I needed to go see Terri. I tried to say to Debbie and the nurses, "She looks so peaceful," but the tears were pouring from my eyes and I began to sob. I leaned over the bed and cradled Terri in my arms.

Finally, I got up and limped down the hall to the room they'd set aside for me until Terri died. The doctor came in, examined my knee, and suggested that I might want to go for a CT scan. I told her I'd be fine if she would give me something for the pain. A few minutes later she came back with some Motrin, and also set a little glass on the desk, saying, "That's for later." After everyone left, I looked at the glass a bit closer. She'd provided me the ingredients for a scotch-and-Motrin cocktail.

I'd called Brian and asked him if he could drive up to bring me some clothes and food. Brian said he'd call when he got to the place and I could meet him at the back door. I told him, "It's not like that, Brian. I can't go anywhere. I have an armed guard with me everywhere I go."

When he finally got to my room, Brian and his wife, Donna, had brought about ten or twelve grocery bags full of food, and of course, I only had a tiny refrigerator in this small room. The Schiavos are used to eating a lot—but my appetite was gone. Over the next couple of weeks I probably lost fifteen or twenty pounds.

In the middle of all this, the legal battle was still going on. As soon as the Florida Supreme Court had upheld Judge Greer's denial of the congressional committee motions, they appealed to the U.S. Supreme Court. Justice Anthony Kennedy could have taken it upon himself to make a decision, but he opted, instead, to refer the matter to the entire Court, which wasted no time in denying the committee's request for an injunction. Instead of having just one Supreme Court justice to rail against, Randall Terry, Tom DeLay, Bill Frist, Jeb Bush, and the zealots they encouraged could now add nine more names to their list of judges who needed to be brought to heel.

Committee on Government Reform
of the U.S. House of Representatives, Applicant
v.
Michael Schiavo, et al.
Lower Ct: Supreme Court of Florida

Date	Proceedings and Orders
Mar 18 2005	Application (04A811) for injunctive relief, submitted to Justice Kennedy.
Mar 18 2005	Application (04A811) referred to the Court by Justice Kennedy.
Mar 18 2005	Application (04A811) denied by the Court.

That night, I left the hospice grounds with police bodyguards and went to a hotel, where George and I appeared on CNN with Larry King. Our appearance was followed by Terri's sister and one of the Schindlers' attorneys. It was a waste of time, for both me and the viewers. In the world of twenty-four-hour news and talk, facts don't seem to matter, only opinions stated as fact do. In five years, the Schindlers had lost in every single court; they'd lost in the U.S. Supreme Court twice. And yet they continued making the same claims, denying that Terri had expressed her end-of-life wishes, denying that she was in a persistent vegetative state, denying that as her husband, I had the legal right to make decisions for her. They were wrong medically and wrong legally. That was incontrovertible fact. So they resorted to innuendo and insinuations.

Suzanne told King, "We have evidence that something may have happened pretty ugly the night that she collapsed." But Larry King didn't stop her in her tracks and ask her to produce the evidence. As a result, viewers could leave the program saying, "Oh, there's evidence Michael did something to Terri . . ."

Suzanne also told King, "We don't believe Terri is in the condition some doctors are saying she's in. We see Terri as a vibrant, fairly healthy [woman], except she's severely brain damaged." Did you ever look up what the word "vibrant" means? Its synonyms are "lively," "vivacious," "animated," "exciting," "pulsating," "energetic," and "effervescent." Could you honestly apply any one of those to the videotaped images of Terri that the Schindlers themselves had released?

There wasn't much to do at the hospice besides sit in either my room or Terri's and watch C-SPAN or other news channels. The level of ignorance displayed by elected officials was discouraging. House majority leader Tom DeLay used the Schiavo case to try and distract Americans from the fact that he was soon to be indicted for ethics violations. A few days earlier he'd said, "In my opinion, the sanctity of life overshadows the sanctity of marriage. I don't know what transpired between Terri and her husband, all I know is Terri is alive and this judge in Florida wants to pull her feeding tube and let her starve for two weeks. That is barbaric. And unless she had specifically written instructions in her hand and with her signature, I don't care what her husband says."

DeLay's intellectual approach reminds me of the guy who was asked about the difference between ignorance and apathy, and he answered, "I don't know and I don't care." But DeLay ran the House of Representatives, and even though it had already adjourned for the Easter recess, he called them back for a special session to rubber-stamp what could be called a federal version of Terri's Law, the Florida measure that had been ruled unconstitutional.

On the night of March 20, I watched in astonishment as elected members of the U.S. House of Representatives told lies, displayed ignorance, and generally made fools of themselves while debating the federal Terri's Law. These people ranged from religious zealots to political demagogues. Those who shouted the loudest revealed the greatest ignorance.

It was only the bill's opponents who pointed out that elected law-makers were not qualified to make a medical diagnosis or second-guess decisions made by Florida courts. "We're not doctors, we just play them on C-SPAN," quipped Rep. Barney Frank, a Democrat from Massachusetts.

Not too long before the 12:30 A.M. vote that approved the measure by a vote of 203–58 (many congressmen had already gone back to their districts for the Easter holiday, which explains why 174 members didn't vote), the speaker of the House, Dennis Hastert, proved him-self to be a really deep thinker when he said, "We have heard very moving accounts of people close to Terri that she is, indeed, very much alive." I was astounded listening to the debate that these people were talking as if they knew Terri. Hell, they were talking as if they'd known her for years. How could they know whether Terri would want to live this way? Even calling her "Terri" as though they were on first-name terms with this now-forty-one-year-old adult was offensive.

But watching the Congress for three hours was nothing compared to seeing our president break off his vacation at the ranch in Craw-ford, Texas, and return to Washington in order to be available to sign the bill once it had been approved by both houses of Congress. Here's a man who didn't think Hurricane Katrina was reason enough to skip a political trip to Arizona and California to go see for himself what was happening to our Gulf Coast until aides made him watch a DVD of the news coverage, but he spends a couple hundred thousand of our tax dollars to ride Air Force One back to Washington just to stage a bill-signing photo op in his pajamas at 1:11 A.M.

Sitting there in my room at the hospice I thought, *This is weird. My problems are being discussed by the president of the United States. Aren't there more important things that he needs to worry about? This man has no clue what fifteen years of court hearings and trials did. He's ignorant.*

New York Times multi-Pulitzer Prize–winning writer Thomas Friedman wrote, "Our president and Congress held a midnight ses-sion about the health care of one woman, Terri Schiavo, while ignor-ing the health crisis of 40 million uninsured." NBC White House correspondent David Gregory said Bush's surprise flight back to the White House was "being seen as either an attempt to defend innocent life or a crass act of political theater." Gregory said Bush's "aides deny a political motive on the president's part, saying as long as there is a dispute about Terri Schiavo's intent—whether she wants to live or die—every effort must be made to protect her." I need to take something for nausea every time I read that line.

The good news in all this is that the American public didn't fall for it. An ABC News poll showed 70 percent called it inappropriate for Congress to get involved in this way; 67 percent thought the elected officials were trying to keep Terri alive more for political advantage than out of concern for her or the principles involved.

A CBS News poll indicated that 82 percent of Americans believed neither Congress nor the president should be involved in the Schiavo case. Eighty-nine percent of Democrats felt that way compared to 72 percent of Republicans. Asked, "Why do you think Congress got involved?" 13 percent said "they cared about Terri Schiavo" while 74 percent said Congress was "trying to advance a political agenda."

And speaking of hypocrisy, in 1999 then-Texas governor Bush signed the Texas Futile Care Law. It created a legal mechanism to allow attending physicians and hospital ethics boards to pull the plug on patients, even if that act specifically contradicted patient or family wishes. If Terri had been in Texas, that law would have applied to her.

I made the same offer to the president that I'd made to his brother. The media quoted me as saying, "Come down, President Bush, come talk to me. Meet my wife. Talk to my wife and see if you get an answer. Ask her to lift her arm to shake your hand. She won't do it. She won't, because she can't." The president's response was identical to Jeb's. Confusing oneself with the facts can be so messy. Why bother?

The next night, the Pinellas Park police took me out of the hospice and over to George's office, where I was going to appear on *Nightline*. The police department's tactical plan was designed to make certain that the demonstrators outside never knew when—or how—I left, or when I returned. And to their credit and my everlasting thanks, they pulled it off beautifully.

George and Debbie were working with the ACLU attorneys to be ready for the inevitable motion that the Schindlers would file with federal district court judge James D. Whittemore of the Middle District of Florida. The new law essentially ordered the federal court to hear the case and ignore any claims that the Florida courts had already settled the matter. Within hours of the president signing the law, the Schindlers filed a motion claiming that Terri's constitutional rights were violated when the feeding tube was withdrawn, and asking that the court grant a temporary restraining order and a permanent injunction requiring Judge Greer to rescind his order to withhold food and water from Terri, and to refrain from issuing any further orders that would cause her death. And just for fun, they asked the judge to require us to pay their damages, costs, and attorneys' fees. The next day, Judge Whittemore issued a thirteen-page order that concluded:

This court appreciates the gravity of the consequences of denying injunctive relief. Even under these difficult and time strained circumstances, however, and notwithstanding Congress' expressed interest in the welfare of Theresa Schiavo, this court is constrained to apply the law to the issues before it. As Plaintiffs have not established a substantial likelihood of success on the merits, Plaintiffs' Motion for Temporary Restraining Order must be **DENIED**.

Of course the faithful of the religious right were ready to string Judge Whittemore up on the same gallows they wanted to hang Judge Greer—who, by the way, was now being protected around the clock by U.S. marshals because of increasing death threats. But if they had bothered to read the bill that Congress passed, they'd see that the chief sponsor of the measure, Senator Mel Martinez of Florida (the same one who was exposed for sending out a memo suggesting to Republicans that they could politically exploit the

Schiavo case for votes) screwed up when he allowed a change from "the Federal court *shall* issue a stay of State court proceedings pending determination of the Federal case" to "the Federal court *may*" stay the proceedings.

It was Michigan Democratic senator Carl Levin who proposed the change, got an assurance that the bill would not mandate a stay, and then magnanimously said, "In light of that assurance, I do not object to the unanimous consent agreement under which the bill will be considered by the Senate. I do not make the same assumption as the majority leader makes about what a Federal court will do. Because the discretion of the Federal court is left unrestricted in this bill, I will not exercise my right to block its consideration."

Within hours, the Schindlers appealed Judge Whittemore's decision to the Eleventh Circuit Court of Appeals in Atlanta, which heard the case, and the following day turned them down on a two-to-one vote. They immediately asked for a hearing by all twelve judges of the eleventh circuit, and they lost there as well.

The religious right went berserk; the Republicans in Washington were outraged. How dare these federal judges follow the law but not reach the conclusion they wanted them to reach? The radicals writing at blogforterri.com preached anarchy and murder (and poor spelling):

> If our laws permit Terri to be starved to death then we need to burn down EVERY courthouse in this country and start our justice system anew! This is a GRAVE injustice. Posted by: kate abbott at March 23, 2005 03:22 PM

> I agree. If Terri dies I believe we will see wide spread rioting and the courthouses may indeed be burned to the ground. Michael, his comman law whore, his to out of wedlock children, and all those in the legal profession responsable for Terri's death would probably be strung up by the people. Posted by: michael Barron at March 23, 2005 03:29 PM

At our home in Clearwater, the demonstrations intensified. Now, in addition to the Catholic brothers in the potato sacks, Randall Terry showed up. Jodi was well aware of his reputation for inciting protests that resulted in mass arrests, and she grew more concerned for our family's safety.

The Clearwater police made it clear to everyone in front of our house, demonstrators and media alike, that if they came onto our property, they could be arrested for trespassing. Most of the time they paid attention. Sometimes they didn't. Actually, the television camera crews often seemed to be the most obnoxious. There was one instance in which several of them decided to set up on our lawn. John went into the garage, flipped the sprinkler control to manual, and turned the water on full force.

Perhaps the scariest moment came when a foreign television reporter walked up to the front door with his cameraman and tried to open the door, as though he was just going to walk right in. The police quickly explained to him that our concept of "free press" didn't allow for that.

Some of the local TV people were the worst. They'd just ignore the NO TRESPASSING signs, and at ten or eleven o'clock at night, they'd walk up to the front door with the cameras on their shoulders and the lights on, and knock on the door as though they actually expected Jodi to open it up and invite them in. It was much easier for them to show some meaningless video than to actually take the airtime to explain to their audience why the courts consistently ruled in our favor.

On the same day that the entire Eleventh Circuit Court of Appeals denied the Schindlers' motion, Governor Jeb Bush sicced the DCF dogs on us once again. Bush reported that a neurologist associated with the famed Mayo Clinic claimed that Terri was not in a persistent vegetative state. DCF attorneys rushed breathlessly into Judge Greer's courtroom waving a seventeen-page motion to intervene. Their claim was that the hotline was ringing off the hook with reports that I'd abused Terri, and the last seven pages of the motion was Dr. William Cheshire's résumé.

His seven-page, single-spaced affidavit came to the conclusion that Terri might be in what's called a "minimally conscious state." He reached this conclusion by visiting—but not examining—Terri for ninety minutes, and by reviewing her medical records. He also reviewed affidavits that were provided by some of the long-distance diagnosticians like Chicago speech pathologist Sara Mele. And he watched the videotape of Dr. Hammesfahr's examination of Terri. You'll never guess what he saw fit to cite in his affidavit as evidence that Terri might be responsive. Remember the leg-raising parlor trick? Cheshire wrote, "In the taped examination by Dr. Hammesfahr from 2002 . . . she did appear to raise her right leg four times in succession each time she was asked to do so."

In an analysis of Cheshire's affidavit, Dr. Ronald Cranford, who *did* examine Terri and reviewed all her records and test results, wrote, "Cheshire completely ignores the flat EEG's and makes no mention of them whatsoever."

Cranford also said, Cheshire's "most glaring contradiction from a neurological standpoint is point # 7 in his affidavit, 'Although Terri did not demonstrate compelling evidence . . . of verbalization, conscious awareness, or volitional behavior [words of a good neurologist], yet the visitor had the distinct sense of the presence of a living human being who seems at some level to be aware of some things around her [words of a good theologian].' " Cheshire received his M.A. in bioethics from Trinity International University and is a member of the Ethics Commission of the Christian Medical Association. However, he prepared his affidavit as a neurologist, not a theologian, and it failed to impress Cranford, who wrote, "Unlike previous opinions from the doctors representing the Schindler family, this is by far the most professional, learned, comprehensive, impressive, detailed and credible *bogus neurological report* in the entire Schiavo matter."

The Mayo Clinic appeared to be equally unimpressed. On the same day Cheshire's affidavit was released, Mayo sent out a memo to the media that noted that the doctor had not conducted an examination of Terri. It went on:

> Mayo Clinic recognizes that the standard of care for the evaluation of a comatose patient includes a detailed review of the patient's history and previous evaluations as well as the performance of a comprehensive neurological examination. In some instances, electrophysiological and imaging studies may be used to establish a diagnosis.
>
> The views expressed by Dr. Cheshire in the case of Terri Schiavo do not represent the opinion of Mayo Clinic or its Departments of Neurology. The Mayo Clinic Departments of Neurology do not have opinions regarding the diagnosis of Terri Schiavo because they have not performed an evaluation as described above.
>
> Dr. Cheshire is not available for interviews.

Later that same afternoon, George received an excited call from the attorney for Morton Plant Hospital. The lawyer said that the hospital had been called by the Florida Department of Law Enforcement and told to be ready for them to bring Terri in, and to have people standing by to reinsert her feeding tube and begin treatment. The DCF was poised to snatch Terri out of the hospice. George immediately dropped everything and headed for the courthouse. He knew that the only person who could stop this nonsense was Judge Greer.

At the same time, I was in my hospice room with my brother Bill. We'd been watching for news from Tallahassee, where the Florida Legislature was taking up a new version of Terri's Law, one that had been rewritten in order to try to get past the constitutional objections that had sunk the previous version. The bill failed to pass in the state Senate by a vote of 18–21. This time, Senate president Jim King corrected his earlier mistake, and worked against the measure.

But that didn't turn out to be the day's big Schiavo news. The program we were watching was interrupted by a breaking story. It was Jeb Bush saying that he had a report from a neurologist—it was Cheshire—saying that Terri had been misdiagnosed. I could feel myself immediately getting agitated. I jumped up, my eyes got big and my jaws clenched. "What an asshole he is!" I couldn't shout because of where we were, but I probably spit the words through my teeth. I was talking to the television. "The guy never even examined Terri!"

And then Bush said that the FDLE is accompanying agents from the Department of Children & Families to take custody of Terri and remove her from the hospice. My temperature must have spiked ten degrees. It was like I could feel myself boil, I was so angry. The DCF couldn't keep track of the kids they were supposed to be protecting, and they were worried about Terri Schiavo. I knew that I had to find Debbie immediately. She and George had agreed that one of them would have to remain at the hospice at all times in case something bizarre happened. And it just had!

With Bill right behind me, I hobbled down the hall toward the social worker's office that Debbie had been using. I found Debbie already talking with the hospice administrator on duty, with police Captain Michael Haworth, and a couple of other people whom I had a feeling were higher up the governmental food chain. It turned out that the hospital had received the same call that the lawyer for the hospital had received.

"Do you know that FDLE is coming to grab Terri? What the hell is this? Do you know what's going on?" I said, not waiting for an answer between questions.

She said, "I'm just hearing it now." She was using her "I'm dealing with it, you can calm down" tone of voice. Sometimes it worked.

Debbie turned to Haworth and the others, and said, "Guys, the only thing that stands between FDLE and DCF coming in and yanking Terri out of here is you. What are you going to do?"

One of them responded, "We'll take care of it." I was too steamed to recall the details, but Debbie said he got on the phone to FDLE and said, "Unless you're bringing Judge Greer down here to tell us to turn her over to you, we're not turning her over." Apparently, the FDLE guy said he'd get back to him.

In the meantime, at the courthouse, George Felos had spoken to

Judge Greer, who immediately issued a restraining order prohibiting the Department of Children & Families from removing Terri from the hospice or otherwise reinserting her feeding tube. That happened late on Wednesday afternoon. An appeal by Bush's attorneys seemed inevitable, but it couldn't be filed until the following morning.

I was still pacing the hall, going back and forth between my room and the office. I'd watch the news reports—they were covering the action in the Legislature and the possibility of a real confrontation. I'd go back and interrupt Debbie, who was constantly on the phone, with my demands to know what was going on. It was a very long two hours. Finally, an FDLE official called and told the hospice administrator, "We're not coming." So, they backed off.

For a while, I'd been thinking, *My God, we're going to have a shoot-out* between the guys guarding me and Terri, and Jeb's personal police force. Fortunately, our governor blinked first and called off the raid to grab Terri, an act that would earn him the scorn and condemnation of the pro-life people he'd been courting with his save-Terri campaign. Remember that e-mail from the congressman to Raquel Rodriguez, Jeb's general counsel? The one that said he was looking into whether a Florida governor had ever defied a court order? I'd guess that Jeb didn't have enough courage to be the first.

He also didn't have attorneys smart enough to figure out how to get around Judge Greer's order. And there was a way. The next morning, the DCF lawyers filed an appeal of Judge Greer's order to the Second District Court of Appeals. Because of a technicality in Florida law, the filing of the appeal had the effect of automatically suspending Judge Greer's order—unless he, himself, vacated the suspension. As it turned out, it took three hours for Greer to do so. In those three hours, the DCF could have grabbed Terri and there wouldn't have been anything we could have legally done to stop them.

With each court decision that went against the Schindlers, it seemed that the volume of hate mail increased and got uglier. We could never quite understand how people saying "every life is precious" could also say that we should be killed. At home, Jodi's brother would stay with her during the day, and my brothers Steve and Bill, who had flown down from Pennsylvania, would stay there at night. During the day, they'd be with Brian and me at the hospice.

I'd spent my time either in my room or Terri's, occasionally wandering the halls and talking to the families of other dying patients, all of whom were extremely supportive even though our presence there caused them massive inconvenience. It truly pained me that while their relative was dying, they had to run a gauntlet of security, first to even pull into the hospice parking lot, and then to show a photo ID and have it matched to a name on the list before they could enter the building. The security was so tight that a young woman who was trying to get to her grandfather's bedside before he passed away didn't make it in time. When I heard about it, I felt absolutely terrible.

All that access was controlled by the Pinellas Park police, who were also quite sensitive to the animosity between my friends and family and the Schindlers. I can only remember one instance in the final two weeks—and it was at the very end—in which I came within eyesight of any of the Schindler family. The police would come and tell me when one of them wanted to visit with Terri, and they'd escort me to my room before allowing them inside.

Every so often, a voice would come on the hospice intercom system and say, "Lockdown. Lockdown." Seconds later, an officer would show up to escort me to my room if I wasn't already there, and he or she would stay with me until the all-clear was sounded. I was told it meant that someone had penetrated the outer security perimeter and gotten onto the hospice grounds. Since there was no way of knowing whether the intention of the intruder was to shoot me or to deliver food and water to Terri, all these incidents were handled as though they were serious threats.

By March 24, seven days had passed since Terri's tube had been removed. We could see subtle changes in her appearance. Her face was drawn, but she was still very much at peace. As a nurse, I could see that the dying process had begun, especially by observing her breathing.

But as her husband, watching the process put me through a variety of emotions. I didn't want Terri to die. But I also didn't want her to be in the position she was in. I never doubted that I was doing what she wanted, but that didn't provide much comfort as I sat and held her or stroked her arm. She was still my wife. She was a part of me. Terri was the first person who made me realize what love was all about.

———

On March 25, federal authorities announced the arrest of a man who had offered $250,000 to anyone who would kill me, and $50,000 for the murder of Judge Greer. The e-mail sent out by Richard Alan Meywes of Fairview, North Carolina, referred to the recent killing of a judge in Atlanta, and the family members of a federal judge in Chicago, and it suggested that I should be tortured before I die.

Local police arrested a man who drove to Florida from Illinois, visited the hospice, and then went to a gun store with a box cutter in order to steal a gun so he could "take some action and rescue Terri Schiavo." The man got away from the gun-toting gun store owner— go figure—but only after breaking the glass in several display cases. Police charged him with attempted armed robbery, aggravated assault, and criminal mischief. Over the next few days, the crowd of demonstrators outside the hospice seemed to grow larger as Easter approached. Bobby Schindler made a point of suggesting that the protestors were appreciated, but that they should consider spending the holy day at home with their own families.

After attending Easter Sunday church services, Governor Jeb Bush proved to both sides in this dispute that his mouth was bigger than his cojones. "I cannot violate a court order. I don't have powers from the United States Constitution—or for that matter from the Florida Constitution—that would allow me to intervene after a decision has been made." Perhaps it's appropriate to note here that among the fifty-five people arrested outside the hospice, there were a couple of kids, one ten, the other twelve, who said that they wanted to make a statement for Terri. I guess when you're thinking about running for president, like Jeb was, you have to rein in any inclination to take a principled action for which you might later pay a price.

Jeb said, "I'm sad that she's in the situation that she's in. I feel bad for her family. My heart goes out to the Schindlers and, for that matter, to Michael." To Terri's parents, who, along with Randall Terry and other pro-life zealots, had said Bush should do more to help their daughter, the governor said, "I can't. I'd love to, but I can't."

It was on the Monday after Easter that the Reverend Jesse Jackson showed up, drawn to Pinellas Park by the lure of the television cameras and, if we're to take him at his word, an invitation from Mary Schindler to come pray with them. Jackson arrived in a white stretch limousine and sent his advance man to tell the police guarding the hospice that Reverend Jackson wanted to pull up to the front door and go inside to pray with Terri and me. The police politely suggested that the limo be parked a block or two away where the ordinary folks parked, and that Reverend Jackson could walk in just like everyone else.

Brian and I had heard that a new act had joined the circus outside the hospice, so we went across the hall to the hospice library, which had a window that overlooked all the action. You would have thought that the president or the pope had arrived. TV camera people were falling all over themselves, walking backward in front of Jackson as he strode toward the hospice. It was the silliest thing we'd seen in a long time—if you don't count the Juggler for Christ—but it was about to get even sillier.

A few minutes later, one of the off-duty Pinellas Park policemen hired by the hospice to keep order inside the building came down to find me. He said, "Mr. Jackson would like to talk with you."

I said, "I have nothing to say to Mr. Jackson."

And the officer, just doing his duty, said, "Well, he'd like to come in and pray with you."

I said, "I'm fine. I'm praying, and I'm good."

The officer made the next request with a look on his face as though he was certain what the answer would be. "Reverend Jackson would like your permission to come in and pray with Terri."

A few days earlier, Terri had received Holy Communion from the hospice chaplain and from Monsignor Malinowski, who immediately went outside and talked about how he'd put wine on Terri's tongue but was unable to give her a communion wafer because her tongue and throat were so parched. I knew that Terri was right with her God, and politely told the officer that Reverend Jackson's request was denied.

Not long afterward, Brian and I looked out the window and saw the Schindlers with Jackson, performing for the cameras. Talk about a tension reliever. The two of us broke into laughter at the sight of Bob Schindler, Sr., being comforted and supported by one of the best known black men in the world.

As we watched the Schindlers' performance, it was Brian who observed that it was almost as though the Stockholm Syndrome had set in between them and the media—only he wasn't sure who were the hostages and who were the hostage takers. It probably switched back and forth. But there was clearly a bond that had formed between those two groups: The cameras needed the Schindlers and the Schindlers needed the cameras. After one of these little lovefests one day, a couple dozen of the hard-core demonstrators began wrestling to get their signs in front of the cameras. One of the policemen outside the hospice said to some media types, "If you guys just left, most of them would go away." He was stating a version of the Heisenberg Uncertainty Principle—observing an act changes it. Our view through the hospice window absolutely confirmed it.

One group of people who unexpectedly suffered the consequences of having a circus outside the hospice were the families of the children who attended Cross Bayou Elementary School just down the block. Fortunately, the week the tube was removed, the kids were on spring break. But after vacation ended, officials made arrangements to move the youngsters to classes in four different area schools. They didn't want them to have to confront demonstrators and media twice a day. I felt bad that they were being inconvenienced, but given what we could see out of the hospice window, it was a good decision.

The next day, Terri's last full day on earth, saw the United States Supreme Court once again refuse to review the latest decisions of Florida courts that had continued to deny the Schindlers' motions. Among those motions, now, was a demand that I not cremate Terri's body, which I'd planned to do. And they were also insisting that an autopsy be performed. I'd gone back and forth on that one, but came to the conclusion that it had to be done, and George already had made contact with the medical examiner's office. What neither I nor the Schindlers knew at the time was that the decision on whether or not he would conduct an autopsy was his, not ours.

Walking into Terri's room on March 30, I could immediately see that the end was relatively close. She wasn't in any distress and still looked peaceful. The nurse in me quickly assessed the physical changes that had taken place—she'd breathe very fast, and then break out of it. She wasn't blinking regularly and her eyes were sunken. Her extremities—the ones that weren't locked—were more relaxed. There were mottled, purplish blotches on her legs and arms. Her skin wasn't shriveled, in fact, it was very smooth.

That's what Michael Schiavo, R.N., could see. But Michael Schiavo, the husband, was going through an emotional upheaval. It's difficult to put this into words that truly convey the awfulness of the situation. Alone. Sad. Empty. It creates a numbing pain deep inside. An aching feeling in my heart. I looked at Terri and knew that the end wasn't that far away. I realized we used to be a couple, and now we weren't going to be one anymore. Half of that was going away. If you've experienced a loss like this, you understand. If you haven't, you're fortunate, but someday you will, and then you'll know what I was feeling.

As a nurse and a respiratory therapist, I'd been with family members when they were experiencing what I was going through, so the emotions didn't surprise me, but that's of no consequence.

I feel compelled to say something about the charge that we were starving Terri to death. The short response is, it wasn't happening. While she wasn't receiving nourishment, she was not being starved to death. That was the catchphrase that was being used on the street, in Congress, and on right-wing radio and television. It's an emotional appeal, and it's also inaccurate. Anyone who's had a relative die of cancer knows the truth. Often, perhaps three weeks before death, the patient voluntarily stops eating. That doesn't mean they die of malnutrition. It's part of the natural process. If you're interested in understanding the process in all its variations, take the time to read *How We Die: Reflections on Life's Final Chapter*, a wonderful book by Dr. Sherwin B. Nuland.

Late in the afternoon of March 30, both Debbie and George arrived at the hospice together. They'd brought with them a beautiful flower arrangement that someone in California had been thoughtful enough to send. They were reasonably certain that the legal proceedings were over based on an assurance from Schindler attorney David Gibbs that he wouldn't be filing anything else. Terri's father and her brother and sister were in and out for a few minutes at a time on the final day. Bobby and Suzanne would spend a few minutes, and then go outside and tell the crowd that their sister was in agony, gasping, and dying a horrific death, a theme they would repeat ad nauseum in the months to come on the pro-life lecture circuit. Mary Schindler stayed home, telling the media she was unable to visit Terri as she died. George felt that he and Debbie should stay the night because it was apparent that Terri could go at any time.

Even with Gibbs' assurance, Debbie couldn't relax. She said, "We were always looking over our shoulder for something that was going to blindside us."

At one point I wondered where the Schindler family was; it just seemed strange that they hadn't been around, hadn't asked to see Terri. I was told that Mr. and Mrs. Schindler were in their condo. They'd left a couple of phone numbers and told the hospice to call them if anything happened.

That evening, the hospice ordered pizza and salad for us and the police, and for several hours, Brian, Debbie, George, and I camped in the room with Terri, whose breathing was becoming more labored.

The lights had been turned down low. We were playing some Celine Dion, and then some soft background music. The air smelled of lavender with a hint of lilies from the bouquet. A couple of candles were burning. It was nice, no one bothered us. I sat in the chair and held Terri's hand most of the night. George and Brian pulled some chairs together and kind of put their feet up, and we waited. Debbie was exhausted. She finally put a blanket and pillow on the floor of Terri's room and slept for several hours.

Brian and I told stories about things that happened when I first met Terri. The episode at the dry cleaners, her first Schiavo family birthday party that looked like it was getting out of hand. We remembered her laughter, and the joy it was to be around her.

Every time Terri's breathing would change, we'd all get up and gather around her. Around seven in the morning, one of the police officers knocked on the door, and said that Bobby and Suzanne had shown up with Father Pavone, and wanted to see Terri. Pavone was the founder of Priests for Life who had accused me of murdering Terri.

Nevertheless, we left Terri's room so they could visit. Brian, George, and I went down to my room, taking the opportunity to stretch a bit and grab a cup of coffee. Debbie stopped in the office to take care of some business.

At 8:45, the staff went in to do an assessment of Terri. They asked Bobby, Suzanne, and Pavone to step out. Terri's sister and the priest left, but Bobby decided that this was the time to pick a fight. "No, I'm going to stay here. My sister's dying." And they said, "No, you have to leave." The policeman on duty outside the room did his best to get Bobby to leave quietly, but he continued arguing so the officer walked him down the hall to the hospice lobby.

Moments later, Becky McDermott, the hospice vice president, came into my room and said, "Mike, if you want to be with Terri, you need to go there now, right now." Brian, Debbie, and I jumped up and ran to her room. Actually, I hobbled. I'd taken off the large brace they'd given me for my knee, and hobbling was the best that I could do. As we were walking, Becky said, "I want you to know that Bobby's down there, and he just got into an altercation with the police officer because he wanted to stay. He's out there arguing with him now."

Then George asked me, "Do you want Bobby in the room or not?"

I thought for a second. *He's out there arguing with a police officer, and they're telling me to come see my wife, who is dying, right now.* My answer was, "No, he can deal with his argument out there. I'm not going to be in the middle of that and have it brought into Terri's room." Going through the lobby a few seconds later, I saw Bobby, still having a loud argument with a couple of people. It was the only time I can recall seeing one of the Schindlers inside the hospice—that's how good a job the Pinellas Park police did at keeping us separated.

When we got to the room, I could see that the end was very close. Terri was gasping for breath, with long periods between breaths. This cycle happened several times, and then—no more than thirty seconds after we got there—it stopped. It was 9:05 A.M. I was kneeling next to the bed, cradling Terri, and I remember Brian behind me, with his arm on my shoulder. Tears were streaming down my face and I was sobbing as I tried to tell Terri that it was okay now, it was finally over. I remember saying, "You can be at peace now. I love you."

I looked up and saw Debbie standing near the door with four of the nurses who had cared for Terri the longest. All the nurses were crying, which is unusual for hospice nurses. I said, "Debbie, this is it, this is the end. I'm so sad. I didn't know how I would feel, but I didn't think I would feel this way."

Asked to recall the moment, Debbie said, "It was just the most touching look on his face. If there was ever any doubt that Michael loved his wife, anybody who saw that look—their doubts would have vanished. It was definitely a bittersweet moment. This is something that all of us knew Terri wanted, we all had worked hard for, and we all believed in. And when it happened, it was a sadness, but a relief and also a joy for her."

The hospice workers who had been wonderful to us throughout the five years Terri had been at Woodside were especially wonderful that morning. Debbie remembered one man in particular, a big, burly guy. "I was just kind of standing by the door and he came over to me and put his arm on my shoulder and said, 'Is there anything that I can do for you?' and I said, 'No,' and then just burst out crying. And he grabbed me and gave me a big hug, and I said, 'Well, I guess there is.'"

One by one, everyone left the room until only Brian and I were there with Terri. The door was closed, and it was very quiet except for the music in the background. I took a rose from the vase on the dresser and put it in Terri's hands, and we stayed there for a while.

About twenty minutes after we left the room, the Schindler family arrived to say their good-byes. They stayed for ten minutes, and then the hospice workers went in to bathe Terri.

I was touched that nearly all the hospice people who'd been on duty throughout the night, the nurses and the nursing assistants, had stayed because they knew Terri's death was imminent. Those people were wonderful; they took incredible care of my wife under very difficult circumstances, and there's no way I could find words adequate enough to thank them all.

Once Terri was bathed, Brian and I went back in the room with her. She was at peace. There was a calmness I hadn't seen in fifteen years. I knelt down, gave her a final kiss, and whispered that I loved her, and we'd see each other again. And then we left and went back down to my room.

George had gone outside to make the official announcement that Terri had died, and he'd come back in and told me that there was still a sizable crowd outside. Because there were still security concerns—there'd been a story making the rounds that crazies were going to try to steal Terri's body—special plans had been made by the police and medical examiner. Outside the exit door at the far end of the hospice, near the room that George, Debbie, Brian, and I were in, two identical white vans were parked. One would take Terri's body; the other was a decoy. Both would leave the hospice with police escorts.

Hospice has a tradition of escorting a deceased patient out of the building with their head uncovered. They believe it's one way of saying that death is a normal part of life, that it's not to be hidden away, as though there's something unnatural about it. I didn't see what happened with Terri, but George told me about it. He said about forty hospice workers gathered in the hall outside Terri's room, held hands, and prayed. The chaplain said a few words, and then they all walked her down the long corridor out to the waiting van. Every last one of them.

I was in no rush to leave the hospice. I just wanted to sit quietly, wait until most of the people outside had packed up and gone home, and then go see Jodi and the children. The police were still concerned about my security, and they weren't unhappy that I'd decided to take things slowly. Around two in the afternoon, Captain Haworth helped us get packed and told me the plan.

Brian was going to pull his SUV up to the same door they'd used for Terri. The police would help Brian put everything in the car, and then we would wait another forty-five minutes. When they said everything was clear, they escorted me out and I climbed into the back of the vehicle, they threw some blankets or stuff over me, and Brian drove out. We went to his home. A few hours later, Jodi and the kids arrived. I began crying, walked out, and gave her a huge hug right in the middle of the street. I just threw my arms around her and held on.

That day, I felt like I was in another world. I was exhausted. My cell phone never stopped ringing. I know that the family members and friends who called meant well; they each had been supportive of me through this entire fifteen-year ordeal. But I found that I didn't have it in me to talk with them, to relive the events of the past days—or years. Each new conversation caused my emotions to well up and overflow. Sometimes, I think, it's important to be alone with your sorrow—at least for a while. I missed Terri so much, yet as strange as it seems to say it now, I was happy for her. She was finally free.

———

On April 12, we returned to the hospice for a memorial gathering in the same wooded area where Brian had seen a bush move. We'd invited about a hundred people: family, friends, coworkers who sat with Terri, hospice workers, the police officers who'd been with me through the final weeks of the ordeal. It was a beautiful spring day, with a gentle breeze blowing.

I thanked everyone for what they'd done for me and for Terri, and I presented a sculpture of an angel to Becky McDermott, saying "You are our angels, and I want you to know that." A handful of people spoke—one of Terri's nursing aides, the hospice chaplain, two priests, George, and Brian.

While my brother was talking—or rather crying his way through his remarks—a gust of wind came and blew down the framed photo of Terri on the table behind him. Brian laughed, and said, "There she is, right behind me, as usual." He continued his remarks, and things got very sad. All of a sudden, this beautiful monarch butterfly, orange, gold, and black, flew in and hovered over Terri's photo. We all thought the same thing. *It's Terri.* And the butterfly flew off. I released a white dove, and we played Celine Dion's song "Fly."

Before Terri died, the Schindlers had filed motions with the court demanding that Terri not be cremated, as I'd planned to do, and that she not be buried in the Schiavo family plot near Philadelphia. The court rejected the motions. I'd planned to bury Terri near the graves of my mom and dad, which seemed quite appropriate. However, when word of that plan got out, the media went nuts. There were TV news helicopters hovering over the cemetery, and a week later *People* magazine ran a photo of my parents' gravesite. It made me ill.

As a result, I changed plans and made arrangements to bury Terri's ashes in Sylvan Abbey Memorial Park in Clearwater. The cemetery owners showed me a peaceful gravesite overlooking a small pond. It was beautifully landscaped, and I knew it was perfect. When I ordered the grave marker, I also ordered a polished stone bench inscribed SCHIAVO.

The bronze plaque on the granite gravestone reads:

SCHIAVO
THERESA MARIE

BELOVED WIFE
BORN DECEMBER 3, 1963
DEPARTED THIS EARTH
FEBRUARY 25, 1990
AT PEACE MARCH 31, 2005
I KEPT MY PROMISE

Although I didn't realize it when I ordered the inscription, the marker at the grave of Nancy Cruzan, whose parents fought the

Missouri Department of Health all the way to the United States Supreme Court for the right to remove her from life support, also lists three dates. Cruzan had been in a persistent vegetative state for nearly eight years when the high court ruled that she had a right to refuse medical treatment—a right to die. Her parents got the idea for the three dates—born, departed, at peace—from a political cartoon about the case.

As for the I KEPT MY PROMISE inscription on Terri's marker, it had been my mantra for the twelve years that I battled to keep my promise to Terri. I felt it was an appropriate expression of my love for her.

Not surprisingly, the Schindlers took exception to it, and at one point made public threats to sue me because of it. Bobby released a statement that said, "This clearly illustrates the spiteful lengths to which Michael Schiavo will go in order to purposely hurt those that loved Terri unconditionally—her family." To the very end, the Schindlers couldn't grasp that this was never about them.

On June 20, 2005, we buried Terri's ashes. Before the service began, I'd placed her wedding ring inside the urn, and I put several of the stuffed animals that had been with her for years in the grave. Father Tony conducted the service, which was held under a canopy during a torrential downpour accompanied by thunder and lightning. When the service ended, my friends and family went back to their cars and left me alone to sit with Terri and say my good-byes. I told her I'd never forget her, that she would always be a part of who I am. It was the first time we'd been alone together in years. And the last.

Epilogue

If there's one thing we've learned from The Schiavo Case—I say *we*, because now it's about Jodi and me—it's that it will never be over. I think the first time I realized that was when I heard the president of the United States speak Terri's name. Now, the world knows *Schiavo*. You can say just that one word to people, and if they had a pulse in 2005, they also have an opinion.

You know something? At this point, the opinions don't matter anymore. All that matters is whether people learned anything from *Schiavo*. Actually, let me set the bar a little higher. What matters is whether people learned anything that will make their life, or that of their loved ones, better. If the only legacy of *Schiavo* is bitterness that whichever side you're on didn't win, then Terri's loss is more tragic than I could have possibly imagined.

It's relatively easy to say that one lesson has to do with end-of-life directives, living wills, durable powers of attorney for health care—they go by many names, and each one means something a bit different. If you don't have one, and if everyone you know over the age of seventeen doesn't have one, you didn't learn much from *Schiavo*. Our ugliest battles were fought because Terri hadn't expressed her wishes in writing. Had she done so, odds are you wouldn't know her name.

Unfortunately, what the final years of the Schiavo war revealed was that there is a segment of our society that has decided that it doesn't matter what *your* wishes are, or your wife's, or husband's, or father's or mother's, or son's or daughter's. These are the zealots who believe that our country has got to be a Christian nation—but they don't concern themselves with being Christ-like. Can you imagine carrying a passport from The Christian Republic of the United States of America? It would be the equivalent of the Islamic Republic of Iran. Nonbelievers in the majority religion become second-class citizens.

These people are promoting legislation that would allow them, and people like them, to intervene in any case where a decision is being made to remove a patient from artificial life support. It won't matter what the next-of-kin wants; it won't even matter if the patient left written directives. These fanatics need to be stopped, and the only way to do that is by electing politicians who are not beholden to the extremists. There's a mid-term election this year; there'll be a presidential contest two years from now. I guarantee you that these enemies of real American freedom to worship and believe as you choose will be making every effort to keep the demagogues in office.

I've made just one speech since Terri died. The case had been out of the headlines for almost half a year, yet when I arrived at the hotel in Minneapolis, the radicals with their picket signs were out there, led by clergy who have a perverted view of the Bill of Rights. These are the people who will show up at the political rallies, who will write checks, and who will knock on doors to keep the demagogues in office. And the demagogues will do whatever is necessary to pander to them.

That includes Senate Majority Leader Bill Frist diagnosing illnesses on the floor of the Senate from doctored videotape, and Governor Jeb Bush, unhappy that the autopsy report proved that everything we'd been saying about Terri's damaged brain was absolutely correct, sending e-mails saying, "What about the hour gap between her collapse and the call to 911?" and then ordering the county prosecutor to investigate me for murder. If you learned anything from *Schiavo*, it's that you can't let them get away with it again. You have to match them rally for rally, dollar for dollar, and door for door.

I had never been involved in any political causes before my name became a household word. But now, that's changed, because I see the threat. Terri, Jodi, and I became their target, and there was no effective way for us to fight back. I've started a political action committee to try to prevent what happened in our case from ever occurring again. You can learn more about it at www.terripac.com.

Now, for something apolitical.

What happened to Terri on that early morning in February 1990, was God's will; I can't explain his reasons. But if God had a purpose for Terri's illness and death, perhaps it was to make more people aware of the types of eating disorders such as the one from which she suffered. Going the next step, perhaps that awareness could result in interventions that might save lives. I'm not going to try to change American civilization here, and rail against the bikini culture that pervades the country. But I see the example of a group of mothers who'd lost children to drunk drivers. They finally got that problem taken seriously. They built awareness. They managed to make the term "designated driver" meaningful. And they saved lives.

So I'm going to take a cue from MADD—Mothers Against Drunk Drivers—and try to keep other young girls from following Terri's tragic path. We asked the National Eating Disorders Association to provide us just a few paragraphs whose sole purpose is to save lives. Do us all a favor—don't skip them:

Eating disorders are serious illnesses that can have life-threatening consequences for an estimated 11 million females and males in the United States. If you or someone you care about is struggling with an eating disorder or disordered eating, it is important that you talk to someone about it. Tell a trusted friend, teacher, parent, coach, doctor, counselor, or nutritionist what you're going through. Ultimately, it will be important to seek the help of a professional, or team of professionals, with experience in working with eating disorders.

Referrals for eating disorders specialists across the nation can be found on the National Eating Disorders Association's (NEDA) Web site (www.NationalEatingDisorders.org) or by calling NEDA's Information and Referral Helpline at 1-800-931-2237.

While the exact treatment needs of each individual will vary according to the level of severity of the disorder and the individual's problems, needs, and strengths, treatment generally involves some form of counseling coupled with careful attention to medical and nutritional needs. NEDA provides detailed information on their Web site, including an eating disorders Survival Guide and information on how to help a friend or loved one, and "Questions to Ask" when evaluating treatment providers for your needs and understanding what to expect from treatment. Remember, recovery is possible and help is available.

My aunt, Carol Schiavo, will regret to her dying day the fact that she was certain Terri had an eating disorder, that she spoke with Terri about being too thin, and accepted her denial of any problem without doing more, without telling anyone else. But we don't blame Aunt Carol. That was almost twenty years ago; we weren't as aware back then as we should be now. So please visit the NEDA Web site and pay particular attention to the warning signs.

Throughout this book, we have shown on numerous occasions that the Schindlers, their attorneys, and their supporters played loose with the facts. But just before we went to press, we received a communication that makes us wonder whether some of them actually believed what they were saying, no matter how delusional, especially in light of the autopsy results.

In an effort to determine how the Terri Schindler-Schiavo Foundation was spending the money it had raised, attorney Jon Eisenberg contacted the Gibbs Law Firm, and attorney Barbara Weller. Gibbs had done much of the legal work for the foundation, which, under Florida law, was responsible for providing financial information to anyone who inquired. In a letter dated December 22 to Eisenberg, Weller wrote:

> It is somewhat comforting this year, in the midst of our sorrow and sadness at losing her, to remember what a good Christmas Terri had last year. When I visited with her she was sitting in her lounge chair, dressed in a holiday sweater. She attempted to sing Christmas carols with her family in her room, particularly when she could hear a group of carolers outside her door, however, she could only make vowel sounds so her words were never too precise. But she did try as best she could, and it was obvious that she enjoyed hearing the rest of the group sing the Christmas song.

Attorney Weller is the person who told the world that in her final days, in response to prompting, Terri said, *"Aaaaah wahhhh,"* which Weller interpreted as, "I want to live." Her letter to Eisenberg continued:

> [Terri] understood everything that was going on around her and tried to participate as much as possible, although some days were better than others . . . while in obvious discomfort, she was still trying to communicate with her friends and family.
>
> Interestingly, though, she apparently never attempted to communicate with Michael. I believe that she knew who the people were who were trying to help her.

Weller went on to say, "I do know that people like Ross Perot offered to pay for any rehab Terri would need if we were able to get her out of the clutches of Michael and the court."

Here's something Weller either doesn't know or isn't saying: Ross Perot's representative provided Terri's medical records—and paid a lot of money—to a well-respected neurologist to evaluate them in order to determine whether Terri could benefit from rehabilitative therapy.

The neurologist reported to Perot that, without question, Terri was in a persistent vegetative state. Perot appears not to have pursued the matter further.

So, maybe the question has to be asked: How many of the Schindlers' supporters are delusional true believers who will not let facts get in their way?

Now for something that's easier and much more pleasant to talk about. This book is dedicated to the two loves of my life, Terri, and Jodi Centonze, my companion through the trials—literally—of the past dozen years. Without Jodi, I'm not sure I would have outlived Terri. That's not hyperbole; just fact. I've been depressed since Terri's collapse, and medical science and therapy notwithstanding, I believe it is Jodi who has gotten me to this point.

She often endured the unspeakable to remain with me, and for that, there is no adequate way to express my gratitude. One of the questions I often get asked is, "Why did Jodi stay with you?" Since I don't speak for her, as you've no doubt figured out by now, I asked her. I think her answer boils down to two words—stubbornness, and love. In her own words:

"Why did I stay with Mike? When I look back sometimes, I think I was just stupid. We joke about that. But I loved him, and I don't think any of us could foresee how horrible it would really become. And for me to walk away from Mike because of what he was going through with Terri would have been what the Schindlers were hoping he would do to *her*. Leave just when things got rough. She deserved better, and so did Mike. And did I mention that I love him?"

And I love her. Which probably explains why, on January 21, 2006, Jodi and I were married by her priest in the Catholic church she's attended for years, in the presence of God, our families, friends, and our children, Olivia and Nicholas.

Acknowledgments

To my mother and father; there is not a day that goes by that I don't think of you or mention your names. Thank you for raising me to be a strong person, for teaching me love, respect, and to fight for what I believe in. Thank you for loving me every day of my life. I love you both and miss you so much, but I know that one day we will be together again. Take care of Terri, as I know you will.

My brothers and sisters: Bill, Joan, Steve, Scott, Karen, Brian, Donna, and Pam. Thank you all so much for being so supportive and speaking out. I am so proud to be a part of this family. Every day I thank God that I have all of you. I will never forget what you all did for Terri and me. She loved all of you very much. Never forget that I love all of you.

To Aunt Joan, Auntie Carol, Uncle Dick, Aunt Helen, Uncle John, Aunt Chickie, Uncle Frank, Uncle Mike, Aunt Roe, Mary Lou, Larry, BJ, Kelley, Tommy, Stephen, Lisa, Aleen, Scott, and Ryan, and to all my cousins and their wives. Thank you all for the support you gave me throughout the last fifteen years.

Mom Centonze, I miss your fiery attitude and our talks. You gave me so much support and helped Jodi and me through so much. Even though you are gone I will never forget you. Thank you, Ethel!!

Father Finnegan, Father John, Father Tony, Father Paul, Father Bob, Father Braun, thank you for all your support and guidance.

Debbie Bushnell, thank you for being my attorney, my sounding board, my therapist, and my friend. You have a style that I will never forget, especially when it came to dealing with me. You will always remain special in my heart.

George Felos, you stayed the course and did not let them bring you down. You believed in me, you believed in the process, you believed in the right to die with dignity and respect. I thank you, George, for those beliefs, and I will never forget you and what you have done for Terri and me. She would have been so proud of you. You and I will always have a special bond and we will always remain friends.

Dan Grieco, you started me off and kept me going throughout these many years. You pointed me in the right direction and have continued to be a big influence in my life. Your family, David, Angela, Mr. and Mrs. G., and of course your better half, Diane, will always be greatly appreciated for their friendship and support over the years.

Gary Fox and Glenn Woodworth, you were there at the beginning and remained supportive through the end, and I thank you both very much for your hard work and dedication.

Hamden Baskin III, you came into this case late in the game, but you came in with fire and fortitude. Thanks for coming to the hospice to visit and just to talk, when you could have been spending time with your family.

Cindy Gay, thank you for the assistance you provided to George and Debbie as they fought my legal battles, and for the support you gave me over the last eight years. You are truly an inspiration and a great friend.

The volunteer attorneys of the ACLU of Florida, especially Randall Marshall, the Washington office of Jenner & Block and lead attorney Tom Perrelli, and California attorney Jon Eisenberg, provided timely and invaluable assistance during the crazed final months of The Schiavo Case when the appeals process was moving at the speed of light and Supreme Court briefs were being written in hours, not weeks.

John and Gloria, there is not enough room to thank you both for all you've done. You truly went above and beyond. John—next time you're going over the fence.

Sergeant Steven Sears and the entire Clearwater Police Department, when I couldn't be there, you kept Jodi and the babies safe from people who threatened to do them harm. Words can't possibly express my gratitude.

Captain Michael Haworth and the entire Pinellas Park Police Department, thank you not only for keeping the peace at the Woodside Hospice, and for keeping us safe, but for the consideration you showed for the other families who were dealing with their own family members in the final stage of their dying process. And a special thanks to my PPPD bodyguard, Taichiang Ku, for his devotion to duty.

Sheriff Jim Coats and the men and women of the Pinellas County Sheriff's Office, thank you all for taking care of my family and for all of the support that you gave me by donating your vacation time so that I could take time off to be with Terri in her final months. And a special thanks to my colleagues on the sheriff's medical team for your incredible support during this difficult time.

Dr. Lofty Basta and Project Grace are dedicated to educating healthcare and legal professionals, spiritual leaders, and community groups about end-of-life issues and advance care planning. This work deserves everyone's support.

Dr. Alan and Lisa Shoopak, you've been my friends through good times and bad. If not for you, I'd never have met Jodi. How can I possibly thank you for that? And a special thanks for your love and kindness at the end. I could not ask for better friends.

Russ Hyden, we stuck together through it all and I will never forget our friendship and what that meant as we both dealt with losing our wives.

To the Queen and Kaylor families, Jodi and I are truly blessed to have such wonderful neighbors as you. How can we thank you for putting up with the craziness that went on in front of our homes?

To the Rowley family, and especially Jodi's best friend, Bonnie, thank you for all the chicken wings and M&M's. But mostly thank you for all your support and friendship.

To Bob and Michelle Connington, thanks for your years of support to me and my family. Michelle, thanks for twisting in the ER—Michaelsaurus.

Wilma Mackay, thank you for sitting in the courtroom all of those long days. It was a great comfort to know that you were there for me.

Thanks to three women whose friendship and support meant so much to Jodi during the roughest times, Katie Duchesneau, Kathy Messenger, and Pam Matthews.

A special thank-you to the one media person I could always count on for support, and a fair shot at telling my story, Todd "MJ" Schnitt.

To the entire staff at Woodside Hospice, thank you so much for your support and love over the many years. I could not begin to tell you what each and every one of you meant to me. You are all angels, and there is a very special place for all of you in heaven. I love you all.

To all of the doctors who cared for Terri so skillfully and compassionately over the years, I thank you from the bottom of my heart. The road was long and difficult, and I am especially grateful for your patience with me, especially in the early years.

God bless all of you.

———

This book could not have been written without the invaluable support, both personal and professional, of many people:

Attorney Jon Eisenberg, the author of *Using Terri*, generously shared his insights into the legal technicalities of the case, and read early drafts of the manuscript.

Kathy Kirkland's assistance in the research and writing of *Terri*, and her suggestions as we wrote the manuscript, were invaluable.

The most useful online reference source for *Schiavo*-related legal milestones is the time line maintained on the University of Miami Web site by Kenneth Goodman of the university's Ethics Program, and by Kathy Cerminara, of Nova Southeastern University's Shepard Broad Law Center. Without it, we would never have made our deadline.

Dr. Ronald Cranford provided us with a short course in neurology and brain damage. His help while lecturing half a world away in New Zealand and Australia, and his analysis of the official autopsy report, went above and beyond the call.

Attorney Debbie Bushnell stated from the start that she had no desire to relive The Schiavo Case—and then did just that when we had crucial questions about the way things actually happened. She's the one who said, "*Schiavo* is a tar baby. It won't let you go." She was right.

Anita Kumar of the *St. Petersburg Times* and Dara Kam of the *Palm Beach Post* both covered aspects of the case, and both were extremely generous in sharing their time and insights. We thank Ron Kolwak of the *Tampa Tribune* for taking the time to help us find precisely the right news photos for the book.

Clinical psychologist Elizabeth Heron, Ph.D., gave us what all good psychologists help their patients find—insight. Given the intensity and pressure of the writing process, we might need more than that from her.

Attorneys Richard Aronson, Richard Greenwald, and Ira Furman provided additional explanations of legal procedures and terminology, and with any luck, they won't find any places where we misinterpreted what they had to tell us. Missy Becker and Jennifer Weisberger both read the manuscript and made useful suggestions.

Literary agent Matt Bialer, and his assistant, Anna Bierhaus, of Sanford J. Greenburger, Associates, are two of the best hand-holders an author under the gun can ask for. There'll be no more panicked e-mails—until the next time.

Thank you to attorney Steven Beer for his guidance through the world of New York publishing.

Susan Schwartz, Joseph Mills, and Bob Wojciechowski at Dutton all did a terrific job in putting the book together.

Scott Biel is responsible for the superb cover, and Carla Bolte did an outstanding job designing the book and the remarkably great-looking photo insert.

———

A special thank-you goes to Dutton publisher Brian Tart, who saw the value in this book from the beginning, and who has worked tirelessly to make it a success. His assistant editor, Neil Gordon, is blessed with a very calming and confident persona that was a terrific asset when we were all working under extreme deadline pressure. Neil did a great job staying on top of everything that was needed to make the photo insert the best one we've ever seen in a nonfiction book. And if you've read this far, and you're not related to either of the coauthors, it's probably because of the remarkable work done by Lisa Johnson, Dutton's head of marketing and publicity.

On a very personal note, my coauthor, Michael Hirsh, would like to thank his wife, Karen, their children, Jennifer and Joel Weisberger, and Debbie and Bill Hirsh, and *their* children, Ella, Jack, and Matthew, for putting up with his preoccupation with all things *Schiavo* for several months. He loves you all very much and promises to make it up to you.

Appendix 1
Judge Greer's 2000 Order

IN THE CIRCUIT COURT FOR PINELLAS COUNTY,
FLORIDA, PROBATE DIVISION
File No. 90-2908GD-003

IN RE: THE GUARDIANSHIP OF
THERESA MARIE SCHIAVO,
Incapacitated.

_____

ORDER

THIS CAUSE came on to be heard upon the Petition for
Authorization to Discontinue Artificial Life Support, and Suggestion for
Appointment of Guardian Ad Litem. The case was tried before the court
sitting without jury during the week of January 24, 2000. Before the court
were Michael Schiavo, Guardian of the Person of Theresa Marie Schiavo,
(sometimes referred to as "Petitioner"); George J. Felos, Esquire, and
Constance Felos, Esquire, attorneys for Petitioner; Robert Schindler and
Mary Schindler, the parents of Theresa Marie Schiavo, (sometimes referred
to as "Respondants"); and Pamela A.M. Campbell, Esquire, attorney for
Respondants. The court took testimony from eighteen witnesses, including
the parties, the brother and sister of Theresa Marie Schiavo, (sometimes
referred to as "Terri Schiavo"); the brother and sister-in-law of Petitioner,
and the treating physician for Terri Schiavo. The court also received into
evidence certain exhibits, including CAT scans of Terri Schiavo and, for
comparison purposes, Dr. James Barnhill. The court has carefully reviewed
its notes, the transcribed testimony of those non-parties who testified to
conversations with Terri Schiavo regarding end of life declarations, the
report of the Guardian Ad Litem, the video tape (Respondents' Exhibit
No.1) and the other exhibits introduced as evidence. The court has also
reviewed the case law submitted by and argued on behalf of the parties.
Based upon the foregoing, the court makes the following findings of fact and
conclusions of law.

Terri Schiavo was reared in a normal, Roman Catholic nuclear family
consisting of her parents and her brother and sister. She spent the majority
of her life in New Jersey and moved to Pinellas County, Florida in 1986 with

EXHIBIT 1
PAGE 1 OF 10

1

her husband, Michael Schiavo, whom she married on November 10, 1984. They had dated for a total of two years, being engaged for year prior to their marriage.

Shortly after the move to Pinellas County by Mr. and Mrs. Schiavo, her parents and sister followed. The families on and off lived together, on and off shared expenses and generally functioned well together. Mr. Schiavo had a series of jobs including manager of a McDonald's restaurant. Terri Schiavo, after a brief period immediately following the move, resumed her employment with Prudential Insurance Company.

On February 25, 1990, in the early morning hours, Terri Schiavo suffered cardiac arrest, apparently due to an imbalance of potassium in her system. Michael Schiavo awakened when he heard a thump, found her lying in the hallway and called 911. He then called her brother who was living in the same apartment complex and her mother. The paramedics came, performed CPR and took her to a hospital. She has never regained consciousness and to this day remains in a comatose state at a nursing home in Largo. Terri Schiavo is currently being nourished and hydrated via a feeding tube and by this Petition her husband seeks authority to withdraw such life support.

In 1992, Michael Schiavo filed an action against the physicians who had been treating Terri Schiavo prior to her cardiac arrest. In late 1992, the case was resolved with a settlement and jury verdict, which resulted in Mr. Schiavo receiving $300,000 as regards his loss of consortium claim and the Guardianship of Theresa Marie Schiavo receiving net funds of $700,000 as regards her damages. Those monies were actually received in February of 1993.

During the period of time following the incident of February 25, 1990 the parties worked together in an attempt to provide the best care possible for Terri Schiavo. On February 14, 1993, this amicable relationship between the parties was severed. While the testimony differs on what may or may not have been promised to whom and by whom, it is clear to this court that such severance was predicated upon money and the fact that Mr. Schiavo was unwilling to equally divide his loss of consortium award with Mr. and Mrs. Schindler. The parties have literally not spoken since that date. Regrettably, money overshadows this entire case and creates potential of conflict of interest for both sides. The Guardian Ad Litem noted that Mr.

EXHIBIT 1
PAGE 2 OF 10 000569

Schiavo's conflict of interest was that if Terri Schiavo died while he is still her husband, he would inherit her estate. The record before this court discloses that should Mr. and Mrs. Schindler prevail, their stated hope is that Mr. Schiavo would divorce their daughter, get on with his life, they would be appointed guardians of Terri Schiavo and become her heirs at law. They have even encouraged him to "get on with his life". Therefore, neither side is exempt from finger pointing as to possible conflicts of interest in this case.

By all accounts, Mr. Schiavo has been was very motivated in pursuing the best medical care for his wife, even taking her to California for a month or so for experimental treatment. It is undisputed that he was very aggressive with nursing home personnel to make certain that she received the finest of care. In 1994, Mr. Schiavo attempted to refuse medical treatment for an infection being experienced by his wife. His unrefuted testimony was that his decision was based upon medical advice. Mr. and Mrs. Schindler filed an action to have him removed as Guardian based upon numerous allegations, including abuse. Mr. Schiavo relented and authorized the treatment after which a Guardian Ad Litem appointed by this court found that there was no basis to have him removed. Mr. and Mrs. Schindler ultimately dismissed their petition citing financial considerations as their motivation.

The court heard testimony as to various issues; most of which having little or nothing to do with the decision the court is called upon to make. The court also heard from witnesses who ran the gambit of credibility, from those clearly biased who slanted their testimony to those such as Father Murphy whom the court finds to have been completely candid. The court also has concerns about the reliability of testimony which differed from prior deposition testimony. Vague and almost self serving reasons were given for the changes including reflection, reviewed in another fashion, knowledge that this was a real issue, found a calendar, and so forth, to the extent that at trial recollections were sometimes significantly different and in one case were now "vivid". The court has had the opportunity to hear the witnesses, observe their demeanor, hear inflections, note pregnant pauses, and in all manners assess credibility above and beyond the spoken or typed word. Interestingly enough, there is little discrepancy in the testimony the court must rely upon in order to arrive at its decision in this case.

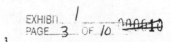

The Petition under consideration was filed on May 11, 1998 and on June 11, 1998 Richard L. Pearse, Jr., Esquire, was appointed Guardian Ad Litem. On December 30, 1998, Mr. Pearse filed his Report of Guardian Ad Litem, a copy of which is in evidence as Respondents' Exhibit No. 2. An issue was made as to the impartiality of the Guardian Ad Litem. Mr. Pearse readily agreed that he has feelings and viewpoints regarding the withdrawal of feeding and hydration tubes and that he did not so advise the court prior to his appointment. It was suggested that he should not have served as Guardian Ad Litem since he possesses feelings on the subject. The court is unable to agree with that assertion since most attorneys who practice in this area of law surely do have feelings one way or the other. For the court to preclude an attorney from serving as Guardian Ad Litem simply because of feelings would deprive the court of this valuable resource. The court finds that Mr. Pearse did a good job but unfortunately he did not have an opportunity to interview all of those persons who testified at trial. However, that is not his fault. Mr. Pearse did testify that his recommendation was a "close call" and that the outcome of his report may have been changed had he found certain of this other testimony heard by the court to be creditable and reliable. Consequently, the court is unable to rely upon his conclusions except for the fact that he felt Michael Schiavo alone, due to his potential conflict of interest, was not able to provide clear and convincing evidence to support the granting of his Petition.

It has been suggested that Michael Schiavo has not acted in good faith by waiting eight plus years to file the Petition which is under consideration. That assertion hardly seems worthy of comment other than to say that he should not be faulted for having done what those opposed to him want to be continued. It is also interesting to note that Mr. Schiavo continues to be the most regular visitor to his wife even though he is criticized for wanting to remove her life support. Dr. Gambone even noted that close attention to detail has resulted in her excellent physical condition and that Petitioner is very involved. Again, these are collateral issues which have little or nothing to do with the decision the court must render.

There are no written declarations by Terri Schiavo as to her intention with regard to this issue. Therefore, the court is left with oral declarations allegedly made to parties and non-parties as to her feelings on this subject. The testimony before this court reveals that she made comments or statements to five (5) persons, including her husband and her mother.

EXHIBIT 1
PAGE 4 OF 10

4

There was a lot of testimony concerning the Karen Ann Quinlin case in New Jersey. Mrs. Schindler testified that her daughter made comments during the television news reports of the father's attempts to have life support removed to the effect that they should just leave her (Karen Ann Quinlin) alone. Mrs. Schindler first testified that those comments were made when Terri was between 17-20 years of age but after being shown copies of newspaper accounts agreed that she was 11 perhaps 12 years of age at the time. A witness called by Respondents testified to similar conversations with Terri Schiavo but stated that they occurred during the summer of 1982. While that witness appeared believable at the offset, the court noted two quotes from the discussion between she and Terri Schiavo which raise serious questions about the time frame. Both quotes are in the present tense and upon cross-examination, the witness did not alter them. The first quote involved a bad joke and used the verb "is". The second quote involved the response from Terri Schiavo which used the word "are". The court is mystified as to how these present tense verbs would have been used some six years after the death of Karen Ann Quinlin. The court further notes that this witness had quite specific memory during trial but much less memory a few weeks earlier on deposition. At trial she mentioned seeing the television movie on Karen Ann Quinlin and had no hesitantly in testifying that this was a "replay" of that movie and she watched such replay at college in Pennsylvania. She also knew precisely what song appeared on a TV program on a Friday evening when Petitioner was away at McDonald's training school. While the court certainly does not conclude the the bad joke and comment did not occur, the court is drawn to the conclusion that this discussion most likely occurred in the same time frame as the similar comments to Mrs. Schindler. This could well have occurred during this time frame since this witness and Terri Schiavo, together with their families, spent portions of summer vacation together which would have included the mid-1970's.

Michael Schiavo testified as to a few discussions he had with his wife concerning life support. The Guardian Ad Litem felt that this testimony standing alone would not rise to clear and convincing evidence of her intent. The court is not required to rule on this issue since it does have the benefit of the testimony of his brother and sister-in-law. As with the witness called by the Respondents, the court had the testimony of the brother and sister-in-law transcribed so that the court would not be hamstrung by relying upon its notes. The court has reviewed the testimony of Scott Schiavo and Joan

Schiavo and finds nothing contained therein to be unreliable. The court notes that neither of these witnesses appeared to have shaded his or her testimony or even attempt to exclude unfavorable comments or points regarding those discussions. They were not impeached on cross-examination. Argument is made as to why they waited so long to step forward but their explanations are worthy of belief. The testimony of Ms. Beverly Tyler, Executive Director of Georgia Health Discoveries, clearly establishes that the expressions made by Terri Schiavo to these witnesses are those type of expressions made in those types of situations as would be expected by people in this country in that age group at that time. They (statements) reflect underlying values of independence, quality of life, not to be a burden and so forth. "Hooked to a machine" means they do not want life artificially extended when there is not hope of improvement.

Turning to the medical issues of the case, the court finds beyond all doubt that Theresa Marie Schiavo is in a persistent vegetative state or the same is defined by Florida Statues Section 765.101 (12) per the specific testimony of Dr. James Barnhill and corroborated by Dr. Vincent Gambone. The medical evidence before this court conclusively establishes that she has no hope of ever regaining consciousness and therefore capacity, and that without the feeding tube she will die in seven to fourteen days. The unrebutted medical testimony before this court is that such death would be painless. The film offered into evidence by Respondents does nothing to change these medical opinions which are supported by the CAT scans in evidence. Mrs. Schindler has testified as her perceptions regarding her daughter and the court is not unmindful that perceptions may become reality to the person having them. But the overwhelming credible evidence is that Terri Schiavo has been totally unresponsive since lapsing into the coma almost ten years ago, that her movements are reflexive and predicated on brain stem activity alone, that she suffers from severe structural brain damage and to a large extent her brain has been replaced by spinal fluid, that with the exception of one witness whom the court finds to be so biased as to lack credibility, her movements are occasional and totally consistent with the testimony of the expert medical witnesses. The testimony of Dr. Barnhill establishes that Terri Schiavo's reflex actions such as breathing and movement shows merely that her brain stem and spinal cord are intact.

Argument was presented regarding the woman in New Mexico who awakened from a coma a few months ago after sixteen years. Dr. Barnhill testified that he would have to believe that patient had a different kind of

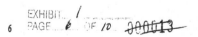

condition or else it was a miracle. Since he knew nothing more than what appeared in the newspaper, any medical explanation would be "speculative". The court certainly would have expected a more complete explanation from the stipulated expert but the unrebutted evidence remains that Terri Schiavo remains in a persistent vegetative state. Dr. Barnhill earlier drew the distinction between comas which are catatonic in nature (no brain damage) and those caused by structural brain damage as in this case. Again, the court cannot speculate on the New Mexico situation as neither party has offered evidence in that regard.

The controlling legal authority in this area is a case which arose in St. Petersburg. A little over nine years ago, the Florida Supreme Court rendered its opinion in a case in which the State of Florida was opposing the withdrawal of feeding tubes. In that case Estelle Browning had a living will and the issue was essentially whether or not an incapacitated person possessed the same right of privacy to withhold or withdraw life supporting medical treatment as did a competent person. In re: Guardianship of *Estelle M. Browning* 568 So.2nd 4 (Fla. 1990). The Florida Supreme Court began with the premise that everyone has a fundamental right to the sole control of his or her person. They cited in 1914 New York decision in holding that an integral component of this right of privacy is the "right to make choices pertaining to one's health, including the right to refuse unwanted medical treatment". The court also found that all life support measures would be similarly treated and found no significant legal distinction between artificial means of life support. Citing its earlier decision of *John F. Memorial Hospital, Inc. vs Bludworth*, 452 So.2nd 921 (Fla. 1984), the Court held that the constitutionally protected right to choose or reject medical treatment was not diminished by virtue of physical or mental incapacity or incompetence. Citing the lower court, the Florida Supreme Court agreed that it was "important for the surrogate decisionmaker to fully appreciate that he or she makes the decision which the patient would personally choose" and that in Florida "we have adopted a concept of 'substituted judgment' ", and "one does not exercise another's right of self-determination or fulfil that person's right of privacy by making a decision which the state, the family or public opinion would prefer".

The Florida Supreme Court set forth a three pronged test which the surrogate (in this case the Petitioner/Guardian) must pursue in exercising the patient's right of privacy, In re: *Guardianship of Estelle M. Browning*, supra. The surrogate must satisfy the following conditions:

" 1) The surrogate must be satisfied that the patient
executed any document knowingly, willingly and without
undue influence and that the evidence of the patient's oral
declaration is reliable;

2) The surrogate must be assured that the patient does not
have a reasonable probability of recovering competency so
that the right could be exercised directly by the patient;
and

3) The surrogate must take care to assure that any limitations
or conditions expressed either orally or in the written
declaration have been carefully considered and satisfied."

The Florida Supreme Court established the clear and convincing test as a
requirement and further held that when " the only evidence of intent is an
oral declaration, the accuracy and reliability of the declarant's oral
expression of intent may be challenged".

The court is called upon to apply the law as set forth in In re:
Guardianship of Estelle M. Browning, supra, to the facts of this case. This is
the issue before the court. All of the other collateral issues such as how
much was raised in the fund-raising activities, the quality of the marriage
between Michael and Terri Schiavo, who owes whom between Michael
Schiavo and Mr. and Mrs. Schindler, Mr. and Mrs. Schindler's access or
lack of access to medical information concerning their daughter, motives
regarding the estate of Terri Schiavo if deceased, and the beliefs of family
and friends concerning end of life decisions are truly not relevant to the issue
which the court must decide. That issue is set forth in the three pronged test
established by the Florida Supreme Court in the *Browning* decision, supra.
The court must decide whether or not there is clear and convincing evidence
that Theresa Marie Schiavo made reliable oral declarations which would
support what her surrogate (Petitioner/Guardian) now wishes to do. The
court has previously found that the second part of that test, i.e. the patient
does not have a reasonable probability of recovering competency, is without
doubt satisfied by the evidence.

EXHIBIT 1 000015
PAGE 8 OF 10
8

There are some comments or statement made by Terri Schiavo which the court does not feel are germane to this decision. The court does not feel that statements made by her at the age of 11 or 12 years truly reflect upon her intention regarding the situation at hand. Additionally, the court does not feel that her statements directed toward others and situations involving others would have the same weight as comments or statements regarding herself if personally placed in those same situations. Into the former category the court places statements regarding Karen Ann Quinlin and the infant child of the friend of Joan Schiavo. The court finds that those statements are more reflective of what Terri Schiavo would do in a similar situation for someone else.

The court does find that Terri Schiavo did make statements which are creditable and reliable with regard to her intention given the situation at hand. Initially, there is no question that Terri Schiavo does not pose a burden financially to anyone and this would appear to be a safe assumption for the foreseeable future. However, the court notes that the term "burden" is not restricted solely to dollars and cents since one can also be a burden to others emotionally and physically. Statements which Terri Schiavo made which do support the relief sought by her surrogate (Petitioner/Guardian) include statements to him prompted by her grandmother being in intensive care that if she was ever a burden she would not want to live like that. Additionally, statements made to Michael Schiavo which were prompted by something on television regarding people on life support that she would not want to life like that also reflect her intention in this particular situation. Also the statements she made in the presence of Scott Schiavo at the funeral luncheon for his grandmother that "if I ever go like that just let me go. Don't leave me there. I don't want to be kept alive on a machine." and to Joan Schiavo following a television movie in which a man following an accident was in a coma to the effect that she wanted it stated in her will that she would want the tubes and everything taken out if that ever happened to her are likewise reflective of this intent. The court specifically finds that these statements are Terri Schiavo's oral declarations concerning her intention as to what she would want done under the present circumstances and the testimony regarding such oral declarations is reliable, is creditable and rises to the level of clear and convincing evidence to this court.

Those statements above noted contain no limitations or conditions. However, as Ms. Tyler noted when she testified as to quality of life being the primary criteria in artificial life support matters, Americans want to "try

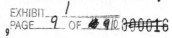

EXHIBIT 1
PAGE 9 OF 9 10 300016

it for awhile" but they do not wish to live on it with no hope of improvement. That implicit condition has long since been satisfied in this case. Therefore, based upon the above and foregoing findings of fact and conclusions of law, it is

ORDERED AND ADJUDGED that the Petition for Authorization to Discontinue Artificial Life Support of Michael Schiavo, Guardian of the Person of Theresa Marie Schiavo, an incapacitated person, be and the same is hereby **GRANTED** and Petitioner/Guardian is hereby authorized to proceed with the discontinuance of said artificial life support for Theresa Marie Schiavo.

DONE AND ORDERED in Chambers at Clearwater, Pinellas County, Florida at the hour of _11:50_ o'clock _a_ m this 11th day of February, AD, 2000.

George W. Greer
Circuit Judge

cc: Pamela A. M. Campbell, Esquire
    George J. Felos, Esquire

Appendix 2
Autopsy Excerpts

JON R. THOGMARTIN, M.D.
CHIEF MEDICAL EXAMINER
DISTRICT SIX
PASCO & PINELLAS COUNTIES
10900 Ulmerton Road
Largo, FL 33778
(727) 582-6800
www.co.pinellas.fl.us/forensics
(The complete report is available at this Web site)

Following are excerpts from the autopsy report released on June 13, 2005:

On March 31, 2005, the District Six Medical Examiner Office began the death investigation of Theresa Marie Schiavo (ME case# 5050439). The chain of events leading to this death investigation began 15 years ago in the early morning hours of February 25, 1990. The determination of her cause and manner of death would include an investigation of the events that occurred and review of available records produced subsequent to that date and time and, regarding some circumstances, extend to a review of events prior to that date.

Could Mrs. Schiavo eat by mouth?

The neuropathologic findings, oropharyngeal anatomic findings, and medical records clearly indicate that Mrs. Schiavo would not have been able to consume sustenance safely and/or in sufficient quantity by mouth. In fact, the records and findings are such that oral feedings in quantities sufficient to sustain life would have certainly resulted in aspiration. Swallowing evaluations and speech pathology evaluations repeatedly record that Mrs. Schiavo was at high risk for aspiration and not a candidate for oral nutrition/hydration. Although in her early rehabilitation, she received speech pathology services, she was later repeatedly evaluated and determined not to be a candidate for speech/dysphagia therapy. According to medical records, she had been treated in the past for aspiration pneumonia. Thus, Mrs. Schiavo was dependent on nutrition and hydration via her feeding tube. Claims from caregivers of past oral feedings are remarkable, and, based on the autopsy findings and medical records, these feedings were potentially harmful or, at least, extremely dangerous to Mrs. Schiavo's health and welfare.

What diagnoses can be made in regards to the brain of Mrs. Schiavo?

Mrs. Schiavo's brain showed marked global anoxic-ischemic encephalopathy resulting in massive cerebral atrophy. Her brain weight was approximately half of the expected weight. Of particular importance was the hypoxic damage and neuronal loss in her occipital lobes, which indicates cortical blindness. Her remaining brain regions also show severe hypoxic injury and neuronal atrophy/loss. No areas of recent or remote traumatic injury were found.

By what mechanism did Theresa Schiavo die?

Postmortem findings, including the state of the body and laboratory testing, show that she died of marked dehydration (a direct complication of the electrolyte disturbances brought about by the lack of hydration). The state of her fatty tissue and laboratory findings indicate that she did not starve to death.

What was the cause and manner of death?

Mrs. Schiavo suffered a severe anoxic brain injury. The cause of which cannot be determined with reasonable medical certainty. The manner of death will therefore be certified as undetermined.

What was the cause of Theresa Schiavo's collapse in 1990?
What caused her hypokalemia (low potassium)?

On February 25, 1990, according to available records, a 911 call was made at approximately 0540hrs. Both Mr. Schiavo and Bobby Schindler were present prior to arrival of emergency responders. They both describe her as lying prone and breathing or at least they describe her as "making gurgling noises." According to her medical records, paramedics began treating Mrs. Schiavo at 0552hrs. The Pinellas County EMS report records her as supine in the hallway with no respiration and her initial cardiac rhythm was ventricular fibrillation. She was intubated within the first 5 minutes. During her resuscitation, she received . . . seven defibrillations. Although a pulse was documented at 0632hrs, a measurable systolic blood pressure was not recorded until 0646hrs, almost one hour after resuscitation was begun. Her time of arrival at Humana Hospital-Northside was 0646hrs. At 0701hrs, her blood was drawn and that sample showed hypokalemia (2.0 mmol/L, normal 3.5–5.0) one hour after her initial collapse and after over 30 minutes of CPR . . . Mrs. Schiavo was in extremis for over 1 hour prior to her initial blood sampling.

If her initial serum potassium is to be regarded as reliable, then multiple etiologies are possible given her nutritional history. Bulimia Nervosa involving bingeing and purging would be high on the list of differential diagnoses. In a young woman concerned with weight loss, use of diuretics, laxatives, or other potassium depleting substances are reasonable possibilities, but no evidence of their use exists.

Her tea drinking habits may also have played a role. Reportedly, she was a habitual consumer of large quantities of tea and may have consumed as much as 1 gram of caffeine per day. Caffeine was not tested for in the hospital toxicology. Caffeine has been somewhat associated with cardiac arrhythmias and hypokalemia. However, considering her activities on the night prior to her collapse and the time of her collapse, caffeine toxicity is unlikely unless some sort of pill or supplement containing caffeine was consumed. No family member or friend reports use of any drugs.

Did she have a heart attack?

The common term "heart attack" is generally reserved to describe the medical condition of myocardial infarction. Mrs. Schiavo's heart was anatomically normal without any areas of recent or remote myocardial infarction.

Was she strangled?

No trauma was noted on any of the numerous physical exams or radiographs performed on Mrs. Schiavo on the day of, in the days after, or in the months after her initial collapse. Indeed, within an hour of her initial hospital admission, radiographic examination of her cervical spine was negative. Specifically, external signs of strangulation including cutaneous or deep neck injury, facial/conjunctival petechiae, and other blunt trauma were not observed or recorded during her initial hospital admission.

Why was a bone scan performed in 1991 and what did the results indicate?

In summary, any rib fractures, leg fractures, skull fractures or spine fractures that occurred concurrent with Mrs. Schiavo's original collapse would almost certainly have been diagnosed in February 1990 especially with the number of physical exams, radiographs, and other evaluations she received in the early evolution of her care at Humana Hospital-Northside. During her initial hospitalization, she received twenty-three chest radiographs, three brain CT scans, two abdominal radiographs, two echocardiograms, one abdominal ultrasound, one cervical spine radiograph, and one radiograph of her right knee. No fractures or trauma were reported or recorded.

By far, the most likely explanation for the bone scan findings in Mrs. Schiavo are prolonged immobility induced osteoporosis and complicating H.O. (heterotopic ossification) in an environment of intense physical therapy. Without the original bone scan and radiographs from that period, no other conclusion can reasonably be made.

Appendix 3
State Attorney McCabe's Report

Memo to State Attorney Bernie McCabe
from Prosecutors Doug Crow and Bob Lewis

To: BMc
From: Doug Crow / Bob Lewis
Re: Governor's Request on Schiavo case
Date: June 27, 2005

Based on what he refers to as "new information" contained in the
Terri Schiavo autopsy report, Governor Bush has requested that our
office take a "fresh look at the case" with no "preconceptions as to
the outcome." Governor Bush's letter noted that the autopsy had not
determined the cause of Mrs. Schiavo's "original injuries" in 1990 and
had in fact cast doubt on the explanation that had been the basis of the
1992 malpractice verdict. He also noted that in 1992, 2003 and 2005
Michael Schiavo had given a time for his wife's collapse that was 40
to 70 minutes prior to the time that his 911 call was received by emergency services.

I believe it is unrealistic to expect, considering the past decade of
increasingly venomous litigation and family members' disparate and
irreconcilable beliefs as to Terri's wishes, that our office has the ability

352 | APPENDIX 3

to resolve or ameliorate this long-standing dispute. This occurrence has been the object of continuing litigation for the past twelve years. Most of the pertinent "facts" are in the public record and have been considered and reconsidered by lawyers, jurors, judges and a myriad of experts. Our office has twice been asked to consider accusations against Michael Schiavo—once in 2003 based upon contact from Mr. and Mrs. Schindler and again at the request of the Governor's staff earlier this year—and found insufficient evidence of any prosecutable offense to justify a criminal investigation.

Having reviewed the report and discussed the autopsy investigation with Dr. Thogmartin and his chief investigator Bill Pellan in detail and having also reviewed transcripts of the 1992 and 2002 court proceedings along with documents previously supplied to us by the Schindler family, it is obvious to us that there is no possibility of proving that anyone's criminal act was responsible for Mrs. Schiavo's collapse. Despite a thoroughly researched and extensive autopsy that included consultations with other expert pathologists and an exhaustive search for and review of all available medical records and other information concerning the events surrounding Terri's collapse, Dr. Thogmartin has been unable to determine why it occurred. He has convinced us that there are no remaining medical records in existence that would assist him in resolving what caused her 1990 cardiac arrest to a reasonable degree of medical certainty.

Without proof of criminal agency, there can be no hope of prosecution. Nor is there justification to use our investigative powers to perpetuate suspicion where, despite extended litigation and a detailed autopsy, we have no proof to suggest that a crime has occurred. Although Dr. Thogmartin did not believe that the cause could be determined with reasonable certainty, there are explanations far more likely and logical than any involving criminal wrongdoing.

Criminal versus Non-Criminal Causes of Terri's Collapse

Although the Governor suggests that the cause of Terri's "injuries" is more in doubt than ever, Dr. Thogmartin's extensive report makes clear that there is no evidence that she suffered any physical trauma. Despite repeated physical exams and radiographs, the hospital records contained no indication of traumatic injury. Dr. Thogmartin indicated the absence of such entries was significant since "contusions, abrasions, recent fractures and particularly healing fractures would have been visualized during the initial months of treatment" if they had been present. Similarly X-rays of her cervical spine that were taken within an hour of her admittance were negative and external signs of strangulation such as cutaneous or deep neck injury, blunt trauma or facial/conjunctive petechiae were not present.

The hypothesis that Terri's low potassium level was a factitious result of medication and fluid administered during her resuscitation is not new but first surfaced in the 1992 malpractice trial. The basis of the 1992 malpractice suit against Terri's gynecologist was that she had eating and nutritional disorders which he failed to detect and which allegedly led to her cardiac arrest causing profound and irreversible brain damage. Terri had sought this doctor's help in 1989 because of difficulty in getting pregnant and up until the time of her death was under treatment for amenorrhea (abnormally infrequent menstrual periods), a well documented result of eating disorders in young women. Terri had lost as much as 100 pounds since adolescence and had lost 20 pounds since her marriage. The suit alleged that her doctor failed to take a nutritional history and to diagnose and treat the eating disorders and nutritional deficiencies that were not only the cause of her menstrual problems but had ultimately led to her collapse.

Three physicians testifying on Terri's behalf concluded—based upon the medical records as well as interviews and statements of family members and co-workers—that Terri had an eating disorder or nutritional deficiency which had contributed to her cardiac arrest. The testimony suggested, without contradiction, this was the consensus opinion of all the doctors who had been involved in Terri's treatment.

The plaintiff did not attempt to specify the eating disorder but suggested that there was evidence to support bulimia and psychogenic polydipsia and that a combination of diet, excessive intake of fluids and compensatory purging behavior had caused both her amenorrhea and her extremely low level of potassium and that the latter condition led to her cardiac arrest. The defendant doctor had admitted that Terri's eating disorder was probably a factor in the amenorrhea for which he was treating her. He acknowledged that, while there are a number of other possible causes, eating and nutritional disorders are known to cause this condition. Additionally, the defense called a psychiatrist who specialized in the treatment of eating disorders; he testified that based upon reviewing the statements of family members, the medical records, the depositions of eleven physicians and the statements of four of her co-workers that Terri suffered from bulimia. This expert did not concede that the eating disorder was responsible for her cardiac arrest. He noted, as does Dr. Thogmartin, that the resuscitation efforts and administration of medication and fluids could explain her low serum potassium after the incident and that this reading did not necessarily reflect electrolyte levels at the time of her collapse. He suggested, however, that Terri's condition was sufficiently severe and at an early enough stage in the disease process that she would carefully conceal her behavior, would not have acknowledged the problem and was not yet amenable to treatment.

Dr. Thogmartin understandably concluded that currently available evidence was insufficient to either definitively rule out the existence of an eating or nutritional disorder or to conclude with reasonable certainty that it was the cause of her collapse. However, all experts in the 1992 proceedings—relying on all available contemporary records and witness recollections—opined that Terri suffered from an eating disorder and the jury unanimously agreed.

While Dr. Thogmartin's report indicated that non-traumatic asphyxia was not impossible, I do not believe that this can be construed to mean that it represents a plausible explanation or one that is equally or more likely than the possible non-criminal explanations for Mrs. Schiavo's collapse. Asphyxiation occurs when the brain is deprived of oxygen and can be accomplished by cutting off the air to the lungs or the flow of oxygenated (arterial) blood to the brain. While not impossible, it would be exceedingly difficult to accomplish this without leaving evidence of a struggle in a surviving victim. (*See Footnote 1 below)

Cutting off the air supply through suffocation would have to continue for approximately four to five minutes before brain damage ensues. The victim will remain conscious for a significant portion of this time. Common sense suggests and experience has confirmed that victims struggle violently when unable to breathe, flailing out at their attacker and whatever is preventing them from breathing and necessitating in turn that the assailant increase the amount of force against a moving, struggling victim. These factors make it virtually inevitable that observable injury will result. It is also possible to cause rapid unconsciousness with simultaneous bilateral compression of the carotid arteries. Based upon our experience, however, it would be virtually impossible for someone without considerable practice in using the technique to incapacitate a struggling victim, who is later resuscitated and survives, without causing visible injury.

Dr. Thogmartin's report also could not eliminate the possibility of subtle trauma in the form of "commotio cordis," a phenomenon that is most commonly seen in young athletes who are struck in the chest directly over the heart with an object such as a baseball. If the chest is sufficiently flexible and the impact occurs precisely during the 20 millisecond interval of the heart's cycle in which the ventricular muscles are repolarizing, ventricular fibrillation (rapid, unsynchronized contractions) can occur. Resuscitation efforts are rarely successful unless the person is defibrillated within two to three minutes. The timing of the impact as well as the hardness of the object, age of the subject and speed of impact are significant variables; it is unknown how often this type of blow to an unprotected chest can cause fibrillation without leaving any identifiable injury in a surviving adult victim. It seems very unlikely, however, that in the course of a domestic argument where one party is intentionally trying to harm the other, they will direct a single blow to the cardiac silhouette that is of sufficient force to cause ventricular fibrillation but not the intended injury.

Dr. Thogmartin also could not exclude the possibility of toxins or drugs being involved. Terri's described condition and the fact that paramedics were able to resuscitate her despite the twelve minute interval between her collapse and their arrival are not inconsistent with the possibility of an opiate overdose. The police officer who responded to the emergency did find a small number of medications in the residence, but did not feel that the drugs he found were relevant to Terri's collapse and did not record what they were. While there is some indication in the discovery materials from the malpractice suit that a prescription bottle of percocet may have been in the residence, Dr. Thogmartin indicated that the drug screen done at the ER would likely have detected the acetaminophen that is combined with oxycodone in that medication. There is of course no affirmative evidence that Terri ingested toxic amounts of any substance or medication and absolutely no basis to conclude they were forcibly or surreptitiously fed to her.

Time Discrepancies Concerning Terri's Collapse

Absent proof that a crime has occurred, neither Michael Schiavo's credibility nor the consistency of his statements would become a critical and material concern. Nonetheless, the discrepancy between his recollection of the time of the incident and the time that paramedics and police recorded receiving the call hardly constitutes new information. Schiavo testified in the 1992 malpractice deposition and trial that he heard a noise around five a.m. and found his wife collapsed near the bathroom door. In a 2003 interview on *Larry King Live* he indicated this occurred at 4:30 a.m., a time he repeated in a recent interview with medical examiner Jon Thogmartin. Schiavo has consistently said he called for emergency help immediately after finding his wife and that fire rescue arrived within a few minutes of the call. To our knowledge he was never asked about or confronted with the difference between his estimation of the time and the records indicating the fire rescue was called at 5:40 and began resuscitation efforts at 5:52.

Understandably, Michael Schiavo is not the only witness who has been inconsistent or had difficulty recalling the timing of events surrounding Terri's collapse and resuscitation. Shortly after finding Terri, Michael Schiavo called his in-laws and told them what happened. It is unclear whether he or the Schindlers called Bobby Schindler who lived in the same complex as Michael and Terri and who immediately went to their apartment and arrived before the paramedics. Although Terri's parents had been awakened in the middle of the night with extremely disturbing news and waited at their house for a subsequent phone call on their daughter's condition, they have no clear idea what time they were called by Michael. They had previously provided our office a time line indicating that they were called as early as 3–4 a.m. but recently told Thogmartin they could not recall the time. Similarly, Terri's brother, Bobby Schindler, told Dr. Thogmartin he could not remember the time that he was called or initially arrived at the Schiavo residence except in relation to the arrival of the paramedics.

It is not contradicted that Michael Schiavo appeared frantic and extremely distraught throughout the incident. Under these extraordinary circumstances, where both Mr. Schiavo and his accusers have similar difficulty in reconstructing exact times, it cannot be credibly argued that this discrepancy is incriminating evidence. Nor, in light of his consistent and uncontradicted claims that he immediately called 911, can his error in estimating the time be considered an admission that he waited over an hour to get help for his wife. It does not appear that Schiavo's error was considered to be of probative value in either the civil suit or in the subsequent guardianship proceedings. Schiavo was not confronted by opposing lawyers (or by Dr. Thogmartin) with the potential inconsistency nor was he given the exact times recorded by paramedics as a point of reference. The most obvious explanation is also the most logical: under the extremely stressful circumstances his attention to and memory of the exact time were faulty—in the same way that the recollections of Mr. and Mrs. Schindler and Bobby are flawed.

Curiously, a delay such as this would further undermine the speculation that Michael Schiavo caused Terri's collapse by assaulting her. Neither the medical examiner nor our assistants were able to identify any plausible manner by which Schiavo—having physically overcome Terri without injuring her or being injured himself—could keep her incapacitated but sufficiently alive that she could still be resuscitated almost an hour later. Additionally, we could discern no rational motivation for attacking one's spouse, allowing her to linger near death for forty minutes or more and then calling for help in sufficient time to save her life so she could potentially name her assailant.

Family members and others who disagreed with Mr. Schiavo's decision to seek court approval to have his wife's feeding tube removed have made repeated attacks on his credibility and accused him of mistreatment of his wife. At least some of these accusations have been shown to be baseless by the autopsy conclusions. We should note, however, that we have also received unsolicited comments praising his honesty, sincerity and devotion to his wife's care. Also, when asked about her son-in-law during the 1992 malpractice trial, Mary Schindler testified, "He's there every day. She (Terri) does not want for anything. He is loving, caring. I don't know of any young boy that would be as attentive. He is . . . he's just unbelievable, and I know without him there is no way I would have survived this."

In the complete absence of any evidence that Terri's collapse was caused by anyone's criminal actions it has been unnecessary for us to attempt to resolve these conflicting portraits of Michael Schiavo's character. It appears, however, that opinions on his culpability derive from disagreement with the Court's decision to allow Terri's life to end and not from any objective consideration of the evidence. If the available facts are analyzed without preconceptions, it is clear that there is no basis for further investigation. While some questions may remain following the autopsy, the likelihood of finding evidence that criminal acts were responsible for her collapse is not one of them.

We strongly recommend that the inquiry be closed and no further action be taken.

Footnote 1

Decomposition of the body can sometimes hide some of the more subtle signs of assault, including petechial hemorrhages. Also, the bruising process effectively ends when the heart ceases to pump blood. This would not be an issue where the victim is resuscitated and survives.

———

June 30, 2005
Honorable Jeb Bush
The Capitol
Tallahassee, FL 32399-0001

Dear Governor Bush:

I am in receipt of your letter dated June 17, 2005, requesting that this office conduct an inquiry into certain questions raised as a result of the release of Dr. Jon Thogmartin's report regarding the autopsy he performed on Terri Schiavo. Further, you urged that this inquiry be conducted without any preconceptions as to the outcome. We have attempted to follow this sound advice, unlike some pundits, some "experts," some e-mail and Web-based correspondents, and even some institutions of government that have, in my view, reached conclusions regarding the controversy surrounding Mrs. Schiavo based upon such preconceptions and/or misinformation.

Enclosed with this letter is a Memorandum which describes the review and analysis that was conducted by two of the most experienced and capable prosecutors in this office. I have separately reviewed this Memorandum and the thorough, professional Report of Autopsy provided by Dr. Thogmartin. As a result, I fully concur with the conclusions contained in the Memorandum.

In summary, while there have been discrepancies that have existed over what time Mrs. Schiavo collapsed relative to what time paramedics were called, all available records indicate that it has been Mr. Schiavo's consistent position that he called 911 immediately after her collapse. This consistency, coupled with the varying recollections of the precise time offered by other interested parties, lead me to the conclusion that such discrepancies are not indicative of criminal activity and thus not material to any potential investigation.

With regards to the fact that Dr. Thogmartin was understandably unable to determine the "manner of death" with reasonable certainty, it is axiomatic that there be some fact(s) or evidence indicating that a criminal act or agency caused death in order to invoke the investigative jurisdiction of this office. A review of the available records, including Dr. Thogmartin's report, reveals no "facts" or "evidence" that indicate a criminal act or agency was causative of Mrs. Schiavo's collapse or subsequent death. As pointed out by Dr. Thogmartin, there are several hypothetical theories that could be advanced, but I have concluded, though not with reasonable certainty, that the most likely hypothesis for the cause of her collapse was the one advanced during the 1992 malpractice litigation, i.e., an eating disorder.

I realize that this review does not provide definitive answers to the questions you sought to have answered. However, I feel comfortable in stating, without preconceptions, that these are the probable answers when one considers all of the records and reports available at this time.

Sincerely yours,

Bernie McCabe
State Attorney

About the Authors

Michael Schiavo's epic battle, first to heal his wife, and then to allow her to die with dignity, was front-page news around the world. To care for Terri, Michael became an EMT, then a registered respiratory therapist, and finally, a registered nurse. Michael has founded TerriPac.com to mobilize voters against candidates who have no qualms about interfering in what should be personal family decisions. TerriPac will also work to encourage everyone over the age of seventeen to have a living will. Michael lives with his wife Jodi, and their two children, Olivia and Nicholas, in Clearwater, Florida.

Michael Hirsh is a George Foster Peabody Award and Writers Guild Award winner as well as an Emmy Award–winning documentary producer and investigative reporter. He is the author of four nonfiction books, including *None Braver: U.S. Air Force Pararescuemen in the War on Terrorism*.